SCOOK

ANNE-SOPHIE PIC

The complete cookery course

Photographer: Michaël Roulier
Food stylist: Emmanuel Turiot

jacqui
small

'COOKING FOR THOSE WE LOVE IS THE GREATEST PROOF OF LOVE.'

With these words, I started my first book, *Scook: recipes for entertaining*. And since in this book I am going back to my roots, I want to begin in the same way.

This complete cookery course contains the essentials of both how I cook and what I cook, and it is filled with dishes inspired by my childhood and my professional experience.

More than anything, cooking is a process of passing on experience and knowledge: childhood memories and family occasions, especially those centred around food, are enormously important. And the reason I want to pass on everything I have learnt is because those who came before me – my father and grandfather, obviously, but also other cookery writers – are the ones who have taught me, and I want to maintain that tradition.

Cooking for those we love is important, but it is equally important to do it for ourselves; to make the most of good ingredients; to make every meal or taste a pleasure; to take the time to cook properly, so that we look after ourselves properly. I use all my senses when I make a dish: it must look beautiful, smell wonderful and make the most of all the ingredients and their textures.

I hope you will enjoy these cooking lessons, which have one very simple purpose: to share the pleasure of giving pleasure.

Everyday

Entertaining

Homemade

Classics

For children

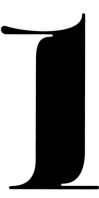

I • ENTERTAINING

Dinner with friends

Roast saddle of lamb with basil and mustard 12
Fresh morels with tarragon and Parmesan cream 14
Sea bass in a Guérande sea salt crust with tarragon hollandaise . 16
Tuna tartlet with sauce vierge 20

Elegant snacks

Baked eggs with turmeric, mushrooms and chestnuts 26
Sardine rillettes with whisky and cauliflower cream 28
Fillet of marinated salmon with petits pois and wasabi mousseline 32
My spaghetti bolognese 34
Saint-Marcellin cheese croquettes 36
Cream of chestnut soup with spices and seasonal mushrooms . . 38
Veal kidneys with gin and pepper 40

Cutting edge

Tomato mozzarella revisited 46
The new pissaladière, with crunchy fennel and onion pickles . . 48
Brown shrimp and citrus verrine 52
Seared red tuna with warm vodka and lemon foam 54
Roast duck breast with black cherry compote 56
Pork fillet with red pepper confit and pineapple 58

Something special

Poached egg with tomato ketchup, capers and black olives 62
Mimolette cheese soufflé 66
Duck liver with seared melon 70
Poached guinea fowl supremes with wakame seaweed cream . . 72
Pommes soufflées re-invented 74

Patisserie

Coconut and lime îles flottantes with banana-
   passionfruit foam 80
Iced vanilla parfait with pineapple 84
Poached vanilla pear with cassis and coffee fondant 86
Cinnamon and cherry clafoutis 88
Rhubarb and tarragon tart 90

II • EVERYDAY

Between friends

Fish terrine with brown shrimp cream 96
Sous-vide cod with lentils 98
Oxtail Parmentier with sweet potato mash 102
Rabbit in white wine with liquorice and petits pois 104
Six-minute foie gras with beetroot 106

Fast and fabulous

Asparagus vichyssoise with fennel seeds 112
Sea bass 'en papillote' with baby leeks, juniper butter
   and lemon zest 114
Tarragon chicken with rice pilaf 116
Ravioli gratin with caramelized onions and
   a light nutmeg béchamel 118
Sardine tempura with Choron sauce 120
Roman gnocchi revisited 124

Cutting edge

Mussel royale with pumpkin cream 130
Mushroom-stuffed squid with creamy tagliatelle 132
Savoury custards: courgette and bay leaf, aubergine
   and coconut milk 134
Lime-marinated scallop carpaccio with mushroom jelly 136
Guinea fowl supremes with walnut crust and a quick jus 140

Something special

Lobster and celery with red fruits 146
Pollock with turnip ravioli and rum sauce 148
Oyster tartare with cheese fondue revisited 152
Roast duckling with saffron-spiced apple 154
Roast veal with potato mousseline and plum chutney 156
Poached egg with snail foam, galangal and artichokes 158

Patisserie

Grandmother's brioche with chocolate hazelnut spread 162
White chocolate fondant with passionfruit and
   chocolate coulis 166
Chestnut cream with pineapple and piña colada sorbet 168
Paris-Valence with red fruits 170
Apricot macaroons 172
Lemon tart with Italian meringue 176

III • CLASSICS

Cold dishes and starters

Soft-boiled egg in lemon jelly with foie gras royale *182*
Lobster 'bellevue' with saffron tomato jelly and
    rainbow tomatoes *184*
Game terrine with red onion pickles *188*
Duck foie gras terrine with rhubarb and tarragon compote *190*
Mixed vegetables with smoked eel *194*
Cold sauces *196*
Jellied ham and parsley terrine *200*

Family favourites

Creamy chicory with ham *204*
Veal paupiettes with mushrooms *206*
Calves' liver soufflé from my childhood, with tomato coulis . . *210*
Eggs Florentine with Beaufort cheese *214*
Crème caramel with muscovado sugar *216*

The great classics of French cuisine

Vol-au-vent *220*
Green asparagus with mint hollandaise sauce *224*
Du Barry velouté with orange *226*
Pot-au-feu with sharp horseradish cream *228*
Breaded whiting with maître d'hôtel butter and fried vegetables *230*
Tarte tatin with tonka bean *232*
Vacherin with vanilla ice cream and strawberry sorbet *238*

Bistrot classics

Spring navarin of lamb. *244*
Mackerel escabeche *248*
Blanquette of veal revisited *252*
Sole bonne femme and crushed potatoes with snails *256*
Pike quenelles with Nantua sauce. *258*
My pommes dauphine *260*
Rum baba with chestnut sauce and vanilla whipped cream *264*

My classic recipes

Mint-marinated langoustines with petits pois cream and
    minted liquorice spring onions *268*
Shoulder of kid goat with sorrel and fondant potatoes *270*
John Dory with cucumber pickle and purée and
    an aniseed sauce. *272*
Roast scallops with spaghettini and rum emulsion *274*
Vegetable tart with young Parmesan cream *276*
Iced Grand Marnier soufflé *278*
Chocolate-mint profiteroles. *280*

3

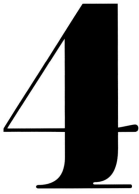

IV • HOMEMADE

The aperitif

Peanut marshmallows 286
A surprise sandwich loaf 288
Melba toast with lardo di Colonnata and Comté cheese 292
Grilled aubergine caviar with turmeric 294
Herb-salt marinated anchovies with Green Zebra tomatoes . . . 296

Lunch with the girls

Beetroot salad with Arabica coffee salt 300
Melon soup with aniseed and goat's cheese cream 302
Quinoa salad with minted yogurt 304
Gravadlax and celeriac remoulade with Meaux mustard 306
Heritage tomatoes with buffalo mozzarella pannacotta 310
Pumpkin soup with Blue Mountain coffee 312

The picnic

Salmon rillettes with tonka bean and green apple 316
Monkfish terrine with prawns and saffron 320
Rabbit rillettes with chorizo and mint 322
Poached egg and piperade with cloves 324
Raspberry shortbread biscuits. 326
Chocolate financiers 328

The afternoon pick-me-up

Pogne de Romans 332
Nathan's favourite fruits in syrup 336
Homemade yogurts: violet, orange flower, jasmine
    and aniseed 338
Almond pannacotta with raspberry confit and crumble 342

One-course dinners

Chard, sheep's cheese and ricotta ravioli. 346
Duck confit with lavender and spices 350
Black rice risotto with bouillabaisse jus 352
Lamb confit and mint tortellini with crushed
    lemon courgettes 356
Tandoori beef bourguignon. 360
Red mullet in aniseed escabeche 362
Vegetable tian with bay leaf butter 364

V • FOR CHILDREN

Fast but good food

Boulangère potatoes with bacon 370
Drôme caillette turnovers 372
Petits pois velouté with horseradish cream 374
Grandma Alice's bulgur wheat with vermicelli. 376
My ratatouille 378
Grandma Suzanne's stuffed tomatoes 380
Goat's cheese and peppermint blancmange with
    aubergine caviar 382

Nurturing a love of fine food

Poached sole and potatoes with sweet spices 386
Mussel risotto 388
Praline cream choux buns 390
Little chocolate pots. 392
Braised beef with red pepper and tomato sauce. 394
Scallops with buttered green cabbage. 396

Childhood favourites

Raspberry Swiss roll 400
Chocolate mousse 402
Glacé fruit cake 404
Glacé grapefruit. 406
Lyonnaise Mardi Gras doughnuts. 408
Pain perdu with strawberry jam 410

1

Entertaining

DINNER WITH FRIENDS

There is nothing more perfect than relaxing around a beautifully laid table with good friends, a lovely bottle of wine and, of course, great food.

In this chapter you will find recipes that are perfect for sharing, dishes that are straightforward to cook and serve to a crowd, even if a little extra something, perhaps an unexpected spice or twist, is never far away. For many of these recipes, some of the steps can be done in advance, leaving you free to spend time with your friends.

Bon appétit!

For 4
Preparation time: 20 min
Cooking time: 20 min

Roast saddle of lamb with basil and mustard

Saddle of lamb is an underrated cut that is well worth trying. More tender than leg, more flavoursome than chops, the meat is exceptional. And it is easily deboned and stuffed – here with mustard. If you have trouble finding the Savora and violette de Brive French speciality mustards, you can substitute any mild mustard, such as Dijon. A great recipe for a special occasion, this one will keep even the most gourmet of guests happy.

The saddle

1 x 600 g/1 lb 5 oz saddle of lamb, deboned (ask your butcher to do this for you)
120 g/4¼ oz white breadcrumbs
2 teaspoons Savora mustard
2 teaspoons violette de Brive mustard
¼ bunch of basil
splash of groundnut (peanut) oil
25 g/1 oz salted butter
fine sea salt, fleur de sel, freshly ground pepper

The chard gratin

3 bunches of Swiss chard (silverbeet)
splash of olive oil
15 g/½ oz salted butter
100 ml/3½ fl oz vegetable stock (see step-by-step method on p. 126)
20 g/¾ oz grated Parmesan
70 g/2½ oz Banon, or other very ripe goat's cheese
70 g/2½ oz sheep's milk Brousse, or other fresh sheep's cheese
80 ml/2½ fl oz single (pouring) cream
fine sea salt, freshly ground pepper

1 ~ The stuffing

Open the saddle widthways, season, then scatter over the breadcrumbs. Spread the mustard all over the meat and strew with the basil leaves. Roll up and tie with kitchen string.

2 ~ The chard gratin

Put the green leaves of the chard to one side. Trim the white stalks, wash in cold water and cut into pieces 3 cm/1¼ in long and 5 mm/¼ in wide. Season with fine sea salt. Heat the olive oil and butter in a frying pan and, when the butter is foaming, add the trimmed chard stems. Stir to coat them in the oil and butter, then cook for 2 minutes. Add the vegetable stock and cook for another 6 minutes, until the chard is meltingly soft. Drain, then place in the bottom of a gratin dish. Mix together all the cheeses and cream, then pour half of this mixture into the dish. Boil the chard greens for 2–3 minutes in salted water, drain well then add to the gratin dish. Pour over the rest of the cheese and cream mixture.

3 ~ Cooking the saddle

Heat the peanut oil and butter in an ovenproof frying pan, then add the saddle and colour it on all sides. Transfer to an oven preheated to 180°C (350°F; gas mark 4) and cook for 6–7 minutes, basting every so often. Remove from the oven and leave to rest for 10 minutes.

4 ~ Plating up

Preheat an overhead grill (broiler). Reheat the saddle for a few minutes in the oven and quickly brown the gratin under the grill until golden. Untie the saddle and cut into slices, then sprinkle with fleur de sel. Serve immediately, with the chard gratin.

Tip | *Pour the pan juices from the lamb over the meat before serving.*

13

For 4
Preparation time: 20 min
Infusing time: overnight
Cooking time: 15 min

} Fresh morels with tarragon and Parmesan cream

You must make this at least once in your life, in the spring, at the height of the morel season. The flavour of tarragon marries so well with morels. A real discovery.

½ bunch of tarragon
300 ml/10 fl oz crème fraîche
 (sour cream)
600 g/1 lb 5 oz morels
1 tablespoon white wine vinegar
1 shallot
20 g/¾ oz unsalted butter
2 tablespoons vegetable stock
 (see step-by-step method on p. 126)
50 g/1¾ oz Parmesan
salt

1 ~ The tarragon cream

The day before, cold-infuse half the tarragon in the cream: just chop half the tarragon, mix it with the cream and leave in the fridge overnight. The next day, sieve the cream to remove the tarragon leaves, then reduce the cream by half over a gentle heat to thicken it.

2 ~ The fresh morels

Remove and discard the morel stalks. Splash the morel caps with vinegar, then wash them in plenty of running water until the water is clear and there is no trace of grit or soil. Leave them to dry on kitchen paper. Finely chop the shallot, then melt the butter in a frying pan and, as soon as it foams, add the shallot and cook for 2 minutes. Add the morels and the stock, then cover and leave to cook for another 3 minutes before adding the tarragon cream. Bring to the boil and stir to coat the morels in the cream. Add a little salt, then finish by scattering over the remaining tarragon and shavings of Parmesan.

3 ~ Plating up

Arrange the morels decoratively on plates and dress with the sauce.

Tip | Raw tarragon has a very different taste from cooked. Before cooking, it is aniseedy and floral, but once cooked it becomes almost spicy. There are several varieties; where possible, try to use the one with small dark green leaves – it is the most fragrant.

15

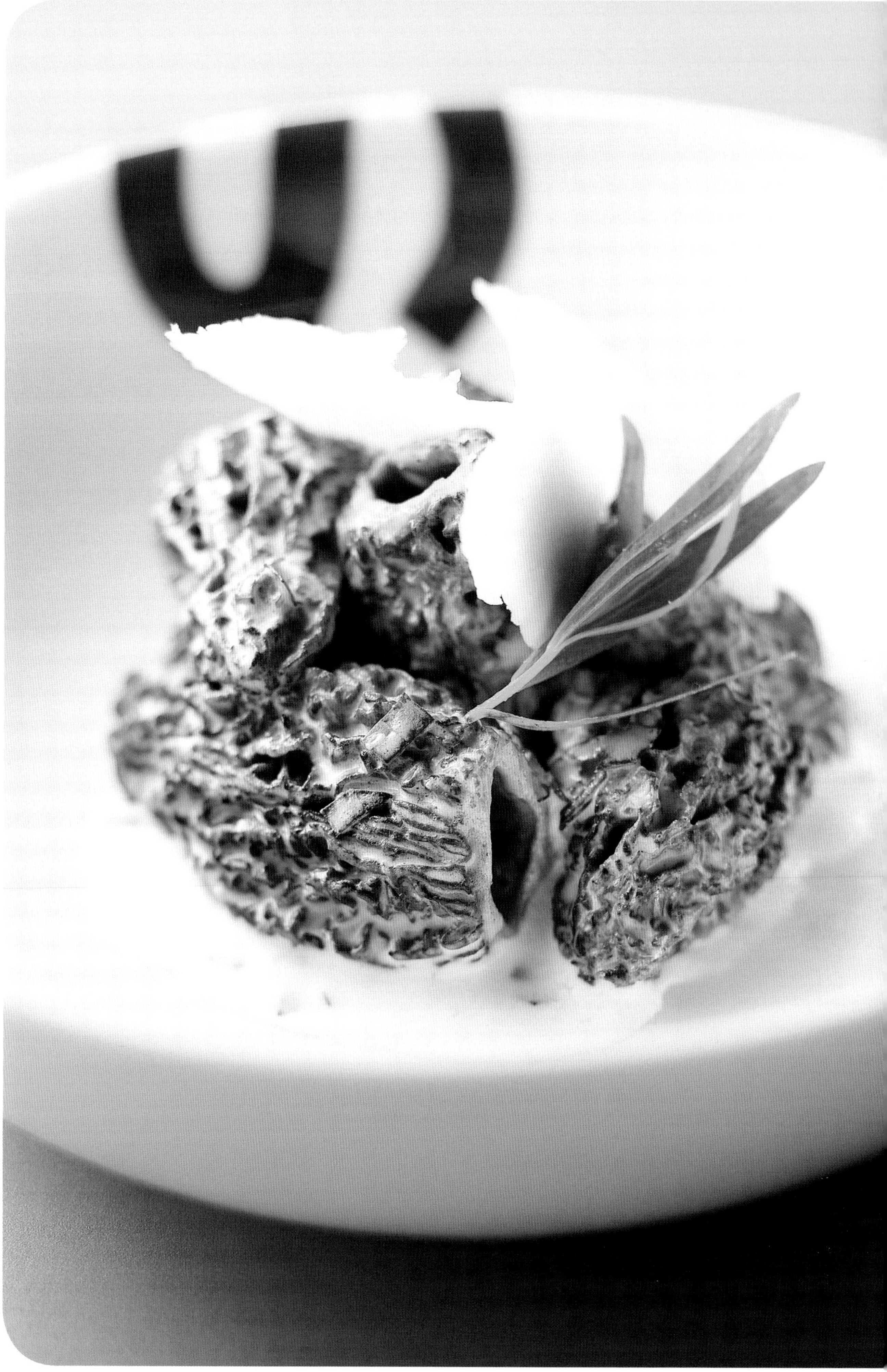

For 4
Preparation time: 15 min
Cooking time: 30 min

}

Sea bass in a Guérande sea salt crust with tarragon hollandaise

This is a recipe that shows how much I love tarragon. Its aniseedy, spicy and fruity flavour deserves much more use in the kitchen. I have even been known to nibble on a few leaves while cooking!

The sea bass

1 x 2 kg/4½ lb line-caught sea bass
sprig of fennel
2 kg/4½ lb Guérande coarse salt
200 g/7 oz plain (all-purpose) flour
large sprig of thyme
large sprig of rosemary
½ bunch of dill
3 teaspoons pink peppercorns
12 egg whites

The hollandaise sauce

3 egg yolks
100 g/3½ oz clarified butter
  (see below right)
juice of 1 lemon
½ bunch of tarragon
fine salt, freshly ground pepper

1 ~ The sea bass

Get the fishmonger to descale, trim and gut the fish for you. Rinse it well, then tuck the fennel sprig into the cavity. Mix the Guérande salt with the flour, herbs and peppercorns. Lightly beat the egg whites with a fork then mix with the salt mixture.

2 ~ The salt crust

Make a layer of the salt mixture, roughly the same dimensions (in terms of length and width) as the fish, in an ovenproof dish. Put the fish on top, then cover with a 1.5 cm/¾ in layer of salt, carefully moulding the salt to the shape of the fish as much as possible. Bake in an oven preheated to 250°C (475°F; gas mark 9) for 30 minutes, or about 1½ minutes per 100 g/3½ oz of fish. (See step-by-step method on p. 18.)

3 ~ The hollandaise sauce

Put the egg yolks and 2 tablespoons of water in a medium-sized bowl. Set the bowl over a saucepan of simmering water over a gentle heat and whisk constantly, using a figure of 8 motion. When the sauce begins to thicken, add the clarified butter in a steady stream, then add the lemon juice and chopped tarragon. Season lightly.

4 ~ Plating up

Break the salt crust using the handle of a very solid knife and remove the fish skin. Serve the fish with the warm hollandaise and a shard of the crust as decoration.

Making it even better | *Serve with these delicious gnocchi. Mix 500 g/1 lb 2 oz cooked and mashed potato with 1 tablespoon chopped parsley, 5 chopped anchovy fillets, a little chopped preserved lemon, 100 g/3½ oz plain (all-purpose) flour, 50 g/1¾ oz grated Parmesan, a pinch of salt and 2 egg yolks. Form into gnocchi 2.5 cm/1 in long, marking them with the tines of a fork, then cook in boiling salted water until they rise to the surface (usually about 2 minutes). Dress with a little olive oil before serving.*

Tip | *To make clarified butter, melt some butter in a bain-marie (that is, in a saucepan placed in another pan filled with simmering water). Skim the foam from the surface, then remove the yellow melted butter, leaving behind the white milk solids. It's as simple as that!*

How to cook sea bass in a salt crust

1 ~ In a bowl, combine the coarse salt with your choice of spices and herbs (see recipe on p. 16).

2 ~ Mix the salt and herbs together well, then add the egg whites and mix again to form a damp, sandy mixture.

3 ~ In an ovenproof dish or baking tray, form a layer of the salt mixture a little bit longer and slightly wider than the fish you are going to cook, pressing it down lightly with your hands.

4 ~ Put the fish on the bed of salt and stuff it with a few sprigs of dried aniseed.Preheat the oven to 250°C (475°F; gas mark 9).

5 ~ Cover the fish with the rest of the salt mixture, starting with the tail and finishing with the head.

6 ~ The fish should be completely covered. Lightly tamp the surface with your hands to make a smooth, even shape. Put in the oven to bake.

7 ~ Remove the baking tray from the oven. The salt should just be very lightly coloured. Leave to cool for a couple of minutes.

8 ~ Carefully break the salt crust to reveal the fish. Remove all the salt and the fish skin, then cut the fish into portions. Serve immediately.

For 4
Preparation time: 15 min
Freezing time: 1 h
Cooking time: 20 min

Tuna tartlet with sauce vierge

Served on a sunny summer's day, this is a complete delight: tempting, refreshing and simply delicious. The combination of tuna, sauce vierge and puff pastry works very well. Choose some beautiful red tuna for this — super-fresh, of course!

The tuna and the pastry

100 g/3½ oz puff pastry
400 g/14 oz fresh red tuna from
the Mediterranean

The tomato concassé

5 vine tomatoes
1 onion
olive oil
1 garlic clove
sprig of thyme
1 small bay leaf
fine salt, freshly ground pepper

The sauce vierge

20 g/¾ oz fresh broad (fava) beans
3 Roma tomatoes
20 g/¾ oz Taggiasche black olives
4 sprigs of basil
3 shallots
100 ml/3½ fl oz olive oil
juice of 1 lemon
fine salt, freshly ground pepper

Finishing off

2 teaspoons black olive tapenade
½ teaspoon Espelette chilli powder
a few leaves of basil
olive oil
40 g/1½ oz Parmesan shavings
Guérande salt

1 ~ The tartlet

Roll the puff pastry out thinly. Cut out four 12 cm x 10 cm/4½ in x 4 in rectangles. Bake them between two sheets of baking parchment, sandwiched between two baking trays, in an oven preheated to 190°C (375°F; gas mark 5) for 10–12 minutes. Leave to cool at room temperature.

2 ~ The tuna

Wrap the tuna in cling film and put it in the freezer for about an hour. As soon as it starts to freeze and solidify a little (but before it gets too hard), remove it from the freezer, slice thinly and keep to one side.

3 ~ The tomato concassé

Peel and deseed the tomatoes. Trim and finely slice the onion, then soften it in a little olive oil, without letting it colour, along with the garlic clove, thyme and bay leaf. Add the tomatoes, then leave to cook and reduce until the liquid has all evaporated. Check the seasoning. (See step-by-step method on p. 50.)

4 ~ The sauce vierge

Cook the broad beans in boiling, salted water for 30 seconds then remove their skins and any sprouts. Peel, deseed and dice the tomatoes (see step-by-step method on p. 22). Quarter the olives lengthways. Chop the basil and the shallots. Mix the broad beans, diced tomato, olives, basil and shallots with the olive oil and a splash of lemon juice, then check the seasoning.

5 ~ Finishing off

Warm the pastry rectangles in the oven, then spread first with tapenade, followed by a layer of tomato concassé, then a layer of tuna. Sprinkle on the Espelette chilli powder, Guérande salt and basil leaves, then drizzle with olive oil. Grill for a few seconds, then scatter over the Parmesan shavings and finish with the sauce vierge.

21

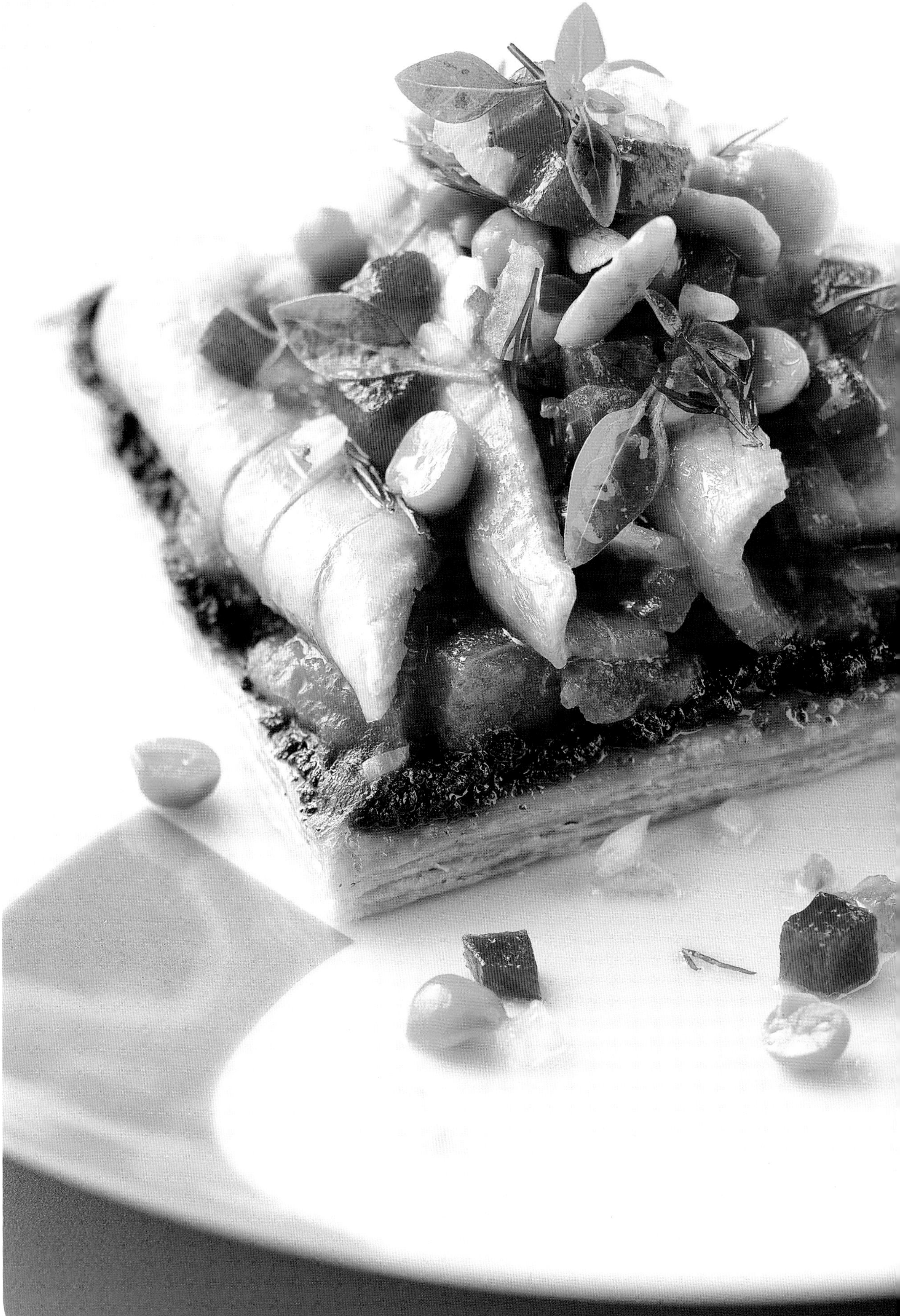

How to peel and dice tomatoes

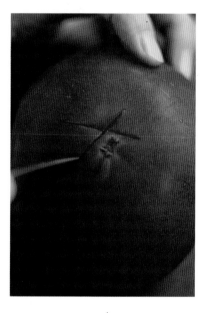

1

With the point of a knife, cut a cross into the base of the tomatoes. It doesn't need to be very deep; it just makes peeling them a lot easier.

2

Plunge the tomatoes into a saucepan of unsalted boiling water. Immerse them for a maximum of 10 seconds, then drain.

3

Plunge the tomatoes into a large bowl filled with cold water and ice cubes. This cools them down quickly and prevents the heat from making them soft. Leave them in the water for about a minute.

4

Remove the tomatoes from the iced water. Starting at the cross, catch the tomato skin between your thumb and the blade of a knife, then pull gently to remove it.

5

Cut around the stalks with the tip of a knife, creating a small cone around the stalk and core, then remove.

6

Quarter the peeled tomatoes. With a knife, remove the seeds as shown, leaving just the flesh.

7

You should now have beautiful tomato segments that you can use to dress dishes and salads.

8

You can also dice the tomatoes with a very sharp knife, then use the dice as they are or to make a tomato concassé (see step-by-step method on p. 50).

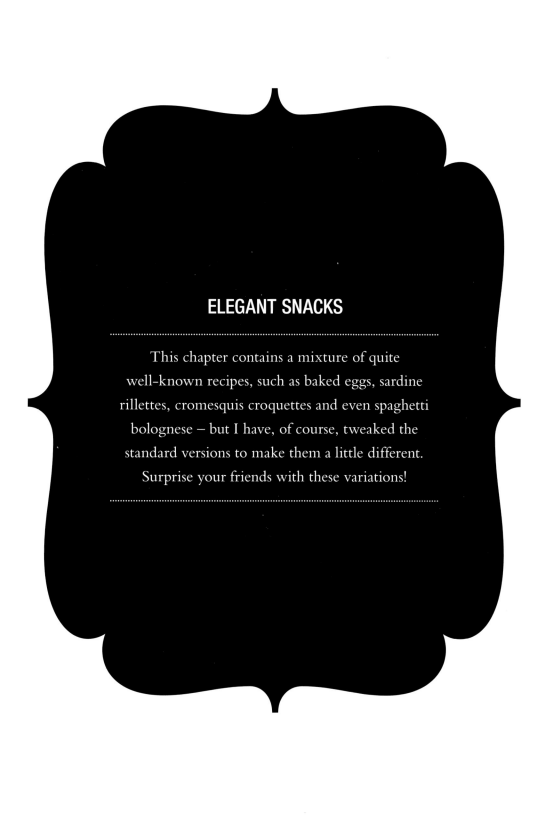

ELEGANT SNACKS

This chapter contains a mixture of quite well-known recipes, such as baked eggs, sardine rillettes, cromesquis croquettes and even spaghetti bolognese – but I have, of course, tweaked the standard versions to make them a little different. Surprise your friends with these variations!

For 4
Preparation time: 25 min
Cooking time: 30 min

}

Baked eggs with turmeric, mushrooms and chestnuts

Turmeric is not just useful for adding a rich yellow colour to dishes; it also has a heady, sophisticated flavour that goes particularly well with eggs. Always buy it in a well-sealed packet, because its flavour fades quickly if it has been badly stored.

8 extra-fresh eggs

The turmeric cream

100 ml/3½ fl oz single (pouring) cream
130 ml/4¼ fl oz milk
1 teaspoon ground turmeric
fine sea salt, freshly ground pepper

The mushrooms and chestnuts

16 small white button mushrooms
knob of salted butter
juice of ½ lemon
3 tablespoons vegetable stock (see step-by-step method on p. 126)
8 cooked chestnuts + extra for decoration
a little flat-leaf parsley
fine salt, fleur de sel

1 ~ The turmeric cream

Pour the cream and milk into a saucepan and simmer for a few minutes to thicken slightly. Remove from the heat and add the turmeric.

2 ~ The mushrooms

Trim the mushrooms, then fry in hot brown butter for 2 minutes. Add the lemon juice and vegetable stock, then leave to cook for a minute. Season with fine salt and drain.

3 ~ The eggs

Make a bain-marie by filling a roasting tin two-thirds full with boiling water then place in an oven preheated to 160°C (325°F; gas mark 3). Break the eggs one by one into small bowls. Use a small paring knife to neatly shape the chestnuts. Evenly divide the mushrooms and chestnuts between 4 ramekins. Carefully add 2 eggs per ramekin, then pour 1 tablespoon of turmeric cream into each ramekin. Place in the bain-marie, checking that the water level reaches the level of the eggs (otherwise they won't cook). Cover each ramekin with foil and cook for 30 minutes.

4 ~ Finishing off

Add another tablespoon of turmeric cream to each ramekin, then top with thin slivers of chestnut (sliced on a mandoline or with a sharp knife) and some parsley leaves. Sprinkle with fleur de sel and serve immediately.

Tip | For egg recipes, always buy organic and/or extra-fresh ones. And before using in this recipe, leave the eggs overnight in the fridge; this will make them denser and easier to place in the turmeric cream.

Good to know | To make brown butter, put the butter in a frying pan, melt it, then let it bubble and colour lightly. That's it!

For 4
Preparation time: 20 min
Cooking time: 10 min

} Sardine rillettes with whisky and cauliflower cream

This recipe is quick yet sophisticated. Combining sardines with cauliflower is really different and the whisky adds a bit of 'oomph'. Try it!

The sardine rillettes

6 large canned sardines
100 g/3½ oz salted butter
2 tablespoons whisky
30 ml/1 fl oz double or whipping
 (heavy) cream

The cauliflower cream

200 g/7 oz cauliflower
85 ml/2¾ fl oz double (heavy) cream
fine salt

The melba toast

6 slices white bread
50 g/1¾ oz clarified butter (see p. 16)

The vinaigrette

splash of sherry vinegar
3 tablespoons olive oil
sprig of coriander (cilantro)
fine salt, fleur de sel, freshly
 ground pepper

1 ~ Sardine rillettes

Lightly crush the drained sardines with a fork. Blend them in a blender or food processor with the softened salted butter and the whisky, then press through a sieve. Whip the cream and delicately fold it through the sardine mixture.

2 ~ The cauliflower cream

Reserve a few of the cauliflower florets and chop them finely. Cook the rest of the cauliflower in salted boiling water until tender, then drain. Blend until smooth, then add half of the cream. Whip the remaining half of the cream until stiff, then gently fold into the cauliflower purée.

3 ~ The melba toast

Use the rim of a small glass to cut out 12 circles from the bread slices. Brush with butter, then bake for 5 minutes in an oven preheated to 180°C (350°F; gas mark 4) until golden. (See step-by-step method on p. 30.)

4 ~ Plating up

At the very last minute before serving, arrange alternate layers of melba toast, cauliflower cream and rillettes in a stack, finishing with a melba toast. Mix the chopped cauliflower with the vinaigrette (made by whisking together the vinegar and olive oil) and the coriander, then place this on top of the last melba toast. Season.

Making it even better | Buy fresh sardines and get the fishmonger to fillet them. Fry the fillets in olive oil for a few minutes and leave to cool, then follow the recipe as above.

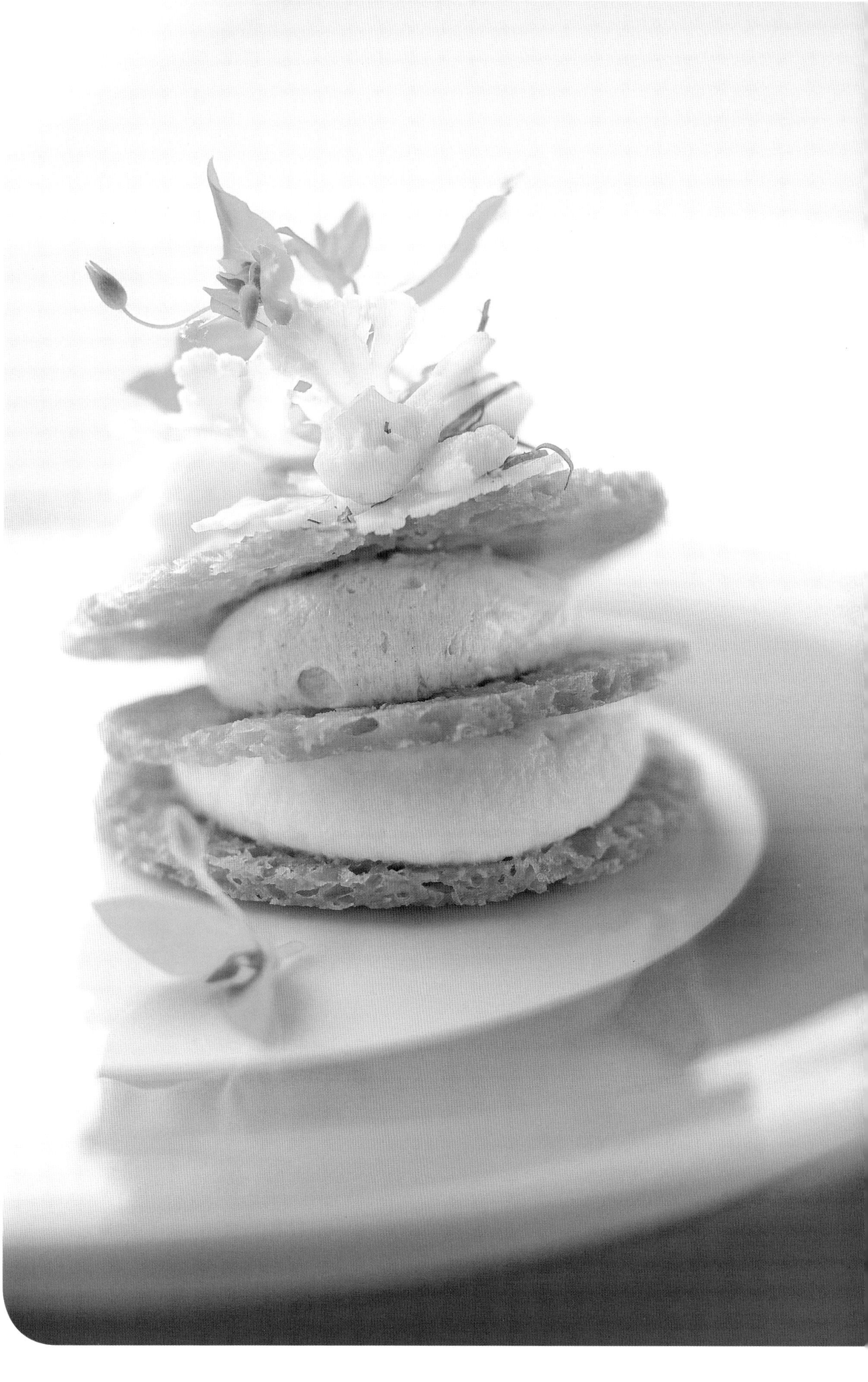

How to make melba toast

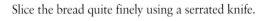

1

Slice the bread quite finely using a serrated knife.

2

Using a pastry cutter (or the rim of a small glass), cut out circles from each slice of bread, avoiding the crust.

3

Brush the bread circles with melted or clarified butter (see p. 16). Be careful not to use too much, or the melba toast will be greasy.

4

Put the buttered melba toast on a baking tray, then cover with a silicone baking mat or, if you don't have one, a sheet of baking parchment.

5

Put another baking sheet on top of the parchment. This is to keep the melba toasts flat, stopping them from puffing up in the oven and losing their shape.

6

Bake in an oven preheated to 180°C (350°F; gas mark 4) for 5–8 minutes. Remove the baking sheet from the oven and transfer the melba toast to a plate or wire rack to cool.

For 4
Preparation time: 30 min
Marinating time: 3 h
Cooking time: 5 min (petits pois)
+ 8 min (salmon)

}

Fillet of marinated salmon with petits pois and wasabi mousseline

In this recipe, the salmon is cooked in oil in the same way as for confit, a method that cooks the flesh evenly at a low temperature, leaving it incredibly soft. Don't worry that the fish will become too oily; the oil doesn't soak into the fish.

The salmon

4 salmon fillets
2 tablespoons fine salt
150 ml/5 fl oz olive oil
1 lemongrass stalk
10 g/⅓ oz fresh ginger

The petits pois and wasabi mousseline

600 g/1 lb 5 oz petits pois
150 ml/5 fl oz vegetable stock, chilled
  (see step-by-step method on p. 126)
small knob of wasabi
fine salt, freshly ground pepper
  and fleur de sel

The cooking oil

500 ml/18 fl oz grapeseed oil
1 lemongrass stalk
10 g/⅓ oz fresh ginger

1 ~ The salmon marinade

Sprinkle the salmon fillets with the fine salt and leave to rest for 6 minutes, then rinse in cold water. Mix the olive oil with the roughly chopped lemongrass and ginger. Immerse the salmon fillets in this marinade, then refrigerate for 3 hours so they fully absorb the flavours.

2 ~ The petits pois and wasabi mousseline

While the salmon is marinating, cook the petits pois in salted boiling water for 5 minutes (they should be very soft), then refresh by immersing them in a bowl of water and ice. Drain the peas, then blend with the well-chilled vegetable stock to make a smooth purée. Keep to one side.

3 ~ Cooking the fish

Put the oil and spices into a saucepan and heat to 60°C/140°F (the oil should be hot, but not bubbling). Carefully submerge the fillets and leave for 8 minutes, maintaining the oil at the same temperature.

4 ~ Finishing off

While the salmon is cooking, warm the petits pois mousseline over a gentle heat, then stir in the wasabi. Season. Serve with the drained salmon, dressed with a little fleur de sel.

Suggestions for garnish | *Decorate the salmon fillets with a few pea shoots or some rocket leaves.*

For 4
Preparation time: 20 min
Cooking time: 30 min

My spaghetti bolognese

This is a very personal take on spaghetti bolognese... unlike in the traditional version, I don't mix the meat with the tomato sauce. If you can find some, use beef (beefsteak) tomatoes because their firm, well-flavoured flesh works perfectly.

The tomato concassé

2 spring onions (scallions)
splash of olive oil
4 tomatoes
sprig of thyme
1 small bay leaf
4 basil leaves + extra for decoration
salt and freshly ground pepper

The meat

4 spring onions (scallions)
splash of olive oil
15 g/½ oz butter
250 g/8½ oz chopped raw beef
½ bunch of coriander (cilantro)
20 g/¾ oz grated Parmesan + some
  slivers for decoration
fine salt, freshly ground pepper

The spaghetti

400 g/14 oz spaghetti
splash of olive oil
2 teaspoons coarse salt

1 ~ The tomato concassé

Finely slice the spring onions, then cook them in the olive oil for 2 minutes without letting them colour. Add the peeled and diced tomatoes (see step-by-step method on p. 22). Stir well, then add the thyme, bay leaf and basil leaves. Leave to cook, uncovered, for 20–30 minutes over a gentle heat, so that the tomatoes release all their liquid and it evaporates to make a thick sauce. Check the seasoning. (See step-by-step method on p. 50.)

2 ~ The meat

Brown the finely sliced spring onions in a little olive oil and the butter for 6–8 minutes, until they are a lovely coppery colour, then leave to cool. Mix with the meat, coriander and Parmesan, then season with fine salt and freshly ground pepper. Form into round patties and cook in a frying pan with a little olive oil, turning halfway through the cooking time. Remove from the pan and put on a plate.

3 ~ The spaghetti

Cook the pasta for 7–9 minutes in boiling salted water (or as instructed on the packet). Drain, then refresh in cold water to prevent it sticking together, and mix with a little olive oil.

4 ~ Plating up

Put the cooked meat patties onto plates, top with the spaghetti, then spoon over some tomato concassé. Decorate with basil leaves and slivers of Parmesan.

Spicing it up! | *If you like a bit of heat, add some spices to the meat – such as cumin, chilli, crushed coriander seeds or cardamom – before shaping the patties.*

For 4
Preparation time: 30 min
Cooking time: 20 min
Chilling time: several hours
Freezing time: several hours

}

Saint-Marcellin cheese croquettes

These cromesquis croquettes belong to the great French culinary tradition. I love to tweak and adjust the recipe, as I have here, with cheese – I think this method is quite special.

The béchamel sauce

25 g/1 oz butter
25 g/1 oz plain (all-purpose) flour
250 ml/9 fl oz milk
salt

The cromesquis croquettes

7 gelatine leaves
2 Saint-Marcellin cheeses,
  rinds removed
65 ml/2¼ fl oz cream
oil for deep-frying

'English-style' breadcrumbs

200 g/7 oz plain (all-purpose) flour
5 eggs
500 g/1 lb 2 oz breadcrumbs
25 g/1 oz salt
1 teaspoon ground cumin

1 ~ The béchamel sauce

Put the butter and flour in a saucepan over a gentle heat and cook for 10 minutes, stirring, then whisk in the milk. Cook until the sauce thickens, then season.

2 ~ The cromesquis croquettes

Soak the gelatine in cold water. Heat the Saint-Marcellin cheeses with the cream in a saucepan, then add the drained and squeezed-out gelatine leaves. Off the heat, stir in the béchamel, then sieve the sauce and pour into hemispherical moulds. Leave to set for several hours in the fridge.

3 ~ The moulds

Unmould the hemispheres and stick them together in pairs, to create round, smooth spheres, then freeze them.

4 ~ 'English-style' breadcrumbs

Put the flour in a shallow bowl, half the beaten eggs in another, half the breadcrumbs with a little salt in a third, the rest of the beaten eggs in a fourth and the remaining breadcrumbs mixed with the cumin in a fifth. Dip the still-frozen cromesquis into each of the bowls in turn, in the order above, coating them thoroughly.

5 ~ Cooking the cromesquis

Deep-fry the frozen cromesquis for 4–5 minutes at 180°C/350°F. Shake off the excess oil, drain them briefly on kitchen paper, then sprinkle with fine salt and serve immediately.

Tip | To find out if the oil is at the right temperature, drop a cromesqui (or a small piece of potato) in the oil: it should start frying immediately without colouring too quickly.

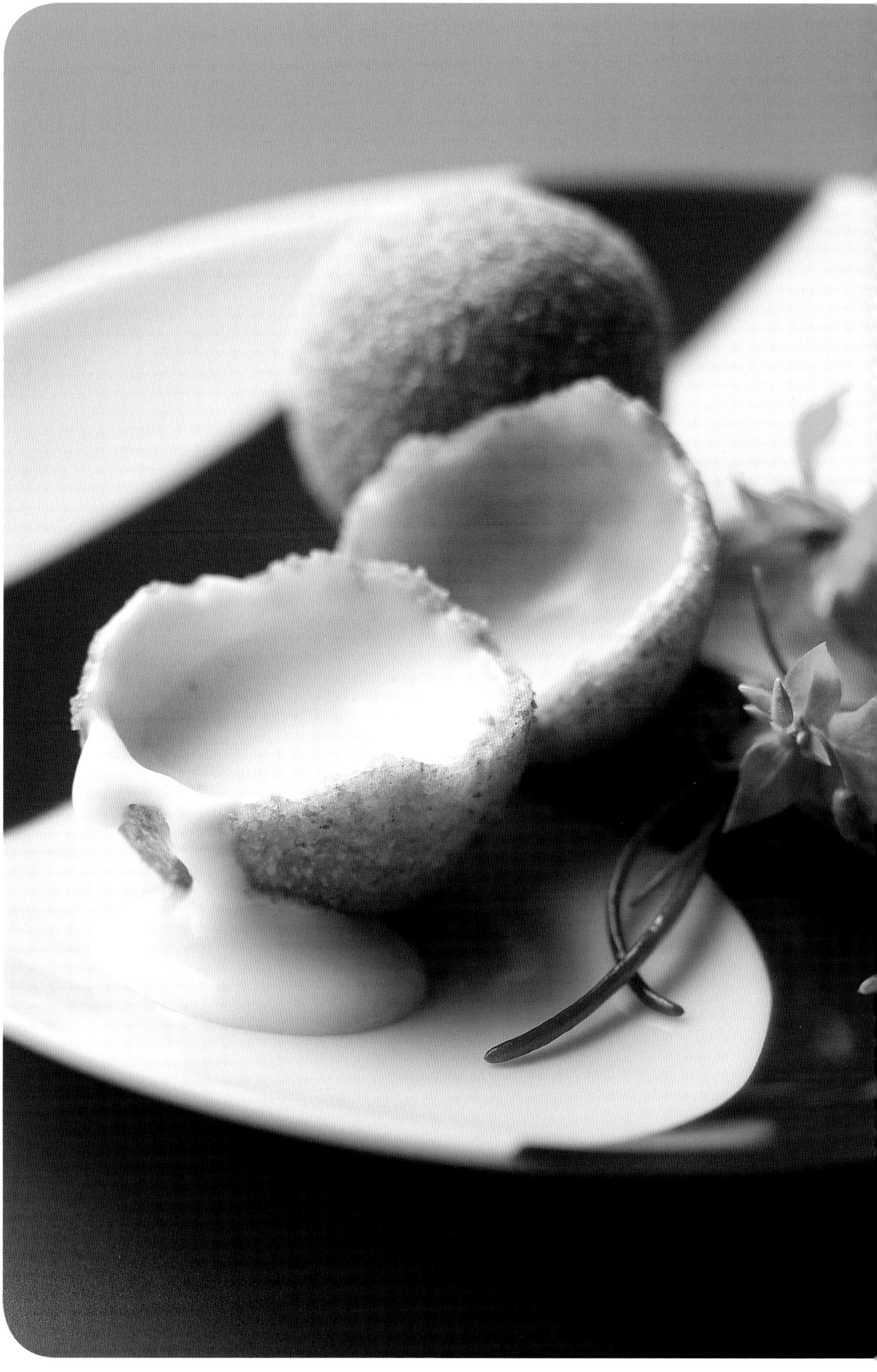

For 4
Preparation time: 30 min
Cooking time: 40 min

Cream of chestnut soup with mild spices and seasonal mushrooms

Finely blended then cooked in vegetable stock, chestnuts make an absolutely delicious cream soup. Out of season you could use frozen or vacuum-packed chestnuts.

The vegetable stock

1 carrot
1 onion
1 leek
1 celery stalk
sprig of thyme
1 small bay leaf
5 white peppercorns
1 clove

The chestnut cream

1 shallot
50 g/1¾ oz salted butter
500 g/1 lb 2 oz raw chestnuts,
    shelled and peeled
mild spices: star anise, cardamom,
    fresh ginger and Szechuan pepper
500 ml/18 fl oz single (pouring) cream

The mushrooms

350 g/12 oz mousseron mushrooms
    or ceps, whatever is in season
1 shallot
1 tablespoon finely shredded parsley
fine salt, freshly ground pepper

1 ~ The vegetable stock

Peel, trim and roughly chop the vegetables. Put them into a large saucepan with the rest of the stock ingredients. Cover with 2 litres/3½ pints of cold water and bring to the boil, then leave to cook very slowly for 40 minutes. Strain through a fine sieve.

2 ~ The chestnut cream

Cook the trimmed and finely sliced shallot in the butter. Add the chestnuts and continue to cook for another 5 minutes, without letting the shallots or chestnuts colour too much. Add the vegetable stock and spices tied in muslin (cheesecloth), just like a bouquet garni. Cover and cook for 40 minutes. Remove the bag of spices, then add the cream. Simmer for 5 minutes before blending until smooth.

3 ~ Finishing off

Fry the mushrooms with the finely chopped shallot and a little salt and pepper, then add the parsley. Put the sautéed mushrooms in the bottom of a serving bowl and pour in the hot chestnut soup. Season to taste and serve immediately.

Tip | I have deliberately not specified how much spice to use – it's up to you! If you want a delicate fragrance, use only a little of each and leave them to infuse for less time. Be careful with cardamom as it has quite a strong flavour, and use fresh not ground ginger. Try adapting the recipe to the season: so in spring, for example, try this soup with girolles and morels; then, in autumn, use ceps and chanterelles.

For 4
Preparation time: 30 min
Infusing time: 30 min
Cooking time: 40 min

Veal kidneys with gin and pepper

Gin is marvellous in cooking, particularly with offal or game. When cooking kidneys be careful not to overdo them: they should remain a little pink.

The confit shallots

8 shallots
large knob of salted butter
pinch of caster (superfine) sugar
fine salt, freshly ground pepper

The pepper sauce

2 pinches of roughly crushed
  white pepper
20 roughly crushed green peppercorns
1 teaspoon roughly crushed
  black pepper
10 roughly crushed juniper berries
200 ml/7 fl oz single (pouring) cream

The veal kidneys

2 large veal kidneys, fat and sinew
  removed, cut into large pieces
large knob of salted butter
100 ml/3½ fl oz gin
fine salt, fleur de sel, cracked
  peppercorns

1 ~ The confit shallots

Peel and trim the shallots and put them on a piece of foil big enough to wrap them up. Dot with butter and sprinkle with salt and sugar. Wrap the foil around them and crimp the edges together to make a parcel. Cook in an oven preheated to 180°C (350°F; gas mark 4) for 20–30 minutes. (See step-by-step method on p. 42.)

2 ~ The pepper sauce

Put all the ingredients in a saucepan and simmer for 2 minutes. Cover the pan, take off the heat and leave the sauce to infuse for 20–30 minutes.

3 ~ The veal kidneys

Season the kidneys with a little salt. Melt the butter in a large frying pan (at least 28 cm/11 in wide) over a high heat until it foams. Add the kidneys and brown all over for 2–3 minutes, no longer. Leave to drain on kitchen paper. Pour out the butter from the frying pan, add the gin and let it bubble for 10 seconds. Add the pepper sauce and simmer for a further minute.

4 ~ Plating up

Finely slice the kidneys and place on the plates, then top with the confit shallots and the sauce. Sprinkle with cracked peppercorns and fleur de sel.

Tip | *Did you know that there is more than one type of pepper? For example, have you heard of Java pepper, with its complex, lingering taste; Sarawak pepper, which is both gentle and hot; or Vietnamese black pepper, which tastes almost smoked? Always have more than one sort in your kitchen, and your cooking will be more varied and sophisticated.*

41

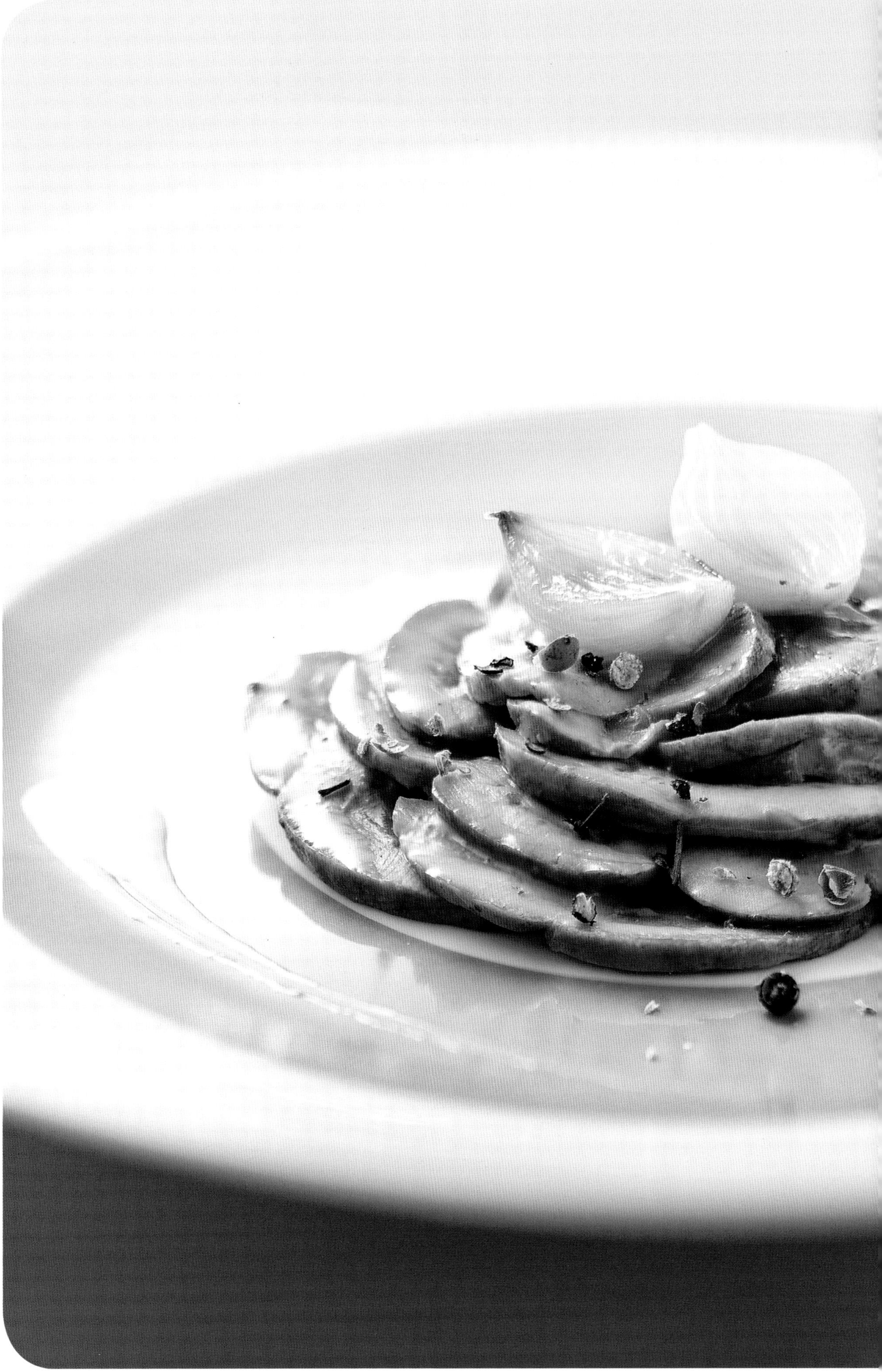

How to cook vegetables 'en papillote'

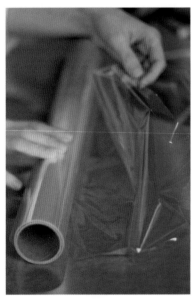

1

Cut the vegetables into slices about 1 cm/½ in thick. You can use peppers, pumpkin or carrots, as well as onions.

2

Cut a 30 cm x 20 cm/12 in x 8 in rectangle of transparent cooking film and place it on a work surface. If you can't get hold of specialist cooking film, use baking parchment or foil.

3

Place the vegetable slices on the foil, keeping them well spaced.

4

Put a dot of butter on top of each vegetable slice, then lightly season with salt and pepper.

5

Cover the seasoned vegetable slices with another sheet of cooking film.

6

Fold the edges of the two pieces of film together, then staple them to create a seal that will keep the flavours of the vegetables inside the papillote parcel. Put the papillote onto a baking sheet.

7

Cook in an oven preheated to 180°C (350°F; gas mark 4) for about 15–20 minutes; the steam created by the vegetables as they cook will make the parcel puff up.

8

Open the papillote with the tip of a knife (be careful – the steam will be hot). The vegetables will be perfectly cooked with a beautiful flavour.

CUTTING EDGE

My cooking style changes continually. I never
think there is a final version of a recipe, and I use
my intuition and imagination in everything I do.
Right now, for example, I am using aniseed
and tarragon in a lot of recipes. I'm also enjoying
working with frothy textures, which is why you
will find a lot of foams in this book. Cooking
is dynamic, a process that is never complete.
So let yourself be carried away by the ideas I give
you and, above all, feel free to experiment
and make them your own. In cooking, freedom
is the key to success.

For 4
Preparation time: 1 h
Resting time: 24 h + 30 min

}

Tomato and mozzarella revisited

Give this new version of an old classic a try: it combines a light mozzarella mousse with tomatoes seasoned with balsamic vinegar. If you can, use buffalo mozzarella, which is softer and has a much better flavour than other types.

The mozzarella foam

200 ml/7 fl oz milk
150 ml/5 fl oz cream
¼ bunch of basil
170 g/6 oz buffalo mozzarella
pinch of agar-agar
splash of olive oil
fine salt, black pepper

The tomatoes

5 tomatoes (red, yellow and green, if possible)
2 tablespoons white balsamic vinegar
6 tablespoons olive oil

The tomato jelly

150 g/5½ oz tomato seeds, from the 5 tomatoes
2 gelatine leaves, soaked in cold water

The garnish

1 ball mozzarella
2 tablespoons toasted pine nuts
4 sprigs of basil
fleur de sel

Equipment

siphon (optional)

1 ~ The mozzarella foam

The day before, infuse the milk and cream with the crushed basil for 24 hours in the fridge. The next day, heat the infused milk mixture, then add the mozzarella and agar-agar and stir to melt. Blend, then sieve. Season with fine salt and a splash of olive oil. Pour into the siphon and insert 2 gas canisters. Chill the siphon while preparing the rest of the recipe.

2 ~ The tomatoes

Immerse the tomatoes in boiling water for a few seconds, then in iced water for another few seconds. Peel the tomatoes and cut into 'petal' quarters, then remove and reserve the seeds. (See step-by-step method on p. 22.)

3 ~ The tomato jelly

Heat 50 g/1¾ oz of the tomato seeds over gentle heat and dissolve the gelatine in the juices. Stir in the remaining cold tomato seeds, then pour the mixture into glasses and leave to set in a cool place for 30 minutes.

4 ~ Serving

Season the tomato petals with balsamic vinegar and olive oil. Place in 4 glasses, layering them with seasoned slices of mozzarella. Put the foam on top, scatter over the chopped pine nuts and finish with sprigs of basil.

If you don't have a siphon | Put 170 g/6 oz mozzarella, 150 ml/5 fl oz cream, some basil leaves and a splash of olive oil into a saucepan. Season with salt and pepper, bring to the boil and then blend until very smooth. Strain the mixture through a very fine sieve, a few times if necessary, until you have a silky infused cream. Chill. Beat the chilled mixture for a few minutes, either by hand or in a mixer, until it thickens (but not for too long, or it will separate and become grainy). Add a few leaves of just-chopped basil and use as instructed in step 4 of the recipe.

Tip | To make sure gelatine dissolves properly, first soak it in cold water then press it between your hands to squeeze out any excess water. This makes it swell then soften, which makes it easier to use.

47

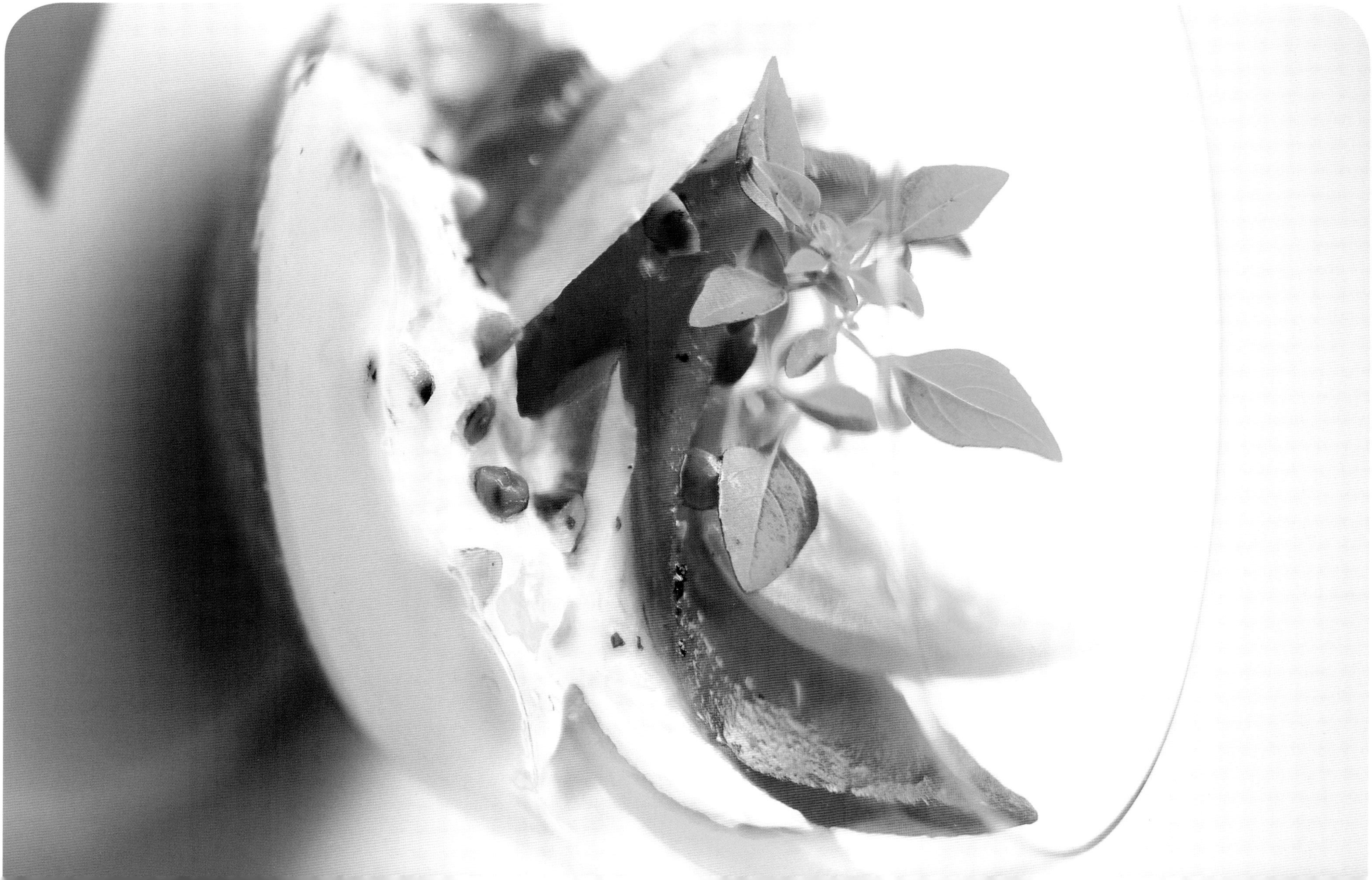

For 4
Preparation time: 1 h
Infusing time: 30 min
Cooking time: 5 min (pastry)
+ 3 min (egg)
+ 30 min (concassé)

}

The new pissaladière, with crunchy fennel and onion pickles

Here is my very personal take on the famous pissaladière. You will notice that I love taking classic recipes and modernizing them. Use the best-quality puff pastry you can find for this.

4 extra-fresh quail eggs
1 fennel bulb

The onion pickles

1 tablespoon grenadine syrup
100 ml/3½ fl oz distilled white
   vinegar
50 ml/1¾ fl oz water
50 g/1¾ oz sugar
2 Cévennes onions

The puff pastry

4 squares of puff pastry

The marinated anchovies

12 fresh anchovies (6 fillets
   per person)
1 teaspoon wild aniseed
2 tablespoons olive oil
2 teaspoons distilled white vinegar
fine salt

The tomato concassé

8 large spring onions (scallions)
splash of olive oil
3 tomatoes
sprig of thyme
1 small bay leaf
1 clove of wet (spring) garlic, unpeeled
pinch of fine salt

1 ~ The onion pickles

Mix all the ingredients except the onions in a saucepan and bring to a simmer, then remove from the heat and leave to infuse for 15 minutes. Peel the onions and slice as thinly as possible. Bring the pickling liquid back to the boil, then pour it over the sliced onions. Chill and leave to pickle (you can keep this in the fridge for up to a week – the longer you leave it, the softer the onions will be).

2 ~ The puff pastry and the marinated anchovies

Cut out a circle from each puff pastry square. Prick the pastry circles all over with a fork and place them first between two sheets of baking parchment, then between two wire grills. Bake in the oven at 190°C (375°F; gas mark 5) for 5 minutes, then transfer to kitchen paper to cool. Marinate the anchovies with the aniseed, oil, vinegar and a little salt for 10–15 minutes.

3 ~ The tomato concassé

Finely slice the spring onions, then soften them in the olive oil for 2–3 minutes, without letting them colour. Add the peeled, deseeded and diced tomatoes (see step-by-step method on p. 22), mix together well, then reduce to get rid of the surplus tomato juice. Add the herbs, garlic and salt, then cover and cook over a gentle heat for 20–30 minutes. Keep reducing the concassé until it is quite thick. (See step-by-step method on p. 50.)

4 ~ Finishing off

Boil the quail eggs for 3 minutes, then peel, keeping only the yolk. Spoon the tomato concassé onto the pastry and arrange the marinated anchovies on top. Add the onion pickles, then put an egg yolk in the middle and decorate with thin slices of raw fennel.

How to make tomato concassé

1

First, peel and finely slice the onions with a very sharp knife.

2

Heat the olive oil in a frying pan or saucepan, then add the onions. Cook over a medium heat, stirring all the time with a spoon.

3

Next, add the diced tomatoes and mix gently.

4

Add the herbs and spices, season and mix again.

5

Cut out a circle of baking parchment and place it on top of the tomatoes. You can also use a lid, but don't completely cover the pan, because some of the steam needs to escape. Leave to cook over a gentle heat for 15–20 minutes.

6

Uncover the concassé and cook until most of the liquid has evaporated. Remove from the heat and leave to cool.

Brown shrimp and citrus verrine

Small brown shrimp are, in my opinion, much better and so much tastier than the more usual and easy-to-find pink prawns. They are harder to peel, but their delicate flavour is unique. I particularly like their iodine tang, which lends freshness to this dish. Here, I've served them with a celeriac remoulade and an orange foam...

The mayonnaise

1 egg yolk
1 teaspoon mustard
200 ml/7 fl oz groundnut (peanut) oil
1 teaspoon white wine vinegar
fine salt, freshly ground pepper

The orange foam

200 ml/7 fl oz double (heavy) cream
1 teaspoon agar-agar
200 ml/7 fl oz orange juice
25 ml/1 fl oz grapeseed oil
fine salt, freshly ground pepper

The brown shrimp remoulade

100 g/3½ oz shelled brown shrimp
1 orange, peeled and quartered
200 g/7 oz celeriac
fine salt, freshly ground pepper

Equipment

siphon (optional)

1 ~ The mayonnaise

In a large bowl, mix together the egg yolk, pepper and mustard. Slowly add the oil, little by little, whisking all the time. When the mayonnaise is thick and glossy and all the oil has been incorporated, whisk in the wine vinegar and a little salt. Check and adjust the seasoning if necessary.

2 ~ The orange foam

Put the cream and agar-agar into a saucepan and bring to the boil, whisking to dissolve the agar-agar, then add the rest of the ingredients. Add a little salt and pepper. Leave to cool for a moment, then pour the mixture into a siphon and insert 2 gas cartridges. Chill in the fridge while you finish the rest of the recipe.

3 ~ The shrimp remoulade

Mix the brown shrimp with the diced orange flesh. Peel and finely grate the celeriac. Add the mayonnaise to make a creamy mixture. Check the seasoning.

4 ~ Serving

Put the remoulade in the bottom of 4 glasses and add the orange foam. Grind over some pepper, then serve immediately.

If you don't have a siphon | Heat the orange juice in a saucepan to reduce it by half, then mix it into the cream. Lightly salt the mixture, then chill thoroughly. Once the cream is cold, whip until fluffy, then use as instructed in step 4 of the recipe.

What is agar-agar? | Agar-agar is a red algae extract that is used as a gelling agent, and is particularly useful for creating different textures like jellies and hot foams. You should be able to find it in health food shops or online.

Making it even better | Heat 250 ml/9 fl oz orange juice, then add a gelatine leaf that has been pre-soaked in cold water. Stir to dissolve, then leave to cool. Pour this jelly into 4 glasses, then chill until set. Serve the remoulade on top of the light orange jelly.

55

For 4
Preparation time: 5–6 min
Cooking time: 20 min

}

Seared red tuna with warm vodka and lemon foam

Vodka and lemon go together very well... and not just in drinks!
I often use this pairing in a very light mousse or in a beurre monté.
It's a combination that works very well with tuna but also with other
fish, such as sea bass.

The tuna

4 x 100 g/3½ oz loin fillets of red tuna
olive oil
fine salt, freshly ground pepper

The foam

50 ml/1¾ fl oz lemon juice
100 ml/3½ fl oz celery juice
50 ml/1¾ fl oz vodka
10 g/⅓ oz sugar
3 gelatine leaves, soaked in cold water
fine salt, freshly ground pepper

The garnish and finishing off

3 teaspoons olive oil
8 celery leaves
fleur de sel

Equipment

siphon (optional)

1 ~ Preparing the tuna

Get the fishmonger to prepare the tuna – be sure to ask for thick loin fillets.

2 ~ The foam

Put all the ingredients except the gelatine in a saucepan. Heat the mixture and dissolve the drained and squeezed-out gelatine leaves in it. Check the seasoning, then pour into a siphon, insert 2 gas cartridges and chill until 30 minutes before serving.

3 ~ Cooking the tuna

Season the fillets, then cook in a little olive oil for 1 minute on each side, making sure each side takes some colour. Leave to cool for a minute on a plate, then slice finely.

4 ~ Plating up

Overlap the tuna slices on the plates, drizzle on a few drops of olive oil and scatter with fleur de sel. Decorate with the celery leaves and serve the foam on the side.

If you don't have a siphon | You really need a siphon to make this warm gelatine-based foam. But here is another recipe to serve with the fish, which is very easy to make and delicious:

Vodka-citron beurre monté | Juice 3 celery hearts, then put the juice in a saucepan with a squeeze of lime juice and a tablespoon of vodka. Bring to the boil and reduce by half, stirring often. Add a tablespoon of double (heavy) cream then, little by little, whisk in 75 g/2¾ oz cold diced butter, beating the mixture well after every addition. Put into a blender with another 75 g/2¾ oz butter and blend thoroughly. Season and serve immediately.

The perfect accompaniment | Trim and peel 4 stalks of celery to remove the strings. Cut the celery into thin sticks, then cook in salted boiling water for 5 minutes. Refresh in cold water, drain and then season with salt, pepper and a little olive oil.

For 4
Preparation time: 25 min
Cooking time: 7 min
(duck breasts)
+ 15 min (compote)

}

Roast duck breast with black cherry compote

A few cherries transform a simple duck breast into a sophisticated and original dish. If you can, use several different cherry varieties for the compote.

4 x 180–200 g/6¼–7 oz duck breasts
fine salt, fleur de sel and freshly
　ground pepper

The blinis

125 g/4½ oz plain (all-purpose) flour
2 eggs
10 g/⅓ oz butter + a little extra
　for cooking the blinis
200 ml/7 fl oz milk
3 tablespoons walnut oil
pinch of fine salt
100 g/3½ oz canned sweetcorn
2 egg whites
oil for frying

The cherry compote

100 g/3½ oz cherries + 4 extra
　for decoration
2 knobs of salted butter
2 tablespoons balsamic vinegar

1 ～ The duck breasts

Remove some of the fat and any sinews or nerves from the duck breasts (or get your butcher to do it). Slash the remaining fat in a criss-cross pattern with a sharp knife, then refrigerate while cooking the blinis and compote.

2 ～ The blinis

Put the flour, eggs, butter, milk, walnut oil and salt into a blender and blend until smooth, then strain through a fine sieve. When ready to cook, add the sweetcorn and the whisked egg whites to the batter. Heat a little oil and butter in a non-stick frying pan and then, when foaming, pour in small circles of batter. Cook over a gentle heat for 3–4 minutes, turning the blinis once or twice as necessary.

3 ～ The cherry compote

Wash the cherries, then remove the stalks and stones. Sauté the cherries for 2 minutes in a frying pan with half the butter. Pour in the balsamic vinegar and leave to cook over a gentle heat for 10 minutes. Take off the heat, then beat in the rest of the butter.

4 ～ Cooking the duck breasts

Season the duck breasts, then brown them in a grill pan or frying pan, starting with the skin side for about 2 minutes. Turn over and brown the meat for 2 minutes. Finish them off in an oven preheated to 180°C (350°F; gas mark 4), skin-side up, for 7–8 minutes. Remove from the oven and leave to rest for 4–5 minutes.

5 ～ Plating up

Finely slice the duck breasts and arrange on the plates. Add a spoonful of cherry compote and a small stack of blinis topped with a cherry. Scatter a little fleur de sel on the meat.

Tip | *Make sure enough fat is removed from the duck: you need to leave a thin layer, only about 2–3 mm/⅛ in. This means the duck breast will still taste delicious but won't be quite so heavy.*

For 4
Preparation time: 20 min
Cooking time: 1 h 20 min

Pork fillet
with red pepper confit
and pineapple

Red pepper confit and pineapple is a sweet-and-sour combination that I particularly love – a classic, but also a little bit different. Cooking the peppers like this removes all of their harshness while keeping their lovely sweet flavour. To make it really vibrant, try using different-coloured peppers: red, green, yellow and orange. You can also serve this with veal or chicken.

The confit peppers

2 red (bell) peppers
splash of olive oil
2 sprigs of thyme
2 garlic cloves

The pineapple

½ pineapple
8 sage flowers
fine salt, freshly ground pepper

The pork fillet

1 x 600 g/1 lb 5 oz pork fillet
splash of groundnut (peanut) oil
20 g/¾ oz salted butter
4 spring onions (scallions)
fine salt, freshly ground pepper

1 ~ The confit peppers

Halve the peppers lengthways and remove the stalk, seeds and white pith. Put the pepper halves on a sheet of foil big enough to wrap them in. Season with salt and pepper, then pour over the olive oil and place a sprig of thyme and half a garlic clove in each pepper half. Close up the foil to make a parcel, sealing the edges so that none of the juices can leak out. Put on a baking tray and cook in an oven preheated to 100°C (200°F; gas mark ¼) for about an hour. Remove from the oven, then open the parcel and cut the peppers into quite thin slices.

2 ~ The pineapple

Peel and trim the pineapple, removing all the brown skin, then dice the fruit. Mix the diced pineapple with the sage flowers. Chill.

3 ~ Cooking the pork fillet

Brown the seasoned meat in the oil and butter for 5 minutes in an ovenproof frying pan or flameproof casserole dish. Add the chopped spring onions and cook for 2 minutes before adding the peppers. Transfer to an oven preheated to 180°C (350°F; gas mark 4) and cook for 8 minutes. Add the pineapple and continue to cook for another 10 minutes. Season to taste.

4 ~ Plating up

Cut the pork into slices and serve with the confit peppers and cooking juices.

Tip | Try not to overcook pork, as it quickly dries out, especially the fillet. And always let meat rest before serving: this allows the cooking juices to redistribute themselves, resulting in meat that's moister and much more tender.

SOMETHING SPECIAL

When you have guests, it's good to know
how to pull out all the stops, and if ever there was
a time when it's worth making something a bit
more complicated, this is it. Some of the recipes
in this chapter come from my à la carte menu but
I have simplified them to make them a bit easier.
While they may require a bit more work, the results
will be worth it. In cooking, every effort pays off,
and it's so lovely when a recipe works and your
guests love it. That is the real heart of cookery –
and the reason we take such pains to get it right.

For 4
Preparation time: 40 min
Cooking time: 22 min
Infusing time: 30 min

}

Poached egg with tomato ketchup, capers and black olives

This might seem a little complicated but all the elements – the eggs, the foam and the ketchup – are actually very easy. And, what's more, you can prepare some of it, including the foam and the ketchup, in advance.

The tomato foam

1 kg/2¼ lb tomatoes
15 g/½ oz fresh galangal
1 gelatine leaf
fine salt, freshly ground black pepper

The tomato ketchup

2 tablespoons sugar
1 tablespoon runny honey
30 ml/1 fl oz white balsamic vinegar
250 g/8½ oz tomatoes
small knob of galangal
½ garlic clove
¼ bird's eye chilli
pinch of fine salt

The eggs and the garnish

4 extra-fresh eggs
50 ml/1¾ fl oz distilled white vinegar
100 g/3½ oz pitted black olives
2 tablespoons capers
fleur de sel

Equipment

siphon (optional)

1 ~ The tomato foam

Blend the chopped tomatoes, then strain through a very fine sieve. Heat the juices with the chopped galangal, then leave to infuse off the heat for 30 minutes. Soak the gelatine leaf in cold water for 5 minutes, then squeeze out and add to the infused juices, stirring to dissolve. Leave to cool, then season. Pour into the siphon, insert 2 gas cartridges and chill.

2 ~ The tomato ketchup

Melt the sugar and honey in a saucepan with the white balsamic vinegar. Bring to the boil and reduce by a third. Add all the other ingredients and cook over a gentle heat for 20 minutes. Leave to cool, then season to taste as required.

3 ~ Cooking the eggs

Crack the eggs into individual ramekins. Boil 1 litre/1¾ pints of water with the vinegar (but no salt). As soon as it simmers, stir briskly with a spoon, then slip in the eggs and cook for 2 minutes. Drain, immerse in iced water, then drain on kitchen paper (see step-by-step method on p. 64). Halve the olives and chop the capers.

4 ~ Serving

Put a tablespoon of ketchup in each bowl, place the egg in the middle, then scatter over the capers and olives. Finish off with the foam and a little fleur de sel.

If you don't have a siphon | Blend the chopped tomatoes, then strain through a very fine sieve. Heat the juice with the galangal and leave to infuse for 30 minutes. Soak the gelatine leaf in cold water for 5 minutes, then squeeze out and add to the infused juice, stirring to dissolve. Leave to cool, then season. Whisk 150 ml/5 fl oz chilled double (heavy) cream, then gently fold it into the mixture to make a mousse. Use as instructed in step 4 of the recipe.

Good to know| You can find galangal in Asian supermarkets. It is easy to recognize because it looks a bit like fresh ginger, though is paler in colour. Its flavour is very distinctive and sophisticated, yet also very powerful. You can also use it in soups and stocks.

Tip | Eggs for poaching must be extra-fresh: that way the white is very viscous and will envelop the yolk properly during the cooking.

How to poach eggs

1

Use very fresh eggs. Crack them into individual bowls – this makes it easier to tip the eggs into the hot water.

2

Heat a saucepan of water. Add a little distilled white vinegar but no salt. Taste the water (being careful not to burn yourself): you should be able to taste the vinegar.

3

Bring the vinegared water to the boil. Lower the heat so that the water just simmers, then stir it rapidly with a spoon to create a whirlpool effect.

4

Hold one of the egg bowls near the surface of the simmering water, then gently slide in the egg: it will start to set immediately. Leave to cook, still at a simmer, for 3–4 minutes.

5

Carefully lift out the eggs using a slotted spoon, then immerse in a bowl of iced water. Leave to cool for 2–3 minutes, no longer.

6

Drain the eggs and, using scissors, trim the rough edges to make lovely round poached eggs.

For 4
Preparation time: 30 min
Cooking time: 11 min

Mimolette cheese soufflé

The secret of a successful soufflé is the dish! It must be perfectly buttered so that the mixture slides over it, which means it will rise properly. Mimolette adds a much more interesting flavour than Gruyère or Cheddar – if possible, use a mature one that has been aged a little.

The soufflé mixture

50 g/1¾ oz salted butter
50 g/1¾ oz plain (all-purpose) flour
500 ml/18 fl oz milk
5 egg yolks
100 g/3½ oz grated Mimolette cheese
  + extra slivers for decoration
pinch of cumin seeds
50 g/1¾ oz melted butter
100 g/3½ oz fine breadcrumbs
8 egg whites
1 teaspoon cornflour (cornstarch)
fine salt, freshly ground pepper

The salad

4 handfuls of rocket (arugula)
3 tablespoons olive oil
1 tablespoon white balsamic vinegar
fine salt, freshly ground black pepper

1 ~ The soufflé

Melt the butter in a saucepan and add the flour. Cook, stirring, over a gentle heat for at least 2 minutes. Whisk in the milk to make a béchamel, then cook, stirring constantly, over a gentle heat for 2–3 minutes. Take off the heat and leave to cool for a few minutes, then mix in the beaten egg yolks, grated Mimolette and cumin. Season, then leave at room temperature while making the rest of the recipe.

2 ~ Preparing the dishes

Butter 4 individual soufflé dishes with the melted butter, then chill in the fridge until the butter is hard again. Repeat two or three times. Coat the inside of the buttered moulds with fine breadcrumbs, then invert and tap lightly to remove any excess. Preheat the oven to 180°C (350°F; gas mark 4). (See step-by-step method on p. 68.)

3 ~ Cooking the soufflés

Whisk the egg whites with the cornflour to form soft peaks, then gently fold them into the béchamel mixture. Fill the soufflé dishes three-quarters full using a tablespoon. Cook the soufflés in the oven for 11 minutes.

4 ~ The salad and serving

Season the rocket with oil, vinegar, salt and pepper. Put a sliver of Mimolette on top of each soufflé and serve with the rocket salad.

Tip | When making soufflés, don't make the common mistake of over-whisking the egg whites. You will find it harder to fold them into the cheese mixture – and their stiffness doesn't mean you have incorporated more air or that the soufflé will rise better. You just need to whisk the egg whites to soft peaks for the recipe to work.

How to butter soufflé dishes

1

Make some clarified butter: melt some butter over a gentle heat, without letting it boil, then remove from the heat and leave to rest for a few minutes at room temperature. Skim the froth off the surface and ladle out the clear golden liquid, leaving behind the white solids at the bottom.

2

Chill the soufflé dishes in the fridge, then use a brush to butter them with the melted butter. Put them back in the fridge until the butter hardens. Do this another two or three times.

3

Tip breadcrumbs into the dishes. It is best to use light-coloured, fine breadcrumbs, if possible.

4

Hold each dish in your hands on its side, then turn it so that the breadcrumbs completely coat the inside.

5

Turn the dish upside down and tap lightly, so any excess breadcrumbs fall out.

6

The surface of the dish is now completely covered with butter and breadcrumbs, which means the soufflé will rise freely, unhindered by the sides of the dish.

For 4
Preparation time: 25 min
Cooking time: 2 min

}

Duck liver
with seared melon

I've always thought that almonds and melon go well together, which is why I came up with this sweet-savoury recipe that I love. The melon adds a fruity sweetness that makes all the difference. Searing the melon quickly over a high heat, without really cooking it, gives it a completely unexpected flavour...

The melon

1 small melon (not too ripe)
8 fresh almonds

The duck liver

4 x 80–110 g/3–3¾ oz duck liver slices
fine salt, fleur de sel, freshly ground
  pepper

1 ~ The melon

Peel and deseed the melon, then cut eight 5 mm/¼ in slices from it. Cut these slices into rectangles. Blend the rest of the melon, then put the purée in a saucepan, bring to the boil and reduce until syrupy.

2 ~ The duck liver

Season the duck liver slices and remove any fat or sinew. Cook them over a high heat in a frying pan for 1–2 minutes, turning once or twice, depending on their thickness. Drain on kitchen paper, then keep warm in a low oven. Wipe out the frying pan, then add the melon rectangles and quickly sear over a high heat, turning them to colour both sides.

3 ~ Plating up

Place 2 melon rectangles on each plate and top with a warm duck liver slice. Dress with a little of the reduced melon purée. Scatter with fleur de sel and garnish with the fresh almonds.

More garnish ideas | Garnish with roughly chopped toasted almonds.

Making it even better | Serve the duck and melon with some delicious almond milk: combine 250 ml/9 fl oz cream, 250 ml/9 fl oz milk, a splash of amaretto, 125 g/4½ oz roasted almonds and a little salt and pepper in a saucepan, then simmer to reduce by three-quarters – you want quite a thick sauce.

Tip | Sear the liver without cooking it completely at the start. Then, when your guests sit down to eat, simply reheat it in the oven.

For 4
Preparation time: 40 min
Cooking time: 25 min
Infusing time: 10 min

}

Poached guinea fowl supremes with wakame seaweed cream

I love cooking with seaweed: it adds a distinctive flavour, unique texture and freshness to any dish. You should be able to find kombu and wakame in organic shops, but if you can only get salted wakame, remember to soak it for a few minutes to remove the excess salt.

The guinea fowl supremes

4 guinea fowl breasts
5 g/0.2 oz kombu
fine salt, freshly ground pepper

The wakame seaweed cream

200 ml/7 fl oz single (pouring) cream
8 g/0.3 oz kombu, in pieces
1 shallot
100 g/3½ oz unsalted butter
20 ml/¾ fl oz white wine
100 ml/3½ fl oz vegetable stock
  (see step-by-step method on p. 126)
8 g/0.3 oz wakame
fine salt, fleur de sel, freshly ground
  pepper

1 ~ The guinea fowl

Cut each guinea fowl breast widthways to make a pouch, then tuck a strip of kombu into each pouch and close up again. Season, then wrap individually in cling film and roll up into a sausage shape. Immerse in a pan of boiling water, then turn off the heat and leave to poach for 25 minutes.

2 ~ The wakame seaweed cream

Infuse the cream with the kombu for about 10 minutes – when the cream has a lovely seaweedy flavour, remove the kombu. In a small saucepan, soften the trimmed and sliced shallot in a small knob of butter without letting it colour. Add the white wine and bring to the boil, then add the vegetable stock and chopped wakame. Leave to simmer for a few minutes, then add the rest of the butter and whisk briskly with a hand-held whisk or stick blender. Pour in the infused cream and whisk or blend for a moment. Strain through a sieve, then season to taste.

3 ~ Plating up

Remove the cling film from the guinea fowl, then slice into beautiful escalopes. Pour over a little seaweed cream, sprinkle on some fleur de sel and serve immediately.

23

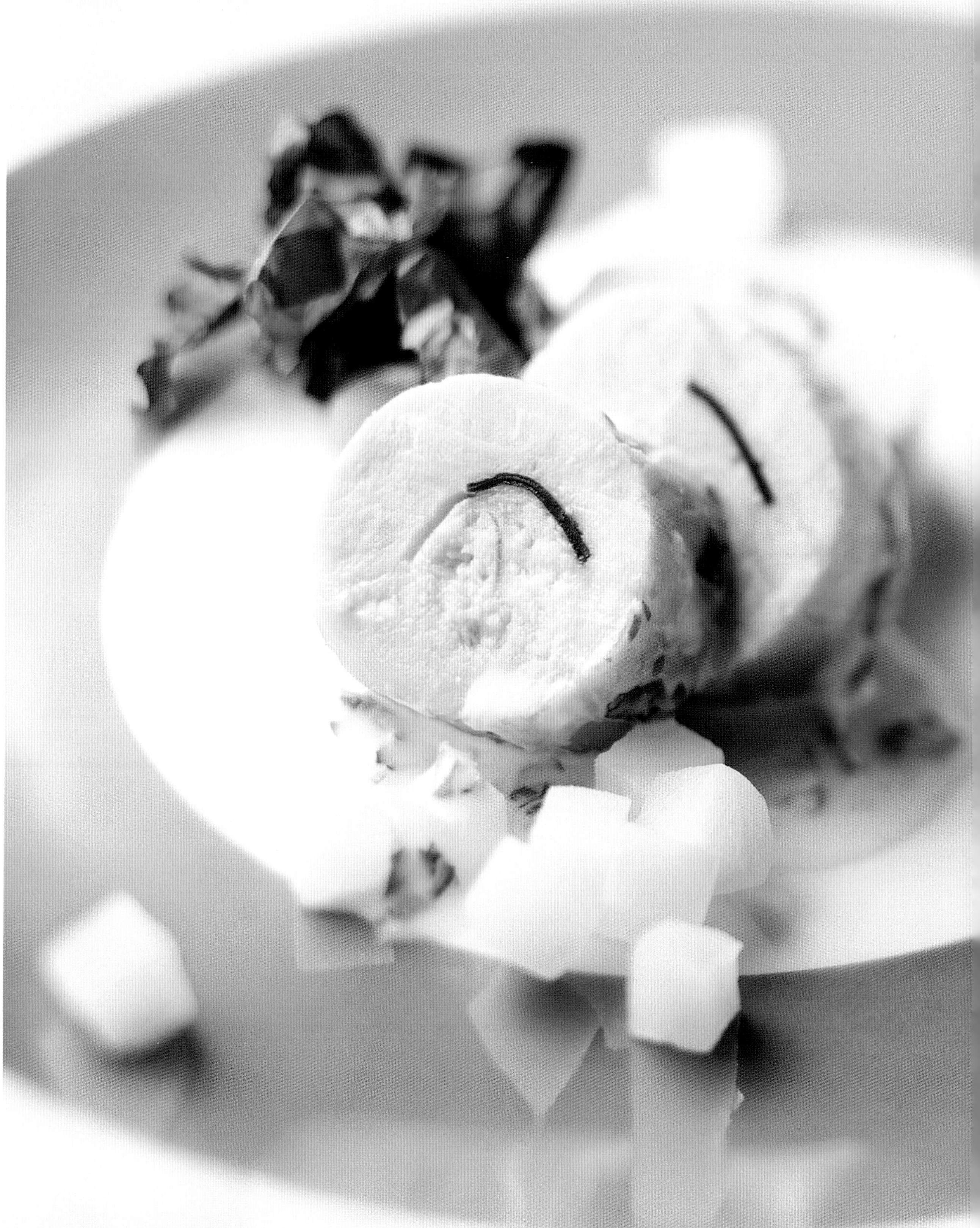

For 6
Preparation time: 25 min
Cooking time: 8 min

}

Pommes soufflées re-invented

There is nothing more delicious or more impressive than a plate of pommes soufflées. It's a very 'cheffy' recipe, but I think that anyone who loves cooking can make them. Pommes soufflés were one of my father's specialities: he would make them at the restaurant for customers' children. I ate them all the time when I was little...

1 kg/2¼ lb Agria potatoes,
  or other floury potato suitable
  for making chips
4 litres/7 pints groundnut (peanut)
  oil, for two oil baths at different
  temperatures
salt

Variations

curry
tandoori spices
paprika
herb salt

Equipment

cooking thermometer

1 ~ Preparing the potatoes

Wash, peel and trim the potatoes. Cut them into slices 3 mm/⅛ in thick, then rinse again and dry thoroughly on a clean tea towel.

2 ~ Cooking the potatoes

Immerse the dry potato slices in a deep-fryer heated to 140°C/275°F. Stir the oil continuously with a spoon or spatula until the potato slices begin to puff, about 5 minutes. Remove with a slotted spoon and immerse them in the second, hotter deep-fryer, heated to 180°C/350°F. Keep stirring, to make them puff up. (See step-by-step method on p. 76.)

3 ~ Finishing off

Remove the pommes soufflées from the oil, again with a slotted spoon, and drain on kitchen paper. Season with salt, then flavour with whatever you like – just dust the pommes soufflées with the spices or salt and toss gently, to avoid crushing them. Then eat them...

Tips |
– You can do the first round of frying in advance – then, when you're ready to eat, you only have to cook them once, in the 180°C/350°F oil.
– You can also freeze the potatoes after their first frying.
– Don't slice the potatoes too thickly, or they won't puff.
– Serve them as soon as they are cooked.
– Never cook these when there are children in the kitchen.
– Always use a dry, firm potato variety.

How to make pommes soufflées

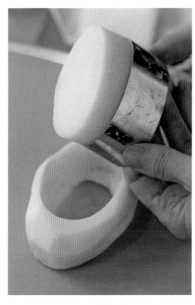

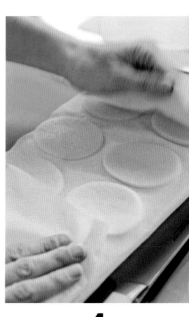

1

Peel and rinse the potatoes. Choose an oval pastry cutter that is slightly smaller than the potatoes.

2

Push the cutter into the potatoes to cut out beautiful neat ovals.

3

Using a mandoline or very sharp knife, cut the potato ovals into slices 3–4 mm/⅛ in thick.

4

Dry the potato slices with a clean tea towel.

5

Immerse the potato slices in a pan of deep-frying oil heated to 140°C/275°F, no hotter, and cook for about 5 minutes, stirring constantly with a spoon or spatula.

6

As soon as the potatoes puff up, remove them with a slotted spoon and immerse them in a second pan of deep-frying oil heated to 180°C/350°F.

7

Remove with a slotted spoon or skimming ladle.

8

Put them straight onto a clean tea towel or kitchen paper to drain, then season with your choice of flavouring. Serve immediately.

PATISSERIE

For me, patisserie should always be written with a capital 'P' because it's so important, and I never tire of discovering different things to make with eggs, flour, butter and sugar! In this chapter I've included a range of recipes, just to help you learn some really useful techniques which, once you have grasped them, will allow you to make lots of things. You'll see that I have, once again, been inspired by the classics then made them my own – I hope you will do the same with my suggestions.

For 4
Preparation time: 15 min
Cooking time: 10 min

}

Coconut and lime îles flottantes with banana-passionfruit foam

You don't need an oven or even a pan for this, just a microwave! These îles flottantes taste and look completely different to the classic version. Try them...

The quick crème anglaise

2 egg yolks
35 g/1¼ oz caster (superfine) sugar
100 ml/3½ fl oz milk
100 ml/3½ fl oz double (heavy) cream

The banana-passionfruit foam

100 g/3½ oz banana purée
100 g/3½ oz passionfruit purée
25 g/1 oz caster (superfine) sugar
120 ml/3¾ fl oz very cold double
  (heavy) cream

The coconut and lime îles flottantes

5 egg whites
60 g/2¼ oz caster (superfine) sugar
zest of ½ lime, chopped
250 g/8½ oz grated fresh coconut

Equipment

siphon (optional)

1 ~ The quick crème anglaise

Put the egg yolks and sugar in a heatproof bowl and mix together for 30 seconds. Warm the milk and cream, then pour into the bowl. Stir, then cook in the microwave at full power (900W) for 1 minute and stir again. Cook for a little longer if the sauce does not have a coating consistency.

2 ~ The banana-passionfruit foam

Mix the 2 fruit purées together, then stir in the sugar and cream. Pour the mixture into a siphon and insert 2 gas cartridges. Chill.

3 ~ The coconut and lime îles flottantes

Whisk the egg whites with the sugar and lime zest until glossy and stiff. Fill plastic moulds 10 cm/4 wide and 3 cm/1¼ in high with the egg whites and smooth the surfaces with a spatula. Cook in the microwave for 30 seconds at full power (900W), then carefully unmould. Leave to cool for 15 minutes, then gently roll them in the coconut. (See step-by-step method on p. 82.)

4 ~ Serving

Pour the crème anglaise into the bottom of 4 glasses or clear dishes. Top with the banana-passionfruit foam, then carefully add a coconut and lime île flottante to each glass. Serve immediately.

If you don't have a siphon | The day before serving, mix 250 ml/9 fl oz double (heavy) cream with the finely chopped zest of a lime. Leave to infuse in the fridge for 24 hours. The next day, whip this cream with 35 g/1¼ oz sugar to make a chantilly. Gently whisk in 100 g/3½ oz passionfruit purée and use as instructed in the recipe.

Speeding things up | Look for ready-made fruit purées in shops specializing in frozen foods or online. Or you could use mixed fresh fruit instead.

Tip | If you make double or triple the amount of crème anglaise, you'll need to microwave it for longer – keep an eye on it and stir it from time to time. If you make more than 4 îles flottantes, you'll also need to increase the cooking time... or just microwave them 4 at a time.

Worth knowing | If the îles flottantes seem too large once they're cooked, just cut smaller pieces out of them using a 4–5 cm/1½–2 in pastry cutter. The presentation will be even more beautiful!

How to make coconut and lime îles flottantes

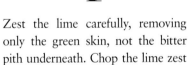

1

Zest the lime carefully, removing only the green skin, not the bitter pith underneath. Chop the lime zest very finely.

2

Separate the eggs. Put the egg whites into the bowl of an electric mixer and add the sugar. Whisk for a few minutes, then add the zest.

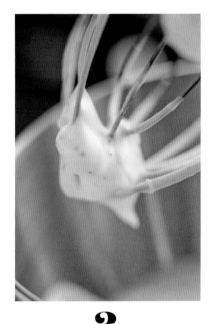

3

Whisk again if necessary: the whites should be stiff and cling to the whisk.

4

Spoon into 4 microwave-friendly moulds or dishes (so plastic or glass not metal), then smooth the surface with a spatula or the blade of a knife.

5

Cook in a microwave on full power (900W) for 30 seconds.

6

Remove from the microwave. Carefully unmould the egg whites, then cut into cylinders using a suitably sized pastry cutter.

7

Carefully remove the egg whites from the cutter.

8

Spread the coconut on a tray or plate, then roll the cylinders in it to coat completely, being careful not to crush them.

For 4
Preparation time: 40 min
Cooking time: 5 min
Freezing time: overnight
Resting time: 2 h

Iced vanilla parfait with pineapple

This delicate mixture of pineapple and vanilla is one of my favourite creations. Use a very ripe pineapple and soft, fragrant vanilla pods. You need to make this a day before you want to serve it.

The iced vanilla parfait

1 vanilla pod (bean)
350 ml/12 fl oz double (heavy) cream
2 egg yolks
90 ml/3 fl oz ready-made sugar syrup

The pineapple dice

40 g/1½ oz pineapple
½ vanilla pod (bean)

The pineapple jelly

200 g/7 oz pineapple
20 g/¾ oz caster (superfine) sugar
5 g/¼ oz gelatine leaves, soaked in
   cold water

The chocolate sauce

25 g/1 oz caster (superfine) sugar
125 g/4½ oz puréed pineapple
110 g/3¾ oz milk chocolate

1 ~ The iced vanilla parfait

The day before, halve the vanilla pod, scrape out and reserve the seeds, then put the pod into the cream. Place the egg yolks in the bowl of an electric mixer. Bring the sugar syrup to the boil, then pour onto the egg yolks and beat until cold and very frothy. Next, whip the infused cream to soft peaks, then fold into the egg yolk mixture. Pour into a hemispherical mould and freeze overnight.

2 ~ The diced pineapple

On the day you want to serve the parfait, dice the pineapple, mix with the reserved vanilla seeds and leave to infuse in the fridge for 1 hour.

3 ~ The pineapple jelly

Blend the pineapple with the sugar, then strain through a fine sieve or chinois into a saucepan. Bring the juice to the boil to evaporate the water, which would prevent the jelly from setting. Add the drained and squeezed-out gelatine leaves and stir well, then add the diced pineapple. Pour into a circular mould or pastry ring and allow to set.

4 ~ The chocolate sauce

Heat the sugar with the puréed pineapple. Melt the chocolate in a bain-marie and then mix it thoroughly into the sugar and pineapple.

5 ~ Plating up

Remove the mould or ring from the pineapple jelly. Put the iced parfait on top of the pineapple jelly, pour over the chocolate sauce and serve immediately.

Tip | Before making a pineapple or kiwi jelly, heat the fruit in a microwave: this removes the enzyme they contain which stops their juice from setting.

Good to know | In step 1, it helps if both the egg yolk mixture and the whipped cream have a similar consistency when you mix them together. So don't overbeat the cream; it shouldn't be too stiff.

For 4
Preparation time: 20 min
Infusing time: overnight
Resting time: 3 h
Cooking time: 30 min

}

Poached vanilla pear with cassis and coffee fondant

This pear is served with a stunning coffee fondant that can be prepared in advance, to save time on the day you want to serve it. Make this in the autumn, when pears are in season and at their best.

The coffee fondant

16 g/½ oz coffee beans
200 ml/7 fl oz milk
3 egg yolks
1 whole egg
160 g/5¾ oz caster (superfine) sugar
2½ gelatine leaves, soaked in
   cold water
2 teaspoons pastis
180 g/6¼ oz butter

The poached pears

150 g/5½ oz caster (superfine) sugar
1 vanilla pod (bean)
150 ml/5 fl oz crème de cassis
4 pears

The vanilla tuiles

30 g/1 oz icing (confectioners') sugar
30 g/1 oz butter
1 vanilla pod (bean)
1 egg white
30 g/1 oz plain (all-purpose) flour

1 - The coffee fondant

The day before, put the crushed coffee beans in the milk and leave to infuse overnight in the fridge. The next day, mix the egg yolks, whole egg and sugar in a saucepan. Pour the infused milk through a sieve into the pan, then mix together. Cook over a gentle heat, stirring constantly, until the mixture coats the back of a spoon. Add the drained and squeezed-out gelatine leaves, stirring to dissolve. Blend, then strain through a fine sieve and add the pastis. Cover with cling film and leave to cool for 15 minutes. Add the softened butter and blend again. Pour the mixture into 4 circular moulds or pastry rings and chill for at least 2 hours.

2 - The poached pears

In a saucepan, boil 1 litre/1¾ pints of water with the sugar, the vanilla pod (cut in half) and the crème de cassis. Peel and trim the pears, then halve lengthways and remove the cores. Immerse in the vanilla-cassis syrup and poach for 20 minutes. Carefully lift out the pears, then reduce the syrup a little.

3 - The vanilla tuiles

Preheat the oven to 200°C (400°F; gas mark 6). Mix the icing sugar with the softened butter and the seeds from the vanilla pod, then mix in the egg white and flour. Spread this mixture in small tuile-shaped ovals on a baking sheet lined with baking parchment. Bake for 6 minutes. As soon as the tuiles come out of the oven, carefully peel them from the baking sheet and drape them over a rolling pin (or clean bottle), so they take on a curved shape once cool.

4 - Plating up

Put the coffee fondants on plates. Press the back of a spoon into the surface of each one, to make a slight hollow, then sit the pears in it. Spoon over a little syrup and serve with a tuile.

Making it even easier | *Put the tuile mixture into a piping bag and use it to make small mounds of the mixture about the size of walnuts on the lined baking sheet. Spread them out a little with a spatula, then cook as instructed in the recipe.*

For 4
Preparation time: 15 min
Cooking time: 15 min

}

Cinnamon and cherry clafoutis

These days I often use cassia bark, a form of cinnamon from China that has a stronger flavour than Indian cinnamon. Used judiciously, I find it leaves a lovely long taste in the mouth, and here I combine it with cherries in a gorgeous, yet noticeably different, clafoutis. If you can, use large Burlat cherries for this.

The clafoutis

12 cherries
knob of butter for frying
1 tablespoon icing (confectioners') sugar
85 g/3 oz unsalted butter, softened
1 teaspoon caster (superfine) sugar
85 g/3 oz icing (confectioners') sugar
4 pinches of ground cinnamon or cassia bark
85 g/3 oz ground almonds
5 g/¼ oz cornflour (cornstarch)
1 egg

The cinnamon cream

150 ml/5 fl oz double (heavy) cream
10 g/⅓ oz icing (confectioners') sugar
4 pinches of ground cinnamon or cassia bark

1 ~ The clafoutis

Wash, de-stalk and stone the cherries. Put a knob of butter in a hot frying pan and sauté the cherries for 1 minute. Sprinkle with icing sugar and cook for a moment longer, then transfer to a sieve to drain. In a large bowl, mix the softened butter with all the other ingredients except the egg to make a smooth batter. Finally, mix in the egg. Butter a shallow baking dish and pour in the batter. Add the cherries and cook the clafoutis in an oven preheated to 175°C (350°F; gas mark 4) for 15 minutes, or until golden. Leave to cool at room temperature.

2 ~ The cinnamon cream

Whip the cream, icing sugar and cinnamon or cassia together until it just starts to thicken. Serve on the side.

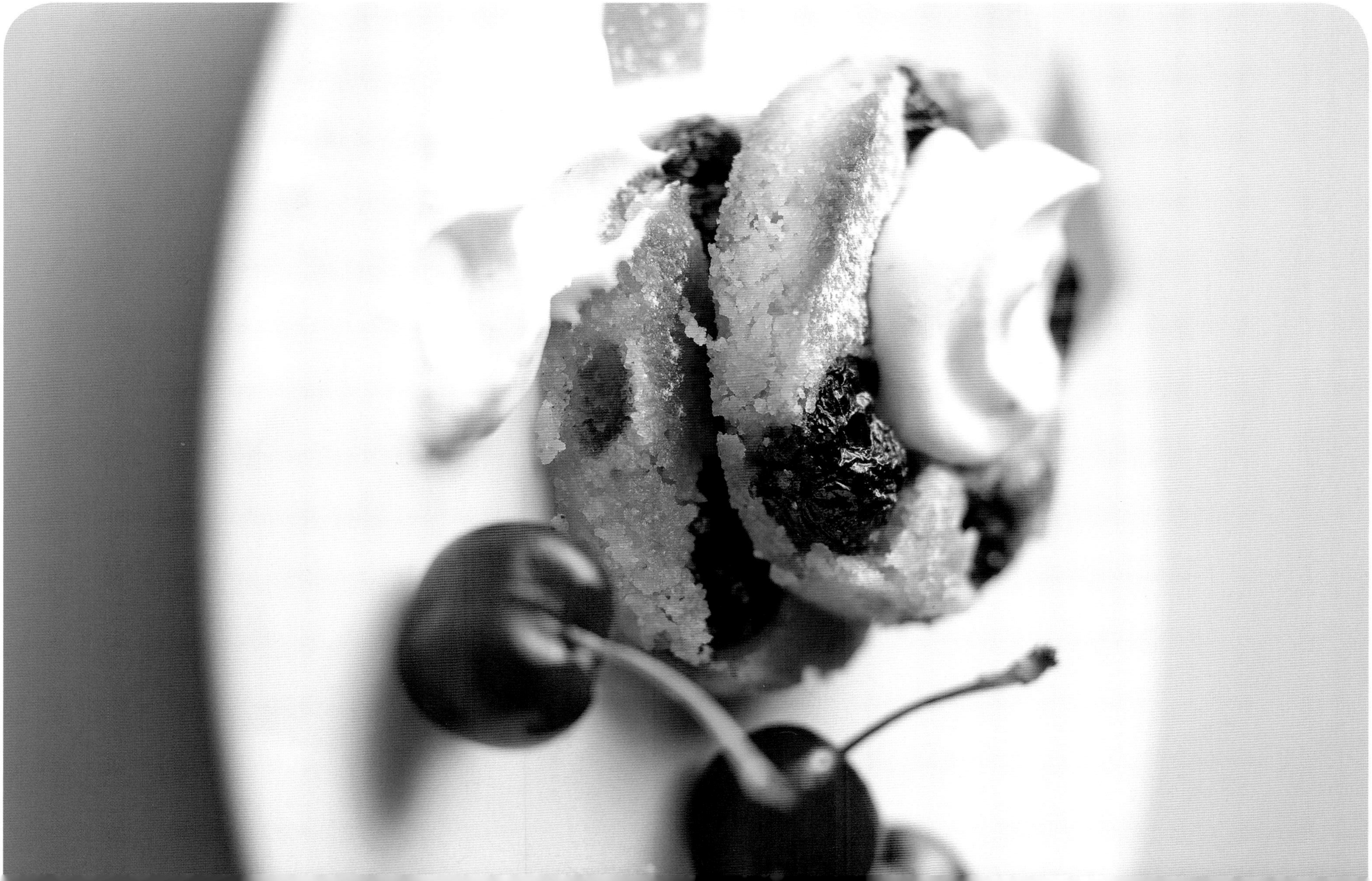

For 4
Preparation time: 25 min
Cooking time: 25 min
Resting time: overnight + 3 h

}

Rhubarb and tarragon tart

This combination of rhubarb and white chocolate foam may seem a little odd but it is very tasty — just remember to start the rhubarb compote the day before. I use tarragon often in my cooking: in salads and main dishes, of course, but also in patisserie. Alas, this marvellous herb is not used as much as it should be. Its unique flavour gives real character to dishes, without overwhelming other ingredients. Give it a try.

The rhubarb compote

350 g/12 oz rhubarb
35 g/1¼ oz caster (superfine) sugar
juice of ½ lemon
¼ bunch of tarragon

The shortbread

40 g/1½ oz salted butter
18 g/¾ oz soft brown sugar
55 g/2 oz plain (all-purpose) flour
¼ teaspoon baking powder
10 g/⅓ oz potato flour

The white chocolate foam

110 g/3¾ oz white chocolate
125 ml/4 fl oz whole milk
5 g/¼ oz caster (superfine) sugar
100 ml/3½ fl oz double (heavy) cream

Equipment

siphon (optional)

1 - The rhubarb compote

The day before, trim the rhubarb and cut into small pieces. Mix with the sugar and lemon juice, then put into a non-metallic colander set over a bowl in the fridge. Leave to macerate overnight. The next day, cook the rhubarb over a medium heat for 25 minutes, stirring every so often. Add the finely chopped tarragon at the end of the cooking time, then leave to cool.

2 - The shortbread

Mix all the ingredients together by hand to make a very crumbly, coarse dough, then spread out on a lined baking sheet or tray. Bake for about 15–20 minutes at 150°C (300°F; gas mark 2) until pale golden. Remove from the oven and leave to cool.

3 - The white chocolate foam

Melt the white chocolate in a bain-marie. Mix together the milk and sugar, then pour this mixture onto the melted chocolate. Beat until smooth, then mix in the cream. Leave to cool in the fridge for 3 hours. Pour into a siphon and insert 2 gas cartridges, then chill.

4 - Serving

Divide the rhubarb compote between 4 glasses or individual dishes and add a layer of crumbled shortbread to each one. Top with the white chocolate foam, then serve immediately.

If you don't have a siphon | Break the chocolate into pieces and melt it in a bain-marie. Combine the milk and sugar, then bring to the boil and pour onto the melted chocolate. Mix together to make a smooth cream. Leave to cool at room temperature. Meanwhile, lightly whip the cream, then carefully fold into the chocolate mixture. Use as instructed in step 4 of the recipe.

Making it even better | For a change, try flavouring the shortbread with a little finely chopped ginger.

16

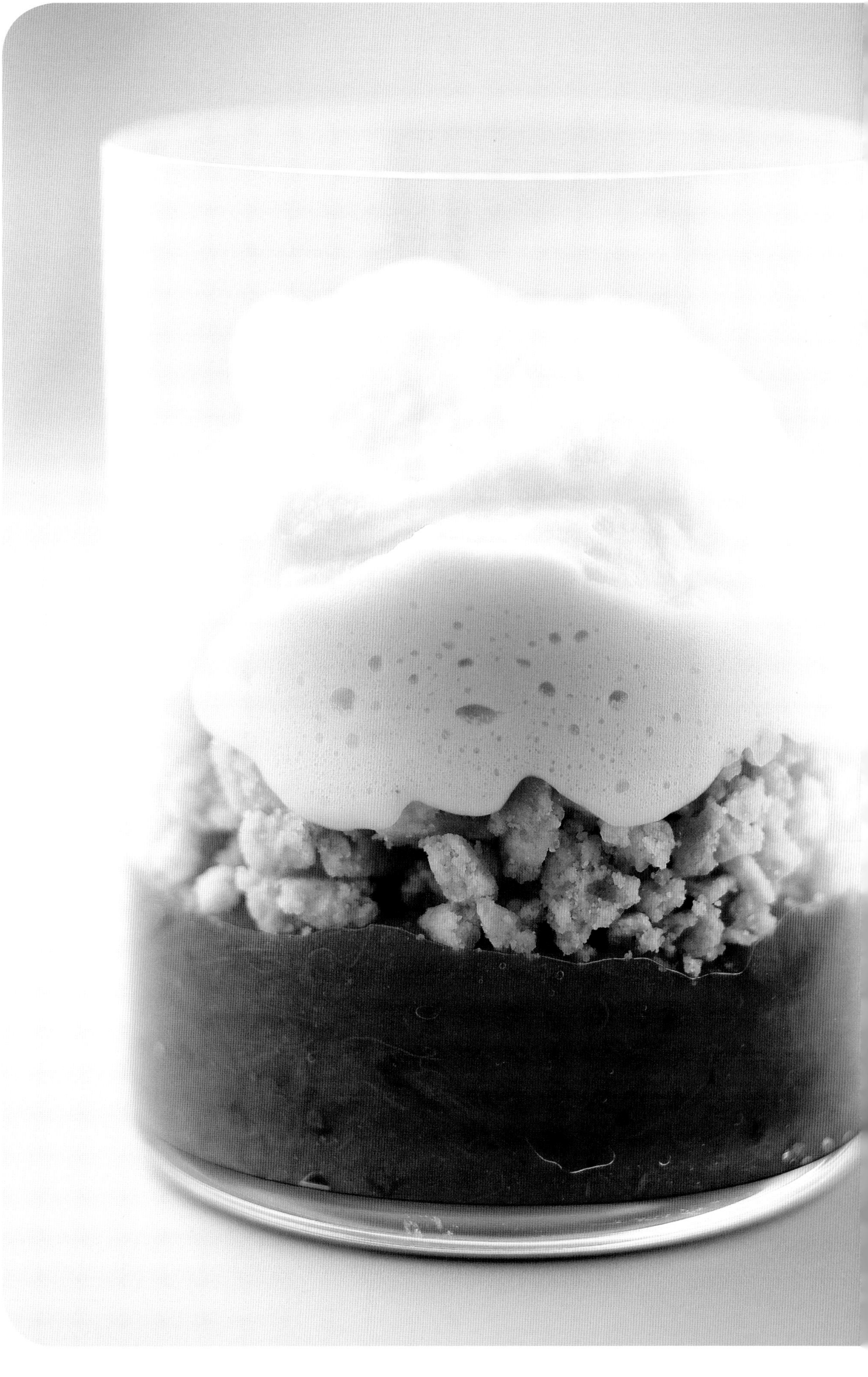

2

Everyday

BETWEEN FRIENDS

Friends are wonderful for lots of reasons,
but especially because they forgive us everything.
Mostly! Which means they make perfect guinea pigs
when it comes to trying out new ideas, seeing what
sort of reaction a new dish provokes, or finding
out whether a new dish is working or not. So yes,
I experiment on my friends, but in the nicest way
possible. Don't worry, these recipes will earn you
plenty of accolades. Between the sous-vide cod and
the six-minute foie gras, you will surprise everyone.
And all without spending ages in the kitchen.

For 4
Preparation time: 45 min
Cooking time: 50 min
Infusing time: 20 min

Fish terrine with brown shrimp cream

Fish terrines are very delicate: their gentle flavour and melting texture makes them unique. So it should go without saying that you need to use the freshest fish possible.

The fish terrine

250 g/8½ oz skinless fillets of white fish (such as cod or pollock), all bones removed

75 g/2¾ oz egg white (from about 3 eggs)

170 ml/5¾ fl oz single (pouring) cream

40 g/1½ oz shelled brown shrimp

fine salt

The brown shrimp cream

100 g/3½ oz whole brown shrimp

splash of olive oil

knob of butter

½ shallot

50 ml/1¾ fl oz vegetable stock (see step-by-step method on p. 126)

50 ml/1¾ fl oz milk

250 ml/9 fl oz single (pouring) cream

2 pinches of green Szechuan pepper

fine salt

Finishing off

40 g/1½ oz whole brown shrimp

1 sheet of wakame seaweed

Equipment

food processor

terrine mould, preferably silicone

1 - The fish terrine

Put the fish, egg white, cream and a little salt in a food processor and process to a smooth mixture. Butter the terrine mould and put half the fish mixture in the bottom, followed by the brown shrimp, then the rest of the fish mixture. Cover the mould with cling film, making sure it is thoroughly sealed, then place in a large lidded pan or fish kettle. Pour enough water into the pan to come three-quarters of the way up the sides of the terrine mould, then put the lid on the pan. Heat until the water is at a steady simmer (about 90°C/195°F, so that it bubbles but never boils), and cook the terrine in this bain-marie for about 50 minutes.

2 - The brown shrimp cream

While the terrine is cooking, lightly brown the shrimp in a saucepan with the olive oil and butter. Add the finely chopped shallot and cook for 2 minutes, then add the vegetable stock and milk. Bring to the boil and simmer for 4–5 minutes. Next, add the cream and Szechuan pepper and return to the boil, then remove from the heat. Cover and leave to infuse for 20 minutes before straining through a sieve into a clean saucepan. Taste and add a little salt if necessary.

3 - Finishing off

Gently heat the brown shrimp cream with the 40 g/1½ oz brown shrimp and the finely shredded seaweed – don't let it boil. Remove the terrine from the bain-marie and carefully unmould it. Leave it to cool slightly, then cut into slices and serve with the brown shrimp cream drizzled over the top.

Some technical advice | Temperature is key to the success of this recipe. If the fish mixture gets too hot in the food processor (as a result of friction from the blades), the texture will be grainy. To avoid this, put all the fish terrine ingredients into the freezer for 10 minutes before starting.

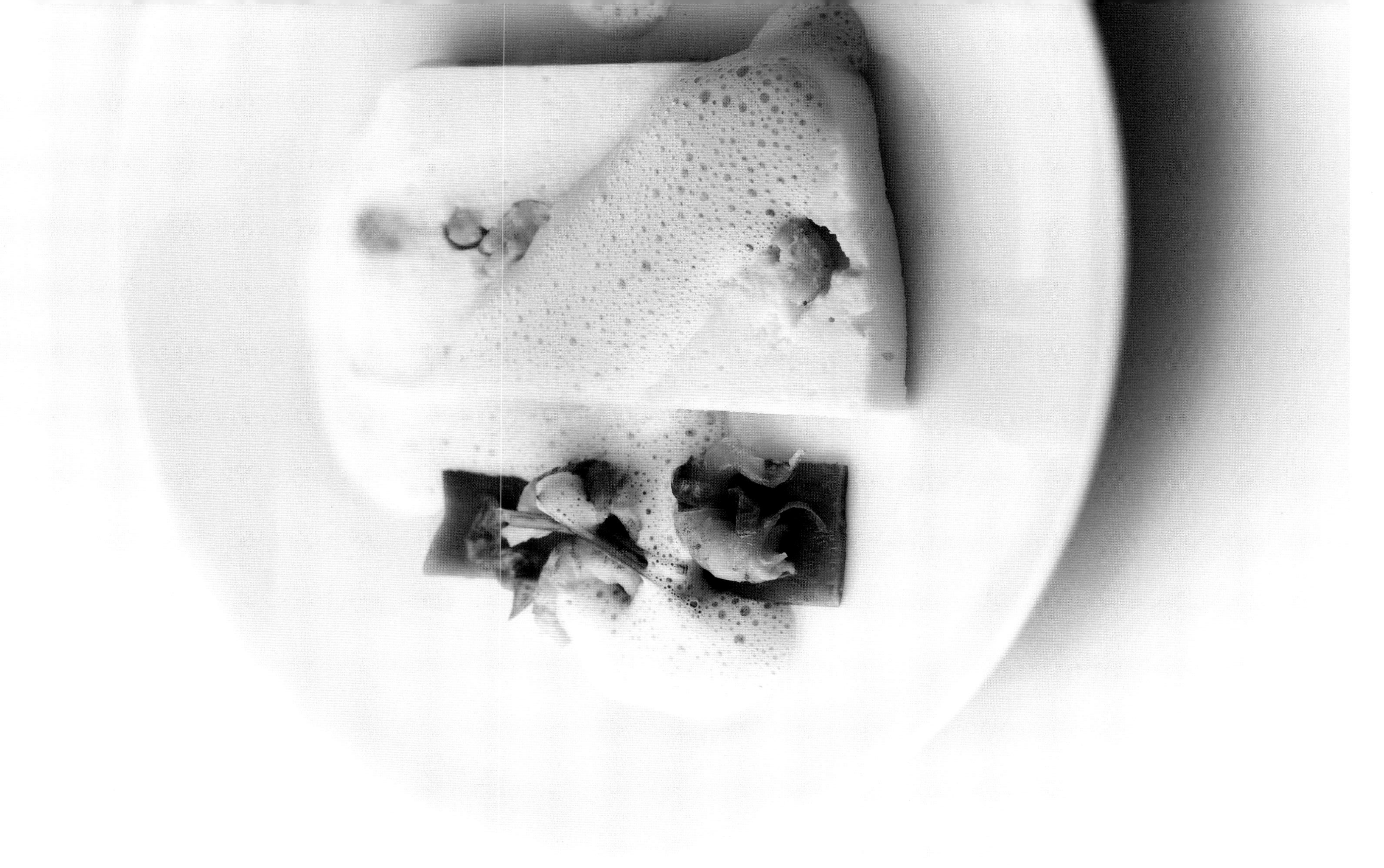

26

For 4
Preparation time: 40 min
Brining time: 15 min
Cooking time: 25 min (lentils)
+ 3 min (fish)
Resting time: 5 min

}

Sous-vide cod with lentils

Here I show you how to cook sous-vide at home, making do with the kitchen equipment you've already got! It's really easy, and such a gentle cooking method perfectly preserves both the delicate flavour and fragile texture of the fish.

The lentils

1 onion, peeled
1 carrot, peeled
1 leek, white part only
1 stalk of celery
knob of butter
250 g/8½ oz green lentils
1 litre/1¾ pints vegetable stock
  (see step-by-step method on p. 126)
4 tablespoons sherry vinegar
40 ml/1½ fl oz olive oil
fine salt

The cod

25 g/1 oz coarse salt
4 x 120 g/4¼ oz cod fillets
pinch of saffron
100 ml/3½ fl oz grapeseed oil

Equipment

zip-lock freezer bags

1 ~ The lentils

Trim the onion, carrot, leek and celery, then cut into large dice. Cook the vegetables in a saucepan with the butter for 2–3 minutes. Stir in the lentils, then add just enough vegetable stock to cover. Leave to simmer for 25 minutes, adding more stock as necessary. Once cooked, drain the lentils if necessary, then season with the sherry vinegar, olive oil and a little salt. Put to one side.

2 ~ The cod

Dissolve the coarse salt in 500 ml/18 fl oz of cold water. Immerse the cod fillets in this brine for 15 minutes. Drain the cod, then put each fillet in a freezer bag with a few strands of saffron and a little grapeseed oil. One at a time, gradually lower the bags into a sink full of cold water to force all the air out (take care not to let any water get inside), then seal them. Bring a large saucepan of water to the boil. Immerse the bags in the boiling water, then immediately take the pan off the heat and let the fish cook in the hot water for 3 minutes. Remove the bags from the pan, and leave to rest for 5 minutes. (See step-by-step method on p. 100.)

3 ~ Serving

Divide the lentils between the plates, open the sous-vide bags and gently place the cod on top of the lentils. Serve immediately.

Some technical advice | *Temperature is vital when cooking sous-vide. Immerse the bags of fish in the water as soon as it boils, then immediately remove from the heat without letting the water return to the boil. If you have a cooking thermometer, use it to check that the temperature is maintained at around 90°C/195°F.*

Important | *Fish cooked this way won't keep, not even in the fridge – eat it straightaway.*

100 | How to cook sous-vide at home

1

Mix the cold water and salt in a bowl, making sure the salt is thoroughly dissolved. Immerse the fish in the brine.

2

Drain the fish, then put a few strands of saffron onto each fillet, place in zip-lock plastic freezer bags (ones with a good hermetic seal, not the sort you tie to close).

3

Nestle the fish into one of the corners at the bottom of the bag, pressing out as much air as possible.

4

Gradually lower the bag into a sink or large bowl full of cold water, keeping the opening at the top and above the water level, to force the air out of the bag.

5

When the water level has practically reached the opening of the bag, and all the air has been removed, seal the bag.

6

The fish is now sous-vide: the plastic is clinging to the surface of the fish and there is no more air.

7

Immerse the bags in a pan of boiling water, then immediately remove from the heat. Leave the fish to cook in the hot water for 3 minutes.

8

Remove the bags from the pan and leave the fish to rest for 5 minutes, then open the bags: the fish should be perfectly cooked.

For 4
Preparation time: 40 min
Cooking time: 30 min (sweet
potatoes) + 45 min (oxtail)
+ 20 min (baking
Resting time: 30 min

}

Oxtail Parmentier with sweet potato mash

Rediscover the great pleasure of a classic that is both homely and sophisticated. Make sure you use oxtail, not another cut of beef – it will make all the difference to the flavour. Brown stock is a very concentrated beef reduction that adds even more depth to the oxtail; you should be able to find it in specialist food stores and some supermarkets.

The oxtail

½ oxtail, cut into slices
oil
butter
100 g/3½ oz diced onion, carrot,
 leek and celery
1 clove
50 ml/1¾ fl oz Cognac
250 ml/9 fl oz red wine
1 litre/1¾ pints brown stock
1 generous tablespoon chopped
 parsley
fine salt, freshly ground pepper

Sweet potato mash

600 g/1 lb 5 oz sweet potatoes
300 g/10½ oz potatoes
2 large knobs of butter
50 ml/1¾ fl oz cream
3 tablespoons breadcrumbs
fine salt

1 ~ The oxtail

In a pressure cooker, brown the oxtail in a little oil and butter for 5 minutes. Add the diced vegetables and cook for 2–3 minutes. Skim off any excesss fat, then add the clove and pour in the Cognac, wine and stock. Follow the manufacturer's instructions for bringing the cooker up to pressure, then cook the oxtail for 45 minutes. Remove from the heat at the end of the cooking time and leave to cool for 15–20 minutes before opening the pressure cooker. Drain the oxtail, reserving the cooking juices, and leave to cool for 15 minutes. Remove the meat from the bones with your fingers, then shred it with a fork. Place the meat in a large bowl and add a ladleful of the degreased cooking juices, along with the parsley. Season with salt and pepper, mix well, then put to one side.

2 ~ Sweet potato mash

Wash and peel both the sweet potatoes and the potatoes. Put them in a saucepan of cold salted water, bring to the boil and simmer for 20–25 minutes, or until tender. Drain, then push through a mouli or potato ricer. Mix with the butter and cream, then season with a little salt.

3 ~ Finishing off

Put the oxtail mixture in the base of a gratin dish, then cover with the mash. Sprinkle over the breadcrumbs and cook in an oven preheated to 180°C (350°F; gas mark 4) for 15–20 minutes. Serve hot.

Tip | The amount of stock added to the beef at the end of step 1 is just a suggestion. You want a smooth mixture that's not too dry, so add as much as you need to get the right consistency.

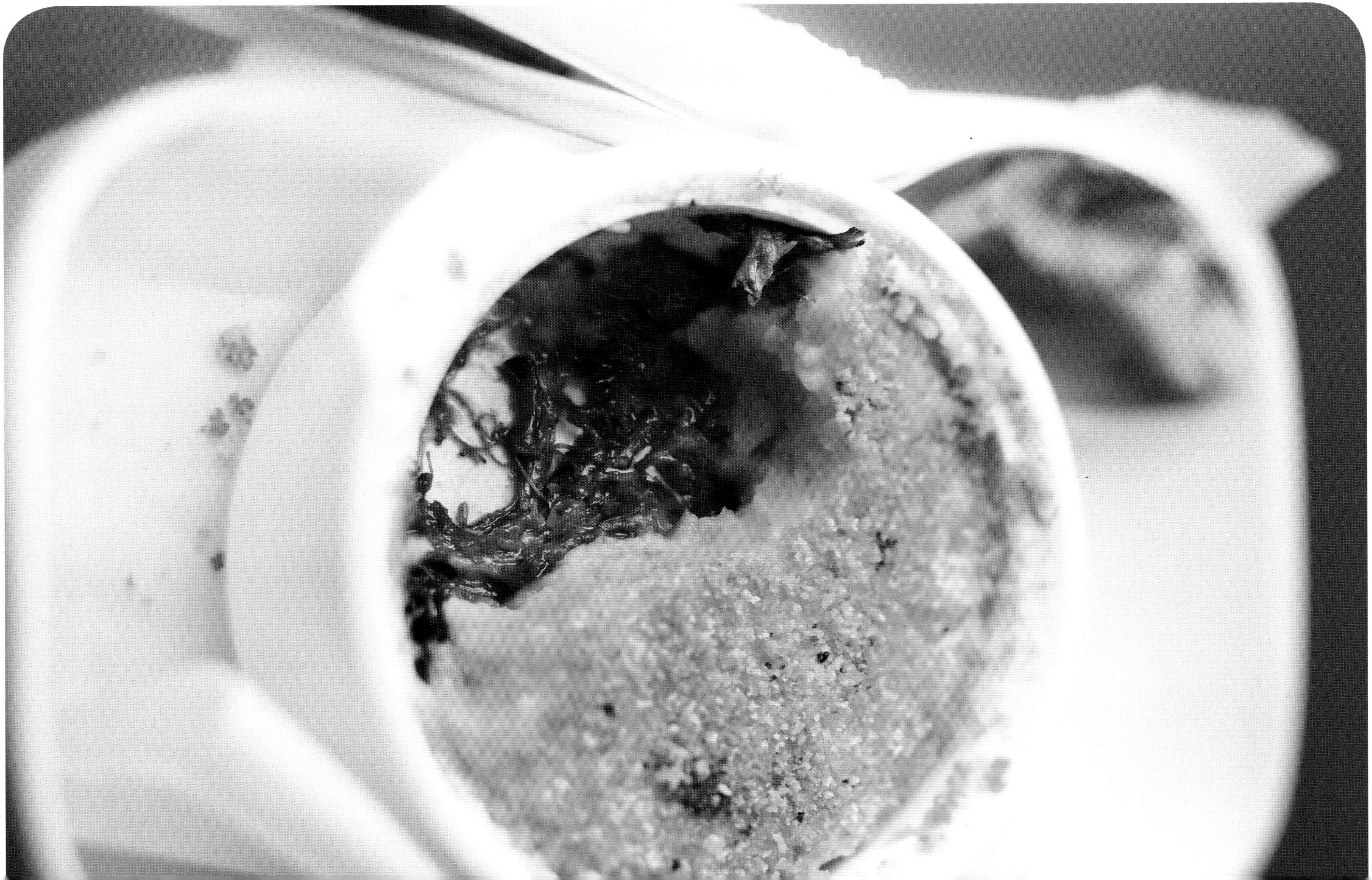

For 4
Preparation time: 25 min
Cooking time: 5 min (petits
pois) + 15 min (rabbit)

}

Rabbit in white wine with liquorice and petits pois

In my version of this classic, I've allowed myself a tiny personal twist, in the shape of a small stick of liquorice. It adds a lovely, just-there aniseed flavour.

The petits pois

200 g/7 oz shelled petits pois
coarse salt

The rabbit

1 x 1.5 kg/3 lb 5 oz rabbit,
    preferably organic or
    free-range, jointed
2 large knobs of salted butter
2–3 tablespoons groundnut
    (peanut) oil
½ onion
50 ml/1¾ fl oz white wine
50 ml/1¾ fl oz vegetable stock
    (see step-by-step method
    on p. 126)
1 stick of liquorice
fine salt, freshly ground pepper

1 ~ The petits pois

Fill a pan with water, add some coarse salt and bring to the boil. Add the petits pois and cook for 1 minute. Drain, then refresh in iced water to preserve their bright-green colour.

2 ~ The rabbit

Brown the rabbit in a lidded casserole dish with the butter and oil for about 10 minutes. Do this in batches if necessary (if you overcrowd the pan, the rabbit won't brown). Add the trimmed and finely chopped onion and cook for another 2 minutes. Skim off as much of the excess fat as possible, then pour in the white wine. Let it bubble for 1 minute before adding the vegetable stock and the liquorice stick, broken into 4 pieces. Cover and leave to cook for 15 minutes over a gentle heat. Add the drained petits pois, then cover again and cook for a further 5 minutes.

3 ~ Serving

Remove the casserole from the heat, then taste and adjust the seasoning if necessary. Serve straight from the casserole dish or transfer to a serving dish. Remember to remove the liquorice stick.

Tip | *It's best to use a farmed rabbit for this dish, as a wild one will take longer to cook.*

Good to know | *Be careful not to overcook the rabbit or it will dry out. There should be about 2–3 cm/1 in of cooking juices in the casserole at all times. If need be, add a little water during the cooking time.*

For 4
Preparation time: 15 min
Cooking time: 6 min (foie
gras) + 25 min (beetroot)
Chilling time: overnight

Six-minute foie gras with beetroot

Who says foie gras is difficult and time-consuming to prepare? Not me! In 6 minutes, you can transform this delicacy into a great dish that can be enjoyed hot or cold.

The beetroot mousseline

3 red beetroot (beets)
zest and juice of 1 orange
2 knobs of butter, melted
1 teaspoon sherry vinegar
fine salt

The foie gras

1 x 500–600 g/1 lb 2 oz–1 lb 5 oz
    foie gras (buy the best quality
    you can get)
fine salt, freshly ground pepper

The cooking liquid

1 litre/1¾ pints light red wine,
    such as Crozes-Hermitage
50 g/1¾ oz sugar
100 ml/3½ fl oz crème de myrtilles
    (blueberry liqueur)
1 cinnamon stick
1 star anise
¼ teaspoon aniseed
1¾ teaspoons salt
2 pinches of freshly ground
    black pepper

1 ~ The beetroot mousseline

Wash and trim the beetroot, then cut into small pieces. Pour 500 ml/18 fl oz water into a pressure cooker, then put the beetroot in its basket and cook for 25 minutes on the 'vegetables' setting, according to the manufacturer's instructions. Once cooked, blend the beetroot with the orange zest and juice in a food processor. Add the melted butter, vinegar and a little salt, then chill in the fridge.

2 ~ The foie gras

Combine all the ingredients for the cooking liquid in a saucepan and heat gently until the sugar has dissolved. Bring to the boil, then leave to cool. Pour the cooled liquid into a pressure cooker, place the seasoned foie gras in its basket and lower into the cooker – the liquid should completely cover the foie gras. Cook, following the manufacturer's instructions, for 6 minutes. Remove from the heat and leave to cool, then carefully open the pressure cooker. (See step-by-step method on p. 108.)

3 ~ Serving

• *To serve hot*: Reheat the beetroot purée and divide between 4 plates. Drain the foie gras, then cut it into 8 slices and place 2 on each plate, drizzled with a little of the cooking juices.

• *To serve cold*: After cooking, leave the foie gras to chill in its marinade overnight. Divide the cold beetroot purée between the 4 plates and dress with a little sherry vinegar and salt. Drain the foie gras, slice and serve on toast.

Tip | If possible, buy the foie gras direct from a farmer or order it in advance from your butcher. It must be as fresh as possible, otherwise it will exude lots of fat when cooked. To make slicing the cooked foie gras easier, run the blade of your knife under hot water.

108 | How to cook foie gras in a pressure cooker

1

Get all the ingredients ready and let the foie gras sit at room temperature for a few minutes.

2

Put the red wine and spices in a saucepan. Bring to the boil, then allow to cool and pour into the pressure cooker.

3

Lightly season the foie gras all over with salt and pepper. Make sure the salt is evenly distributed; you will find this easier if both the salt and your fingers are nice and dry.

4

Put the foie gras into the basket of the pressure cooker. Keep the foie gras whole; don't separate the lobes.

5

Immerse the foie gras in the red wine infusion – it should be completely covered.

6

Set the pressure cooker to 'steam' and bring up to pressure: this gets rid of all the air inside.

7

Immediately adjust the pressure cooker setting to 'vegetables' (lower than 'meat') and leave to cook for 6 minutes. Remove from the heat and allow to cool for 4–5 minutes; opening the cooker too soon can cause a sudden release of pressure that might damage the foie gras.

8

When the pressure cooker has cooled, carefully open it. Skim any excess fat from the sauce with a ladle, if necessary, then serve the foie gras immediately or leave to cool. (See instructions for serving hot or cold on p. 106.)

FAST AND FABULOUS

Sadly, we don't have 48 hours in the day…
With children, family, work, chores and travel
all demanding your time, finding time to cook can
seem almost impossible. However, cooking is not
a waste of time: eating well and spending time
together around a table is essential. So here are
some recipes that are fast and easy to make at home,
with no fuss but plenty of care. For example, the
tarragon chicken can be made inside half an hour,
and adults and children alike will love it. If you
simplify the process as much as possible, only the
best things remain: flavour, friends and family.
Bon appétit!

For 4
Preparation time: 20 min
Cooking time: 30 min
(vichyssoise)
+ 5 min (asparagus)

Asparagus vichyssoise with fennel seeds

I love to cook both white and green asparagus, but although it is the same vegetable, the two types take different times to cook. Green asparagus is best eaten when it still has a little crunch, but white asparagus should be eaten soft. I like fennel seeds with vegetables, particularly green asparagus, but they're also good with cucumber.

The asparagus vichyssoise

½ onion
150 g/5½ oz leeks, white parts only
200 g/7 oz green asparagus
150 g/5½ oz potatoes
splash of olive oil
a few fennel seeds
200 ml/7 fl oz milk
100 ml/3½ fl oz double (heavy) cream
150 ml/5 fl oz vegetable stock
  (see step-by-step method on p. 126)
fine salt

Finishing off

8 spears green asparagus
50 ml/1¾ fl oz vinaigrette (⅓ white
  balsamic vinegar, ⅔ olive oil)
a few fennel seeds
fine salt

1 ~ The asparagus vichyssoise

Peel and finely slice the onion. Wash the leeks and finely slice them too. Trim and peel the asparagus and potatoes, then rinse in cold water. Cook the asparagus in plenty of boiling salted water for 5 minutes, then refresh under cold running water. Put the onion into a frying pan with a little olive oil and cook very slowly. Add the leeks, along with a pinch of salt, and cook for another 5 minutes, then add the potatoes, fennel seeds, milk, cream and vegetable stock. Leave to cook for 30 minutes over a very gentle heat. Add the cooked asparagus, then blend until very smooth. Taste and adjust the seasoning as required, then put to one side.

2 ~ Finishing off

Cook 4 of the asparagus spears for 5 minutes in boiling salted water. Slice the other 4 spears lengthways as thinly as possible, immerse in boiling water for a moment, then put to one side.

3 ~ Serving

Divide the whole asparagus spears between 4 bowls, then pour over the hot soup. Decorate with the slivers of asparagus dressed with vinaigrette, and scatter over the fennel seeds. Serve very hot.

Tip | *Use a mandoline (a very fine slicer) to cut the asparagus spears lengthways – if you cook a lot, it is definitely worth buying one.*

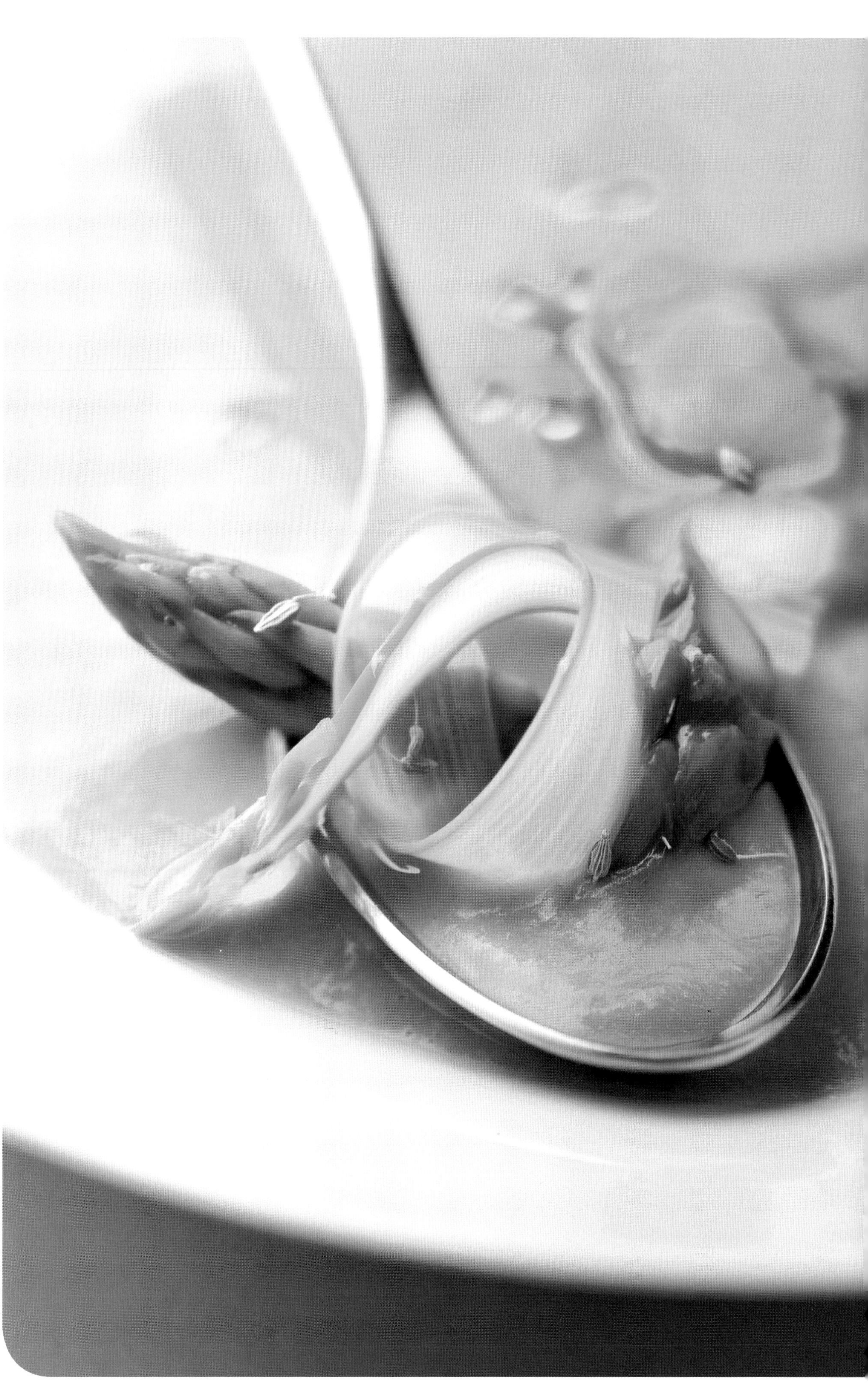

For 4
Preparation time: 20 min
Cooking time: 5 min
(papillotes) + 3 min (leeks)

}

Sea bass 'en papillote' with baby leeks, juniper butter and lemon zest

Cooking fish 'en papillote' helps to preserve and even intensify its flavour – which means that the fish must be really fresh to start with. Sea bass is delicious, meaty and plump, but you could also use pollock, cod or red mullet fillets in this recipe.

The juniper butter

2 teaspoons juniper berries
50 g/1¾ oz unsalted butter

The papillotes

12 baby leeks
4 x 100 g/3½ oz sea bass fillets,
    skin-on
fine salt

Finishing off

lemon zest
fleur de sel

1 ~ Juniper butter

Crush then finely chop the juniper berries. Beat the butter until soft, then mix in the juniper berries. Spread half of the juniper butter between 2 sheets of baking parchment, in a layer about 3 mm/⅛ in thick. Chill for 15 minutes, then cut into small discs.

2 ~ The papillotes

Lay out 4 sheets of baking parchment, each big enough to wrap a fish fillet, on your work surface. Wash the baby leeks well, then cook for 3 minutes in plenty of boiling salted water. Drain, refresh in cold water and drain again. Divide the leeks between the sheets of baking parchment. Lightly season the fish fillets with salt, place on top of the leeks and cover with the remaining juniper butter. Wrap the baking parchment around the fish, folding the edges together to seal, then bake in an oven preheated to 180°C (350°F; gas mark 4) for 5–7 minutes, depending on the thickness of the fish.

3 ~ Finishing off and serving

At the end of the cooking time, open the papillotes. Place a few strips of lemon zest and a little fleur de sel on top of each piece of fish, followed by a disc of juniper butter. Serve immediately.

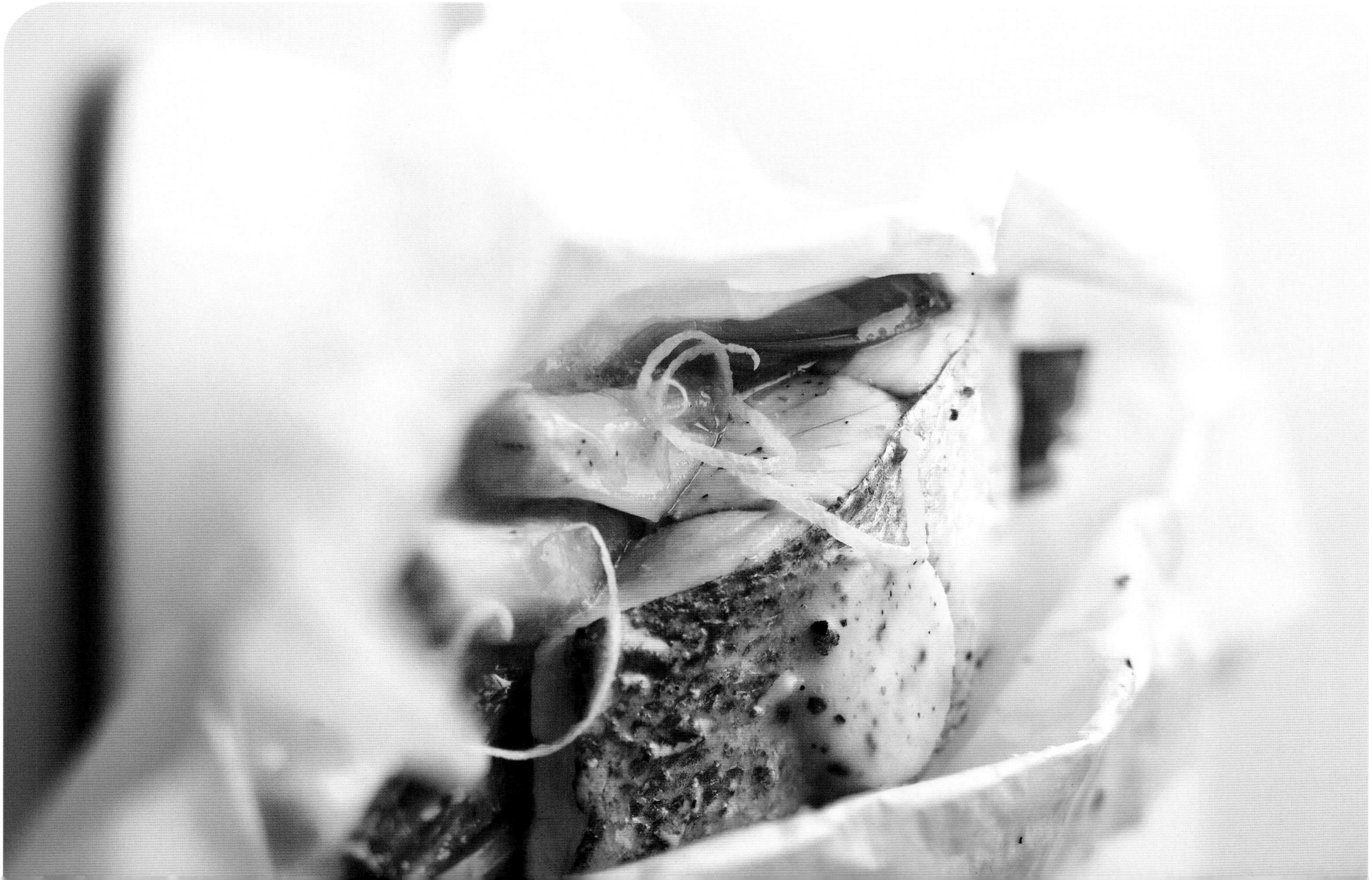

For 4
Preparation time: 25 min
Cooking time: 25 min
(1 min per 100 g/3½ oz and
10 min browning)
+ 20 min (rice)

Tarragon chicken with rice pilaf

Use a really good-quality chicken in this recipe: free-range at the very least or organic if possible. You may come across two types of tarragon in the shops. The first has small, dark green leaves and a very distinct and concentrated flavour; the second has longer, paler green leaves and its flavour is sweeter and aniseedy. Choose whichever you prefer.

The tarragon chicken

1 x 1.4 kg/3 lb chicken

3 sprigs of tarragon + extra chopped
  tarragon to decorate

50 g/1¾ oz salted butter

3 tablespoons olive oil

½ onion

100 ml/3½ fl oz white wine

300 ml/10 fl oz vegetable stock
  (see step-by-step method on p. 126)

fine salt, freshly ground pepper

The pilaf

15 g/½ oz salted butter +
  a few knobs extra

½ onion

250 g/8½ oz long-grain rice

450 ml/15 fl oz vegetable stock
  (see step-by-step method on p. 126)

fine salt

1 ~ The tarragon chicken

Season the chicken inside and out with salt and pepper, then tuck the tarragon inside the cavity. Melt the butter with the oil in a pressure cooker over a medium heat. Brown the chicken all over for 10 minutes, then remove from the pan and tip out most of the fat. Add the chopped onion and leave to cook slowly for 1–2 minutes without letting it colour. Add the white wine, scraping the bottom of the pan with a wooden spatula or spoon to deglaze, then bring to the boil and reduce by half. Pour in the vegetable stock and return the chicken to the pan. Follow the manufacturer's instructions to bring up to pressure, then cook the chicken for 14 minutes. Remove from the heat and set aside to allow the pressure to drop gradually. (If you release the pressure too quickly, it can adversely affect the texture of the meat.)

2 ~ The pilaf

Melt the butter in a saucepan. Finely slice the onion and brown for 2–3 minutes. Add the rice and cook slowly, stirring all the time, for another 2–3 minutes. Pour in the vegetable stock and a little salt, cover and leave to cook for about 20 minutes over a gentle heat. Once the rice is cooked, add a few knobs of butter and leave to rest, off the heat, for a few more minutes. Fluff up with a fork, then check and adjust the seasoning as necessary. Carefully open the pressure cooker and remove the chicken. Cut the chicken into pieces and strain the cooking juices through a sieve into a jug.

3 ~ Serving

Put the chicken in a serving dish, pour the juices over the top and sprinkle with chopped tarragon. Serve hot, with the pilaf on the side.

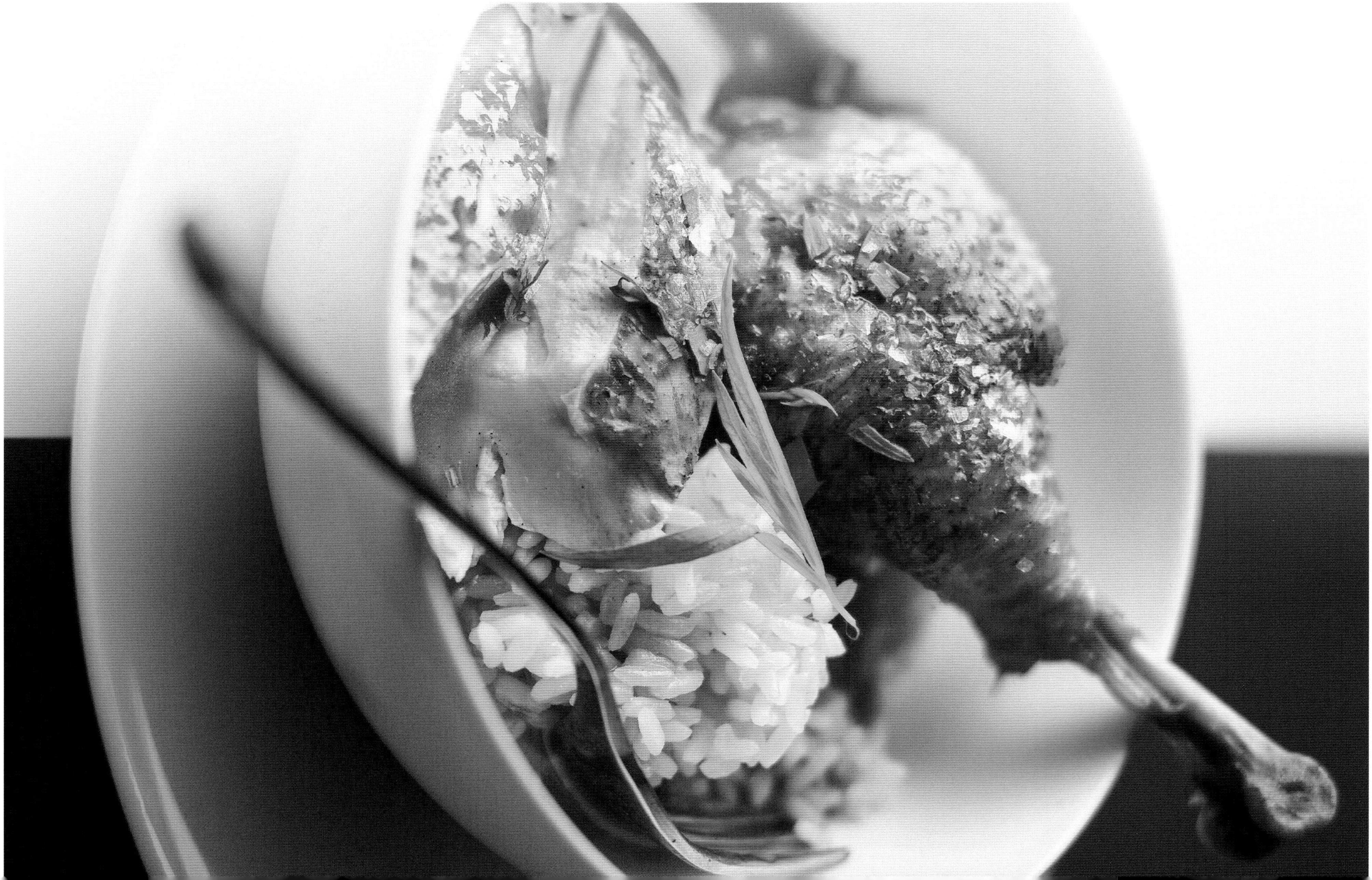

For 4
Preparation time: 20 min
Cooking time: 1 min (ravioli)
+ 5 min (gratin)

Ravioli gratin with caramelized onions and a light nutmeg béchamel

You should be able to find fresh ravioli in good delis, as well as at larger supermarkets, and they come in very handy when you have unexpected guests to feed!

The ravioli gratin

2 onions
splash of olive oil
15 g/½ oz salted butter
4 sheets Dauphiné Ravioli
20 g/¾ oz grated Parmesan
pinch of fine salt

The nutmeg béchamel

20 g/¾ oz salted butter + extra
  for the dish
20 g/¾ oz plain (all-purpose) flour
250 ml/9 fl oz milk
pinch of grated nutmeg
fine salt

1 ~ The caramelized onions

Peel and finely slice the onions. In a sauté pan or large frying pan, heat the olive oil with the butter. Add the onions and season lightly with salt, then cover and cook slowly, stirring often. As soon as they caramelize, remove from the heat and keep to one side.

2 ~ Cooking the ravioli

Cook the ravioli in boiling salted water for 1 minute. Refresh in iced water, then drain.

3 ~ The nutmeg béchamel

Melt the butter, then stir in the flour and cook for 2 minutes until the mixture begins to froth. Gradually whisk in the cold milk, then cook over a low heat, stirring constantly, until the sauce thickens. Take off the heat and add the nutmeg, then season with salt.

4 ~ Finishing the gratin

Preheat an overhead grill (broiler). Butter a gratin dish and spread the caramelized onions in a thin layer over the bottom. Gently mix the ravioli with the béchamel, then place on top of the onions. Sprinkle over the Parmesan, then brown under the grill for about 5 minutes until golden and bubbling. Serve hot.

Good to know | *A regional speciality of south-eastern France, Dauphiné Ravioli are delicate pasta parcels filled with cheese and parsley. You could also use Italian ravioli for this, stuffed with cheese, spinach, mushrooms, pesto or whatever else you like.*

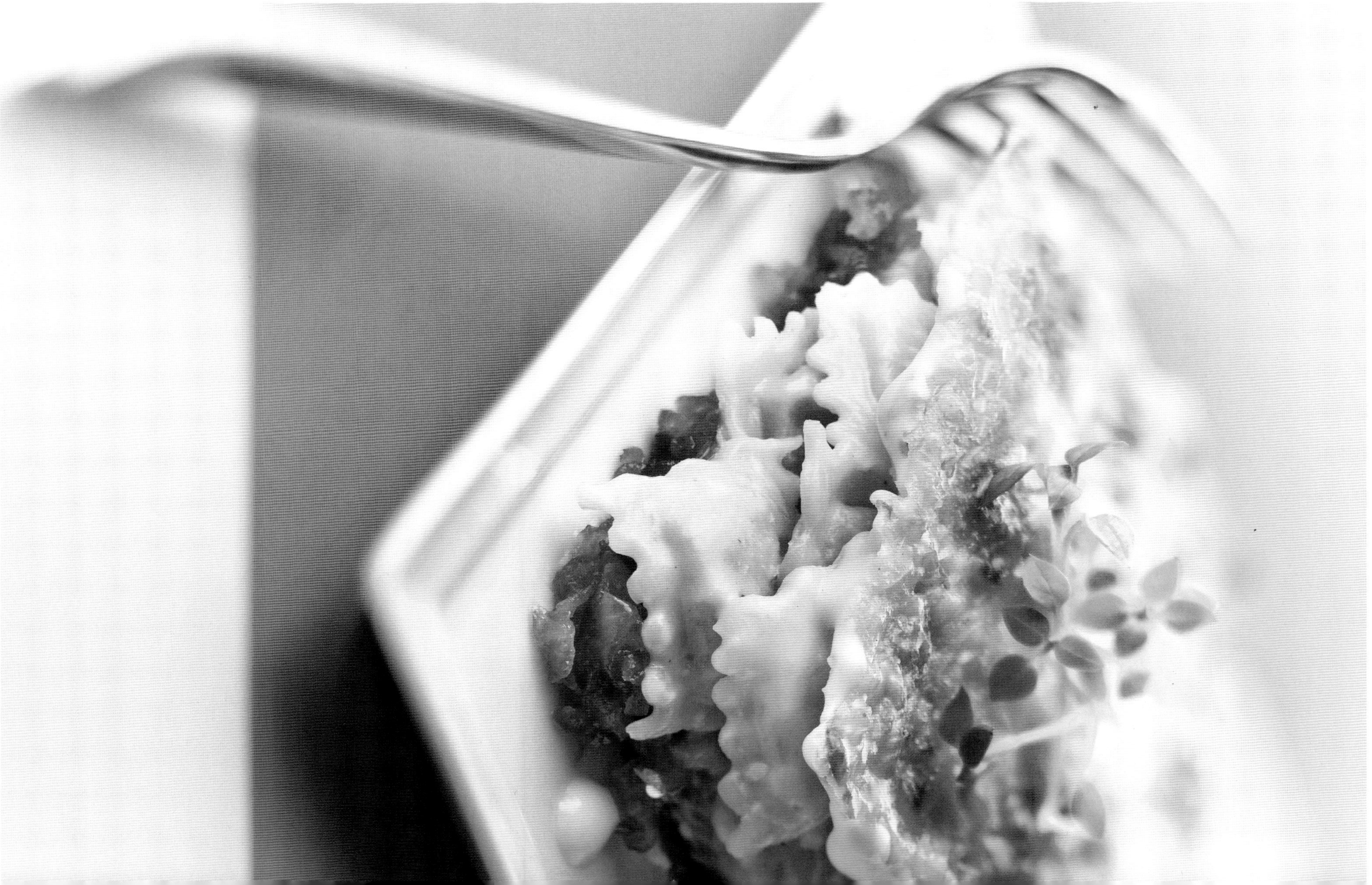

For 4
Preparation time: 40 min
Cooking time: 6 min

}

Sardine tempura with Choron sauce

Japanese tempura is surprisingly easy to make at home. In this version, I've made it with sardines and vegetables. To learn the secret of a perfect Choron sauce, turn to page 122...

The vegetables

2 litres/3½ pints oil for deep-frying
1 courgette (zucchini)
2 carrots
2 baby violet artichokes
juice of 1 lemon

The tempura batter

75 g/2¾ oz fromage frais (quark)
1 egg
125 ml/4 fl oz cold water
15 g/½ oz baking powder
50 g/1¾ oz cornflour (cornstarch)
100 g/3½ oz plain (all-purpose) flour
pinch of fine salt

The fish

24 sardine fillets

The Choron sauce

50 ml/1¾ fl oz white wine
½ shallot
3 sprigs of tarragon
1 teaspoon roughly crushed
   black pepper
2 teaspoons tomato purée
4 egg yolks
150 g/5½ oz clarified butter (see p. 16)
fine salt

1 ~ The vegetables

Preheat a deep-fryer to 180°C/350°F or gently heat the oil in a large saucepan. Wash the courgette, then cut it into matchsticks. Peel and trim the carrots and cut into matchsticks the same size as the courgette. Remove and discard the artichoke leaves, just keeping the hearts. Finely slice the artichoke hearts, preferably with a mandoline, then toss with the lemon juice to prevent them turning black.

2 ~ The tempura batter

Mix all the ingredients together to make a smooth batter.

3 ~ Finishing off

Make the Choron sauce (see step-by-step method on p. 122). Coat the sardine fillets and the vegetables in the tempura batter, then deep-fry in the hot oil for about 2–3 minutes. Remove with a slotted spoon, shaking off any excess oil, then drain briefly on kitchen paper and season with salt. Eat hot with the Choron sauce.

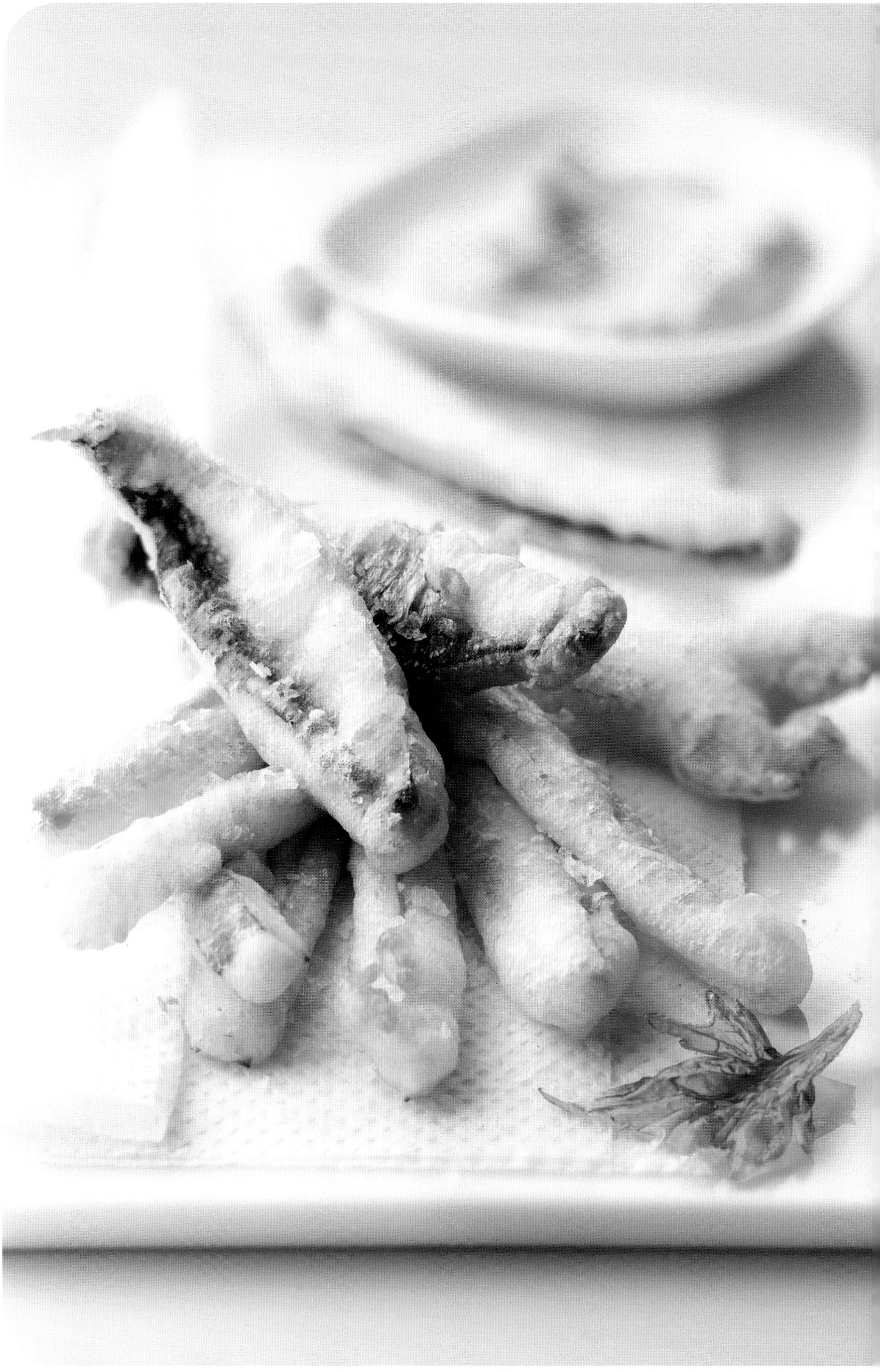

How to make Choron sauce

1

In a saucepan, combine the white wine with the finely chopped shallot, tarragon, pepper and tomato purée. Bring to the boil and reduce by three-quarters, then put to one side.

2

Put the egg yolks in a bowl and add about 25 ml/1 fl oz of water per egg yolk. Whisk until frothy, then transfer to a suitably sized saucepan.

3

Sit the saucepan in a bain-marie or over a very low heat and whisk the yolks thoroughly (you could also use an electric whisk). After about 5–6 minutes, the yolks will be very hot and frothy, and the mixture should be light in colour and texture. As soon as the yolks begin to stick to the saucepan, take it off the heat or out of the bain-marie.

4

Gently melt the butter in another saucepan, without letting it bubble. Remove from the heat, skim the foam from the surface and drain off the clear yellow liquid, leaving behind the white solids. Slowly add this clarified butter to the saucepan, whisking constantly, as if making a mayonnaise. This mixture, known as a sabayon, is the base of the sauce.

Sieve the sabayon to remove any lumps. Now you can make two different sauces.

Béarnaise sauce:

Add the strained and chilled reduction from step 1 to the sabayon. Don't forget to season with a little salt.

Choron sauce:

Make a Béarnaise sauce, then add 1–3 tablespoons of tomato concassé (see step-by-step method on p. 50) and some chopped basil. Season lightly with salt, then mix well.

For 4
Preparation time: 30 min
Cooking time: 10 min

Roman gnocchi revisited

If you have never had freshly made gnocchi, only ones from the supermarket, try this simple and delicious recipe, made with polenta in the Roman style.

The gnocchi

500 ml/18 fl oz milk
40 g/1½ oz butter
20 g/¾ oz grated Parmesan
pinch of fine salt
100 g/3½ oz polenta (cornmeal)
2 eggs

The tomato concassé

2 onions
splash of olive oil
4 tomatoes
1 garlic clove, unpeeled
sprig of thyme
4 sprigs of parsley, chopped
1 tablespoon capers
10 black olives, quartered
4 anchovy fillets, chopped

Equipment

4–5 cm/1½–2 in round pastry cutter

1 - The gnocchi

Combine the milk, butter, Parmesan and salt in a saucepan and bring to the boil. Pour in the polenta, all in one go, stirring constantly, then cook for 5 minutes over a gentle heat, still stirring. Lightly beat the eggs then, off the heat, stir them into the polenta. Pour the polenta onto a baking sheet, spreading it out to a depth of about 1 cm/½ in, then leave to cool until the mixture hardens.

2 - The tomato concassé

Peel, trim and finely slice the onions, then soften in the olive oil for 2–3 minutes, without letting them colour. Peel, deseed and dice the tomatoes. Stir into the onions, then reduce over a gentle heat to get rid of some of the juices. Add the garlic clove and thyme, then cover and cook over a gentle heat for 20–30 minutes. Check the consistency and reduce until the mixture is thick. Blend half the concassé, then return this purée to the rest of the concassé and stir in the parsley, capers, olives and anchovies. Put to one side.

3 - Finishing off

Preheat an overhead grill (broiler). Use a 4–5 cm/1½–2 in pastry cutter to cut out the gnocchi, then place on a baking sheet. Grill for about 10 minutes, turning them halfway through, until golden all over. Serve immediately, with the tomato concassé spooned over the top.

125

How to make vegetable stock

1 onion
2 carrots
1 leek
1 stalk of celery

5 white button mushrooms
1 clove
1 teaspoon white peppercorns
2.5 litres/4 pints cold water

1

Peel, trim and top and tail and wash the onion, carrots, leek and celery, as needed. Dice the carrots and slice the onion, leek and celery.

2

Clean the mushrooms, then slice finely.

3

Put all the vegetables into a large saucepan, along with the clove and peppercorns. Cover with the cold water, then bring to the boil.

You can use this light stock in lots of recipes, especially when making sauces or a more concentrated jus. It is very easy to make, and can even be eaten on its own as a simple broth.

4

Leave the vegetable stock to simmer very slowly, uncovered, for about an hour.

5

At the end of the cooking time, the vegetables will be very well cooked and will have lost some of their colour. The stock should smell rich and be a light amber colour.

6

Take the stock off the heat and strain through a fine sieve, ideally lined with muslin (cheese-cloth) or a clean tea towel. If you're not using the stock immediately, you can freeze it in an airtight container or in ice-cube trays.

CUTTING EDGE

Inspiration is not 'out there', in other people's
heads – it's what happens when you cook!
Try it and you'll see; the more you cook, the more
you'll discover how easy it is, and the more ideas
you'll have. In this chapter I share the recipes I have
really made my own, ones that are definitely off
the beaten track: an aubergine custard, a mushroom
jelly, a nut-crusted guinea fowl supreme. What
I make at any given time depends on the season,
my mood and the products that inspire me. To get
the most out of new ideas in food, you need to let
yourself go a bit and shake off old habits, but always
with the same objective: to make something good
and to make people happy.

For 4
Preparation time: 30 min
Cooking time: 40 min (royale)
+ 15 min (pumpkin)

Mussel royale with pumpkin cream

This recipe has three elements: mussels, royale sauce and pumpkin cream, all of which are very simple and stress-free to make, though the combination is stunning. You can vary it by using different seafood, such as cockles, clams or even razor clams.

The mussels

500 g/1 lb 2 oz mussels
1 shallot
1 garlic clove
200 ml/7 fl oz white wine
sprig of thyme

The mussel royale

100 ml/3½ fl oz mussel-cooking liquid
250 ml/9 fl oz single (pouring) cream
100 ml/3½ fl oz milk
2 eggs
1 egg yolk
50 g/1¾ oz cooked mussels

The pumpkin cream

400 g/14 oz pumpkin
20 g/¾ oz salted butter
olive oil
150 ml/5 fl oz vegetable stock
  (see step-by-step method on p. 126)
100 ml/3½ fl oz single (pouring)
  cream
fine salt

1 ~ The mussels

Clean and debeard the mussels as necessary. Peel, trim and chop the shallot and garlic, then put all three ingredients into a lidded saucepan, along with the wine and thyme. Cover and cook over a gentle heat for 8–10 minutes, stirring a couple of times during the process. Remove from the heat, discard any mussels that haven't opened, then shell the rest and keep the cooking liquid.

2 ~ The mussel royale

Blend all the ingredients together, then strain the resulting purée through a sieve. Carefully pour into 4 glasses, wiping away any smears on the sides, then cook over a gentle heat in a bain-marie (that is, in a saucepan placed in another pan filled with simmering water) for about 40 minutes, depending on the size of the glasses, until set.

3 ~ The pumpkin cream

Whilst the royale is cooking, peel and deseed the pumpkin and cut the flesh into small pieces. Put the butter, a little oil and salt into a saucepan, add the pumpkin and cook for 5 minutes. Add the vegetable stock and cream and cook for another 15 minutes. Blend, season with a little salt and put to one side.

4 ~ Serving

Take the glasses of royale out of the bain-marie. Gently reheat the mussels in their cooking liquid, without letting them boil. Carefully sit the mussels on top of the royale, then pour the hot pumpkin cream over the top, trying not to splash the sides of the glasses (use kitchen paper or a clean cloth to wipe them clean, if necessary). Eat immediately.

Good to know | *When you reheat the mussels in their cooking liquid, do it over a very low heat – if the mussels boil, they will become hard and rubbery.*

Tip | *You can put the pumpkin cream into a siphon, if you want to make it even lighter. Just remember it will need slightly more seasoning.*

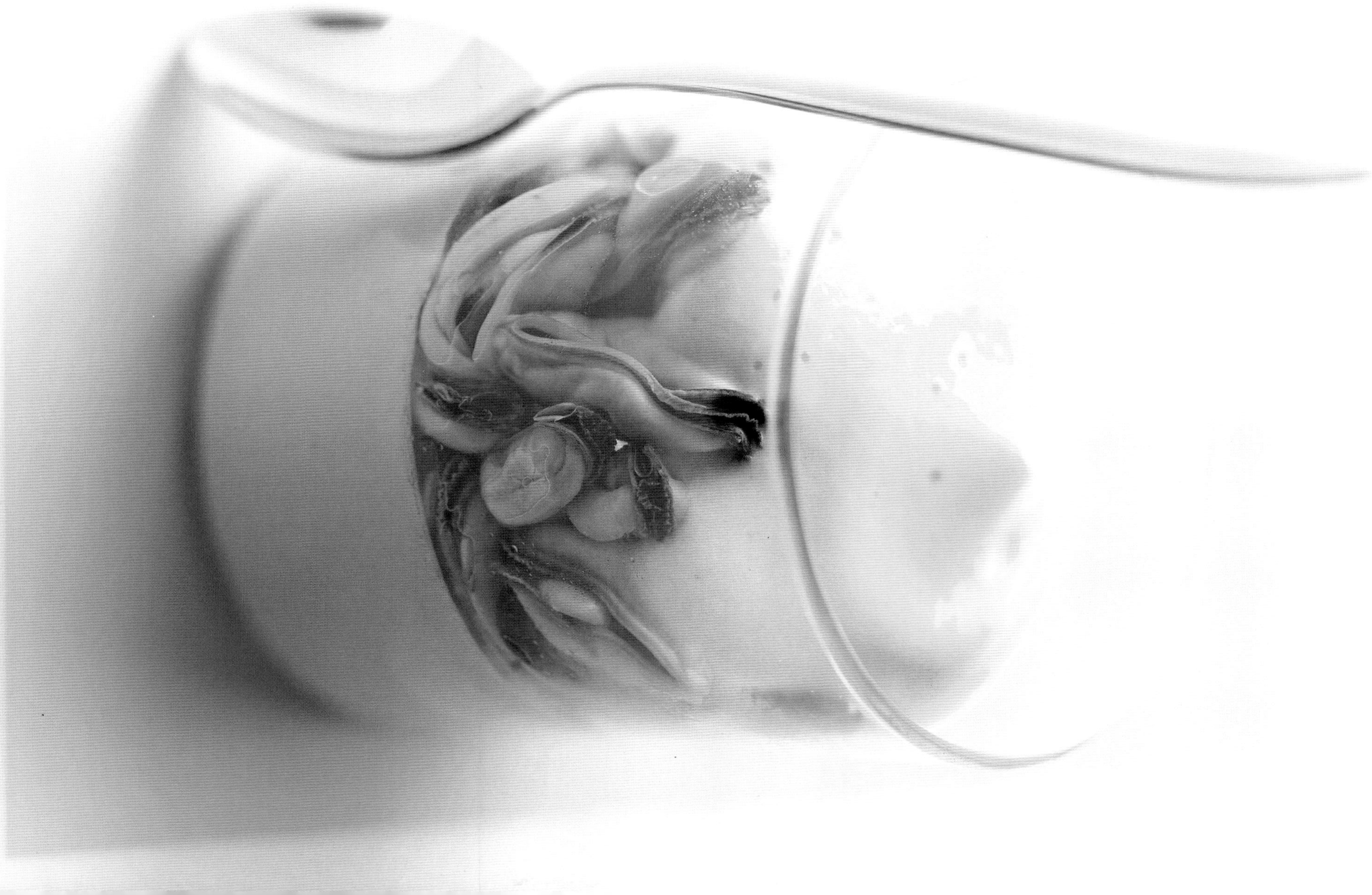

For 4
Preparation time: 1 h
Cooking time: 3 min (pasta)
+ 5 min (squid)

}

Mushroom-stuffed squid with creamy tagliatelle

Don't be afraid of squid. It's much easier to cook than you might think. But it is important to buy the freshest squid you can find: it should be white, shiny and very firm; don't buy squid that seems soft or looks dull.

1 x 500 g/1 lb 2 oz packet
  fresh tagliatelle

The mushroom reduction

2 shallots
2 knobs of butter
8 button mushrooms
juice of 1 lemon
200 ml/7 fl oz double (heavy) cream
fine salt

The squid

1 shallot
knob of butter
6 button mushrooms
juice of ½ lemon
100 ml/3½ fl oz double (heavy) cream
¼ bunch of coriander (cilantro)
2 whole squid, cleaned and quills
  removed (ask your fishmonger
  to do this)
olive oil
fine salt

1 ~ The mushroom reduction

Peel, trim and finely slice the shallots, then cook them with the butter over a gentle heat for 2 minutes. Clean and trim the mushrooms, then slice and add to the shallots, along with the lemon juice. Cook for 2–3 minutes, then pour in the cream. Simmer until the sauce begins to thicken, then remove from the heat, season with a little salt and strain through a fine sieve. Keep warm.

2 ~ The stuffed squid

Preheat the oven to 180°C (350°F; gas mark 4). Peel and finely slice the shallot, then cook in a saucepan with the butter over a low heat for 2 minutes. Clean, trim and slice the mushrooms, then mix with the lemon juice and add to the shallot. Cook for 2–3 minutes, then pour in the cream. Simmer until the sauce begins to thicken, then add the finely chopped coriander and a little salt. Remove from the heat. Stuff the squid tubes with the mushroom mixture and season. Heat a little olive oil in an ovenproof frying pan, then cook the stuffed squid and their tentacles until golden all over. Finish off in the oven for a couple of minutes.

3 ~ Finishing off

Cook the tagliatelle in a saucepan of boiling salted water for 3 minutes (or as per the packet instructions). Drain, then mix with the mushroom reduction in a large bowl. Remove the squid from the oven and halve. Divide the tagliatelle between 4 plates, place half a squid on top and serve immediately.

Tips | To help keep the stuffing inside the squid tubes, close the openings with a cocktail stick or skewer. And don't overcook the squid or it will become tough.

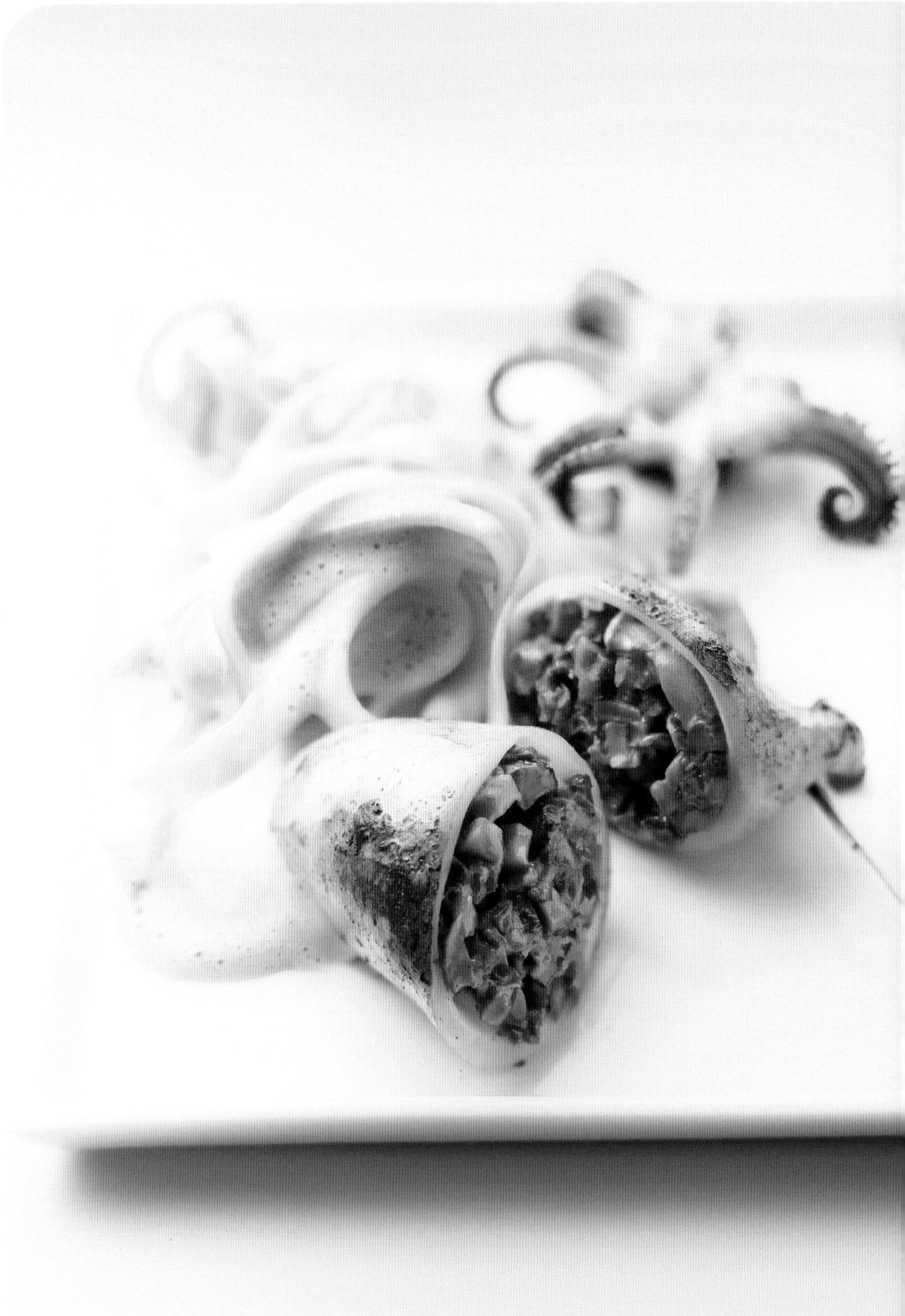

For 4
Preparation time: 45 min
Cooking time: 30 min +
20 min

}

Savoury custards: courgette and bay leaf, aubergine and coconut milk

Have you tried savoury custards? Simple, delicious and healthy, they are a really different way to cook and serve vegetables. These ones can be served as main courses, or as side dishes with chicken or pork. If your children don't like vegetables, you might be able to tempt them to eat them like this!

Courgette and bay leaf custard

80 ml/2½ fl oz double (heavy) cream
30 ml/1 fl oz milk
1 bay leaf
200 g/7 oz courgettes (zucchini)
2 whole eggs
1 egg yolk
20 g/¾ oz melted butter + extra
   for the moulds
fine salt

Aubergine and coconut milk custard

1 aubergine (eggplant)
splash of olive oil
80 ml/2½ fl oz coconut milk
30 ml/1 fl oz milk
2 whole eggs
1 egg yolk
20 g/¾ oz butter
5 g/¼ oz turmeric
fine salt

1 ~ Courgette and bay leaf custard

Heat the cream and the milk in a saucepan. Add the bay leaf and leave to infuse for a few minutes, then remove the bay leaf. Meanwhile, trim and finely slice the courgettes, then cook in boiling salted water for 2–3 minutes. Drain, refresh under cold water to preserve their colour, then drain again. Blend in a food processor with all the other ingredients, then carefully fill 4 buttered ramekins or dariole moulds.

2 ~ Aubergine and coconut milk custard

Preheat the oven to 180°C (350°F; gas mark 4). Halve the aubergine, season the flesh with salt, then drizzle lightly with olive oil. Thoroughly wrap each half in foil, then bake for 30 minutes. Remove from the oven, open the foil parcels, then scoop out the aubergine flesh with a spoon. Blend in a food processor with all the other ingredients, then carefully fill 4 buttered ramekins or dariole moulds.

3 ~ Cooking the custards

Cover the ramekins or moulds with cling film and place in a bain-marie. Cook in an oven preheated to 180°C (350°F; gas mark 4) for about 20 minutes. Keep an eye on them: the cooking time will depend on the size of the moulds used, so insert the tip of a sharp knife to check whether the custards are completely set. Carefully unmould onto plates and eat hot.

Tip | *To cook the custards in a bain-marie in the oven, put the ramekins or moulds into a large baking dish or roasting tin half-filled with water, then put the whole thing in the oven.*

Variation | *Try other flavours: (bell) pepper, pumpkin, spinach…*

For 4
Preparation time: 1 h
Cooking time: 30 min
(mushroom stock)
Marinating time: 10 min

} Lime-marinated scallop carpaccio with mushroom jelly

This subtle marriage of flavours and textures calls for really fresh live scallops.

The mushroom jelly

800 g/1 lb 12 oz button mushrooms
2 onions
25 g/1 oz salted butter
juice of ½ lemon
750 ml/25 fl oz mineral water
2 egg whites
6 g/0.2 oz gelatine leaves,
    soaked in cold water
fine salt

The scallops

8 scallops
100 ml/3½ fl oz white balsamic
    vinegar
1 lime
200 ml/7 fl oz olive oil
4 button mushrooms
fine salt

Equipment

8 cm/3¼ in round pastry cutter

1 ~ The mushroom jelly

Trim the mushrooms and slice half of them. Peel, trim and finely slice the onions, then cook in the butter over a gentle heat for 3–4 minutes. Add the sliced mushrooms and the lemon juice, cook for 5 minutes, then add the mineral water and simmer for about 30 minutes. Strain through a fine sieve, season lightly with salt and leave to cool. Pour the cold stock into a saucepan. Lightly beat the egg whites, then whisk into the stock. Bring to the boil, then lower the heat and cook over a gentle heat for about 10 minutes before straining the stock through a sieve lined with muslin (cheesecloth) or a clean cloth. (See step-by-step method on p. 138.) Reheat 250 ml/9 fl oz of the mushroom liquid, stir in the drained and squeezed-out gelatine then check the seasoning. Pour the jelly onto a plate or tray and leave to set in the fridge for at least an hour. Cut the jelly into rounds with a pastry cutter, then place on 4 plates. Chill again.

2 ~ The scallops

Cut the scallops into slices 2 mm/1⁄16 in thick. Combine the vinegar, lime zest, a little salt and the olive oil to make a marinade, then gently toss through the scallop slices and leave to marinate for 10 minutes.

3 ~ Plating up

Arrange the scallop slices in a rosette on top of the jelly rounds. Decorate with the remaining mushrooms, very thinly sliced (use a sharp knife, food processor or mandoline for this). Serve well chilled.

How to make mushroom stock

1

Thinly slice the mushrooms – they should be very fresh.

2

Cook the mushrooms in the butter with the finely sliced onions over a gentle heat. Stir often.

3

Add the liquid (either vegetable stock or water) and mix in well.

4

Bring to the boil, then lower the heat until the stock is barely simmering.

5

At the end of the cooking time, strain the stock through a fine sieve. Press down on the mushrooms in the sieve with the back of a ladle, to make sure none of the stock is wasted. Leave to cool. If the broth is clear enough at this stage, you can miss out the next two steps.

6

Lightly beat the egg whites, then whisk them into the warm mushroom stock.

7

Bring the stock to a gentle simmer. After about 10 minutes, use a ladle to make a hole in the 'raft' that will have formed on the surface. Every so often, carefully scoop out ladlefuls of the stock and baste the 'raft'.

8

Line a sieve with muslin (cheesecloth) and set over a bowl, or lay a clean cloth over the mouth of a jug. Strain the stock by carefully lifting it out of the pan ladleful by ladleful, disturbing the 'raft' as little as possible.

For 4
Preparation time: 35 min
Freezing time: 15 min
Cooking time: 20 min (15 + 5)

Guinea fowl supremes with walnut crust and a quick jus

We don't use guinea fowl as much as we should. Here I use supremes, which are breasts with their wings still attached; you may need to order them in advance from your butcher. Be sure to use good-quality walnuts for the crust.

The guinea fowl

4 guinea fowl supremes
splash of groundnut (peanut) oil
25 g/1 oz salted butter
fine salt, freshly ground pepper

The walnut crust

100 g/3½ oz freshly shelled walnuts
80 g/3 oz soft unsalted butter
60 g/2¼ oz breadcrumbs
fleur de sel

1 ~ The guinea fowl

Preheat the oven to 180°C (350°F; gas mark 4). Season the guinea fowl with fine salt and freshly ground pepper. Heat the oil and butter in an ovenproof frying pan over a high heat, then add the guinea fowl and brown all over. Transfer the pan to the oven and cook for 10–15 minutes. Remove from the oven, then take the guinea fowl out of the pan and set aside. Carefully spoon as much fat as possible out of the pan, leaving behind the meat juices, then add a little water and stir into the juices to make a quick jus (see step-by-step method on p. 142). Put to one side.

2 ~ The walnut crust

Combine the chopped walnuts and butter, then mix in the breadcrumbs and a little salt. Spread this mixture between two sheets of baking parchment and put the whole lot in the freezer for 15 minutes. Cut pieces of the walnut crust to fit over the guinea fowl supremes, but return them to the freezer (still between the sheets of paper) until you are ready to finish the dish.

3 ~ Finishing off

Preheat an overhead grill (broiler). Peel the paper from the pieces of walnut crust and drape over the guinea fowl, moulding the crust carefully around the meat. Grill crust-side up until golden, about 2–3 minutes, watching constantly to make sure they don't burn. Serve with a little of the reheated jus.

A bit of clarification | *Freezing the walnut crust makes it easier to cut and place on the supremes. But you can also use the mixture straightaway, without freezing it, by simply spreading it straight onto the guinea fowl with a knife; doing it this way uses more, though, which makes the dish slightly richer.*

Tips | *You can replace the walnuts with almonds or hazelnuts. Green asparagus makes a great accompaniment.*

141

How to make a quick jus

1

In a frying pan, cook your meat over a high heat with just a little oil. Small scraps of meat will stick to the pan and caramelize, and it is these that will flavour the sauce.

2

Keep cooking the meat over a high heat: the juices need to continue to cook but without burning. Stir often.

3

At this stage, you can add a little butter or some chopped shallot or onion, if you like. Mix them in well.

4

Still over a high heat, cook for a little longer, stirring frequently to prevent the meat burning. Keep an eye on the colour of the meat: it should never blacken.

5

The meat should now be perfectly browned all over.

6

Now pour in the cooking liquid (water or stock). Bring to the boil, then leave to cook over a very gentle heat.

7

Drain the meat in a sieve set over a clean saucepan, pressing down on the meat with the back of a ladle to squeeze out as much jus as possible. Season to taste.

SOMETHING SPECIAL

In this chapter I have simplified a selection
of the dishes from recent menus at my restaurant.
Some of them require luxurious, and therefore
expensive, ingredients; others are more affordable.
But all of them – and this is the thing to remember
– are easy to make. Just because you've decided
to spoil your guests doesn't mean you should tie
yourself in knots. On the contrary! Many of the
recipe elements can be prepared in advance,
leaving you more time to look after your guests.

For 4
Preparation time: 30 min
Cooking time: 15 min

}

Lobster and celery with red fruits

I find that the iodine flavours of lobster marry very well with red fruits, particularly blackcurrant. The next time you're lucky enough to get hold of some good lobster, make this dish: it's guaranteed to make your tastebuds shiver!

The lobsters

20 ml/¾ fl oz distilled white vinegar
2 x 550–600 g/1 lb 2 oz–1 lb 5 oz
    lobsters
50 g/1¾ oz butter

The celery

½ bunch of celery
knob of salted butter
100 ml/3½ fl oz vegetable stock
    (see step-by-step method on p. 126)
large pinch of green peppercorns
fine salt

The blackcurrant juice

250 g/8½ oz blackcurrants,
    fresh or frozen
25 g/1 oz caster (superfine) sugar

The red fruits

20 blackcurrants
20 blueberries
a little butter for cooking
8 redcurrants
8 raspberries
4 strawberries

1 ~ The lobsters

Bring a large saucepan of water to the boil, add the vinegar and the lobsters and cook for 3 minutes, then drain. Remove the claws from the cooked lobsters, then return the claws to the pan and cook for another minute. Cool the lobsters under cold running water for a few minutes, then shell and chill the meat.

2 ~ The celery

Trim the celery and cut the stalks into strips 1 cm/½ in wide. In a medium-sized saucepan, cook the celery with the butter over a gentle heat for 5 minutes, then add the vegetable stock and the crushed green peppercorns. Leave to cook for 4–5 minutes, or until the stock has practically evaporated and the celery is glossy. Season with a little salt.

3 ~ The blackcurrant juice

Put the blackcurrants and sugar into a saucepan set inside another, slightly larger saucepan filled with water (a bain-marie). Place over a gentle heat for a few minutes. Crush the warm blackcurrants and sugar to release all their juices, then strain through a sieve. Pour three-quarters of the juice into a clean saucepan and reduce over a medium heat until it thickens and becomes syrupy. Keep both the reduction and the remaining non-reduced juice to one side.

4 ~ Cooking the lobsters

Melt the butter in a frying pan, then add the lobster meat and gently reheat – be careful not to overcook it. Halve the lobster tails lengthways.

5 ~ The red fruits

Warm the blackcurrants and blueberries with a little butter in a small saucepan for about 10 seconds. Add the non-reduced blackcurrant juice and cook briefly before adding the other red fruits.

6 ~ Plating up

Brush the lobster tails and claws with a little butter, then place on the plates. Divide the celery and red fruits between the plates, then decorate with drops of the reduced blackcurrant juice.

The secret | Don't overcook the lobster. Its delicate flesh is very sensitive to too much heat: if overcooked, the texture will be ruined and the subtlety of its flavour will be lost. When you take the lobster tail meat from the shells, it should be barely cooked, as it will be finished off in the melted butter when it is reheated (step 4).

For 4
Preparation and
resting time: 45 min
Cooking time: 15 min (turnips)
+ 3 min (fish)

}

Pollock with turnip ravioli and rum sauce

Rum beurre monté is one of my favourite sauces: its complex, creamy vanilla flavour is a real delight, and it goes beautifully with pollock and turnips. Agar-agar is easily found in health-food shops.

The turnip ravioli

6 violet turnips
100 ml/3½ fl oz vegetable stock
   (see step-by-step method on p. 126)
½ teaspoon agar-agar
2 sprigs of mint
coarse salt

The rum beurre monté

½ shallot
1 tablespoon olive oil
20 ml/¾ fl oz golden rum
50 ml/1¾ fl oz double (heavy) cream
150 g/5½ oz unsalted butter
fine salt, freshly ground pepper

The pollock

4 x 110 g/3¾ oz pollock fillets
olive oil
fine salt

Equipment

steamer

1 - The turnips

Wash and trim the turnips. Keep one whole for later, then cut the rest into small pieces and cook in boiling salted water for 15 minutes. Drain well, then blend to a purée. Put the purée in a fine sieve, or in a colander lined with a clean cloth, and leave to drain for 30 minutes. Cut the reserved turnip into 1 mm/1⁄16 in slices and cook in boiling water for a couple of seconds. Drain, then refresh in cold water. Heat the vegetable stock in a small saucepan, add the agar-agar and simmer for a couple of seconds, then remove from the heat.

2 - The turnip ravioli

Lay the turnip slices on a work surface and put a teaspoon of drained turnip purée in the middle of half the slices. Brush the edges of the turnip slices with the vegetable stock (which, thanks to the agar-agar, will work like glue), then cover with the remaining turnip slices. Leave to set for a few minutes without touching them. Allow 2– 3 turnip ravioli per person.

3 - The rum beurre monté

Peel, trim and chop the shallot. Cook in a saucepan with the olive oil over a gentle heat for 2 minutes, then pour in the rum. Bring to the boil, then simmer until reduced by three-quarters. Add the cream and return to the boil, then remove from the heat. Gradually whisk in the diced butter. Season. (See step-by-step method on p. 150.)

4 - The pollock

Lightly season the fish with salt, then steam it for 3–4 minutes, depending on the thickness of the fillets. Remove from the steamer and leave to rest for 2 minutes.

5 - Plating up

Put a piece of fish on each plate and brush with a little olive oil. Next, add 2–3 turnip ravioli to each plate, then spoon over the rum beurre monté. Decorate with a few mint leaves and serve immediately.

Tip | There are different types of turnips – some good, and some not so good. What you want for this dish are small spring turnips, with their lovely white and violet skins, and nice crunchy flesh. Don't try to make it with turnips that are past their best or a bit soft, or you'll be wasting your time.

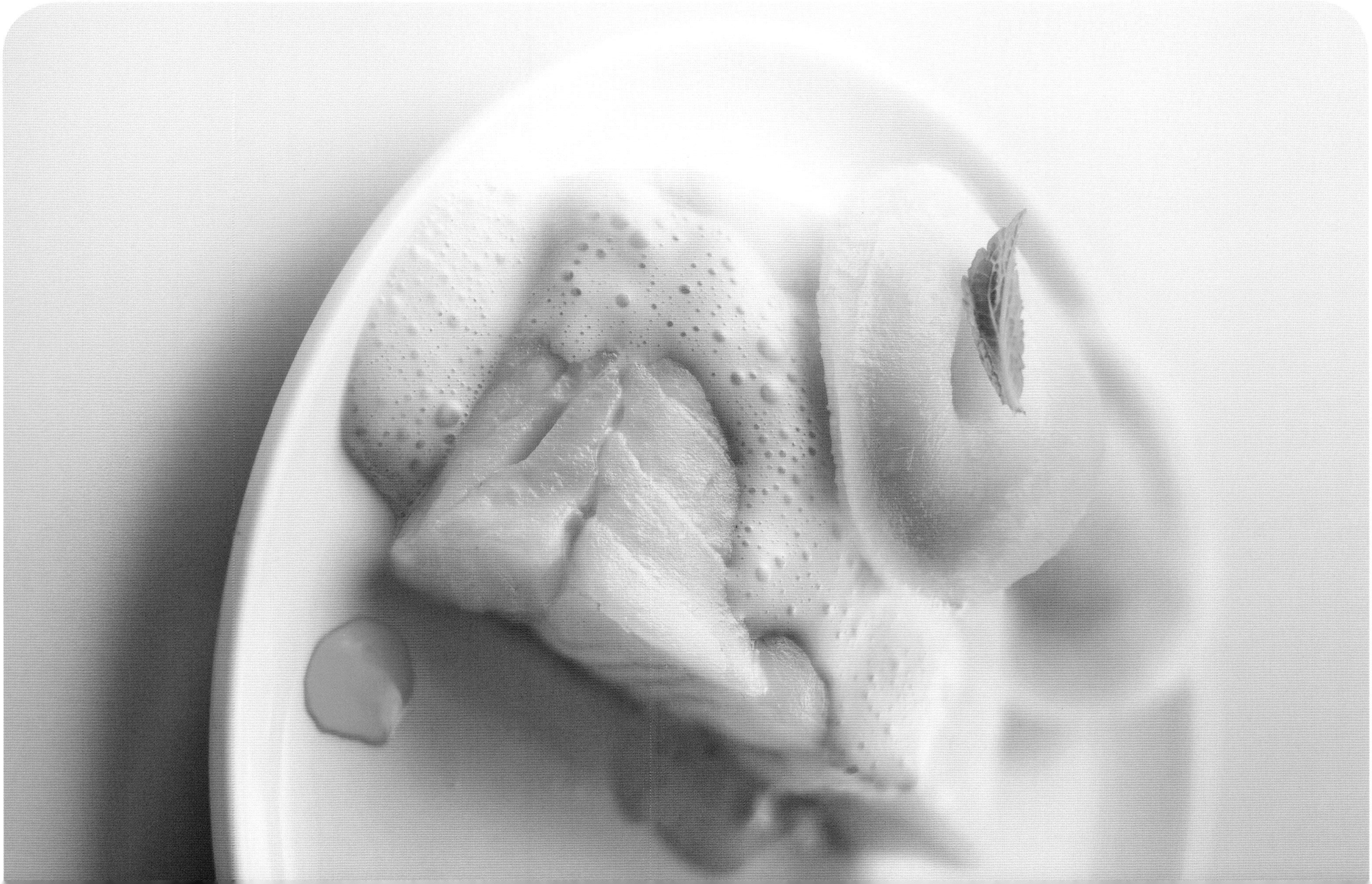

How to make a beurre monté

1

Trim, peel and finely slice the shallots. Cook them over a gentle heat with a little butter, stirring all the time, without letting them colour.

2

Add the alcohol of your choice (rum, for example) and bring to the boil.

3

Pour in a little vegetable stock or cream (just enough to cover the shallots, no more) then bring to the boil again.

4

Reduce the liquid by three-quarters.

5

Strain the reduction through a fine sieve. Press down well on the shallots to extract as much liquid as possible, then discard the shallots.

6

Off the heat, beat the cold, diced butter into the strained reduction.

7

Blend the butter and the reduction well, so that they are completely mixed together. Add a tablespoon of cream to stabilize the sauce.

8

Gently reheat the beurre monté if necessary, but don't let it boil. It needs to be light and frothy. Season to taste.

For 4
Preparation time: 20 min
Resting time: 30 min
Cooking time: 1 min

}

Oyster tartare with cheese fondue revisited

This is one of my newest discoveries! I like using cheese in my cooking and, despite what you might think, combining it with oysters actually improves the flavour of the oysters and makes them the star of the dish.

The oyster tartare

12 medium-sized (no 3) oysters
a few pansies
sprig of tarragon
100 ml/3½ fl oz oyster liquor
  (from the shells)
2.5 g/0.09 oz gelatine leaf,
  soaked in cold water

The cheese fondue

½ garlic clove
50 ml/1¾ fl oz white wine
50 g/1¾ oz Comté cheese
50 g/1¾ oz Beaufort cheese
60 ml/2 fl oz milk
100 ml/3½ fl oz cream
pinch of agar-agar
2 tablespoons kirsch
fine salt, freshly ground pepper

Equipment

oyster knife
siphon

1 ~ The oyster tartare

Shuck the oysters over a bowl, to capture all their liquor, then carefully cut the oysters into small pieces. Place the oyster tartare in the base of 4 glasses with some pansy petals and the finely chopped tarragon leaves. Put 100 ml/3½ fl oz of the oyster liquor into a saucepan and heat for a minute. Add the drained and squeezed-out gelatine leaf and stir to dissolve. Take off the heat and leave to cool, then carefully pour over the tartare. Chill for 30 minutes.

2 ~ The cheese fondue

Rub the inside of a saucepan with the half clove of garlic, then pour in the white wine. Warm over a medium heat, then add the grated Comté and Beaufort and allow to melt. Stir in the milk and blend with a stick blender until smooth, then simmer for 5 minutes, stirring constantly. Put the cream and agar-agar into another saucepan and bring to the boil, then pour onto the melted cheese. Check the seasoning, then stir in the kirsch.

3 ~ Serving

Pour the fondue mixture into a siphon and insert a gas canister. Shake, then keep somewhere warm, such as in a bain-marie. At the very last minute before serving, press the siphon's lever and dress the tartare with the cheese emulsion. Decorate with small pansy flowers, then eat immediately.

Tip | You can change the flavour of this tartare simply by using different types of oysters. If you like a sharper, more iodine-y taste, use flat oysters; for a softer, gentler flavour, use rock oysters.

For 4
Preparation time: 1 h 30 min
Cooking time: 35 min (meat)
+ 20 min (apples)
Resting time: 15 min

}

Roast duckling with saffron-spiced apple

Next time you're in the supermarket, don't just buy a chicken on auto-pilot; move down the aisle a bit, grab a duckling instead and inject a little freshness into your cooking. Sometimes, at least with food, change is really that simple. An easy side dish of spiced apples cooked 'en papillote' is all this needs to go with it. To make the sauce, see the step-by-step method on p. 142.

The apples

30 g/1 oz butter + a little extra
100 ml/3½ fl oz mineral water
1 teaspoon caster (superfine) sugar
4 pinches of ground cinnamon
1 roughly crushed star anise
12 strands of saffron
4 apples, preferably Egremont Russets
50 ml/1¾ fl oz vegetable stock
   (see step-by-step method on p. 126)
fine salt

The duckling

1 duckling, about 1.8 kg/4 lb
4 tablespoons groundnut (peanut) oil
2 large knobs of butter
200 ml/7 fl oz vegetable stock
   (see step-by-step method on p. 126)
fine salt, freshly ground pepper

1 ~ The apples

Preheat the oven to 180°C (350°F; gas mark 4). Melt the butter and pour into a baking dish, along with the mineral water. Mix in the sugar, cinnamon, star anise, saffron and a pinch of salt. Add the apples and toss them in the mixture, then bake for 20 minutes, basting them every so often. Remove the apples from the oven and allow to cool, but leave the oven on at the same temperature.

2 ~ The duckling

Season the duckling. Place the oil and half of the butter in a heavy-based roasting tin over a medium heat and brown the duckling on all sides, then transfer to the oven. Roast for 30–35 minutes, basting the duckling with the juices regularly. Remove from the oven and leave to rest for a few minutes.

3 ~ The jus

Remove the duckling and most of the fat from the roasting tin (keep it for roasting potatoes). Put the pan over the heat and cook, stirring often, for 15–20 seconds, or until the sticky bits of meat and juices in the base of the pan have caramelized. Add the vegetable stock and simmer until the surface appears almost 'beaded' with oil.

4 ~ Finishing off

Reheat the apples for a couple of minutes in a frying pan with the vegetable stock and the extra butter. Slice the duckling and serve with the hot apples and sauce. So simple, yet so good!

Making it even faster | *You can also try this recipe with duck breast, which will take only 10–15 minutes to cook.*

For 4
Preparation time: 1 h
Cooking time: 20 min (meat)
+ 45 min (chutney
and potatoes)
Resting time: 10 min

Roast veal with potato mousseline and plum chutney

Chutneys are really easy to make. Some fruit, a little time and attention, and you're done. And, whether you use plums or mangoes, they are delicious. Here I've made one to go with the subtle flavour of veal fillet.

The plum chutney

250 g/8½ oz red plums
10 g/⅓ oz fresh ginger
½ onion
1 clove of wet (spring) garlic
small knob of butter
2 pinches of ground cassia bark
40 g/1½ oz white balsamic vinegar
65 g/2½ oz caster (superfine) sugar
¼ bunch of lovage, or the leaves from
    a bunch of celery
fine salt

The potato mousseline

400 g/14 oz potatoes
100 ml/3½ fl oz cream
100 ml/3½ fl oz milk
large knob of butter
fine salt

The veal

40 g/1½ oz salted butter
groundnut (peanut) oil
4 x 150 g/5½ oz veal fillet steaks
fine salt, freshly ground pepper

1 ~ The plum chutney

Bring a pan of water to the boil, then immerse the plums in it for 1–2 minutes. Drain and leave to cool, then peel, remove the stones and dice the flesh. Peel and trim the ginger and onion, then dice. Heat the butter in a saucepan over a gentle heat, add the peeled and chopped garlic and the ginger and cook for 2–3 minutes. Add the diced onion and cook for a few minutes without letting it colour. Add the plums, cassia, vinegar and sugar, then leave the chutney to cook over a very low heat for 45 minutes. Finally, add the chopped lovage, season with salt and put to one side.

2 ~ The potato mousseline

Preheat the oven to 170°C (325°F; gas mark 3). Wash the potatoes, but don't peel them. Season with salt, then wrap them all in a large sheet of foil, folding the edges together to make a parcel, and bake for 45 minutes. Remove from the oven, then increase the oven temperature to 180°C (350°F; gas mark 4). Open the parcel and, while the potatoes are still hot, scoop the flesh from the skins. Purée with a food mill or potato ricer, then stir in the cream, milk and butter and season with a little salt.

3 ~ The veal

Heat the butter and oil in an ovenproof frying pan over a high heat, then add the seasoned veal fillets and colour on both sides. Transfer the pan to the oven and roast the veal for 20 minutes.

4 ~ Serving

Remove the veal fillets from the oven and leave to rest for 10 minutes. Serve them with the warm chutney and the hot mousseline.

Spicing it up | *The chutney recipe I've given you here is very mild and gentle, but you can easily add chilli powder, pepper or cumin to give it more personality.*

Tip | *You must use spring or 'wet' garlic (also sometimes called green garlic) for this. Dried garlic would overwhelm the dish.*

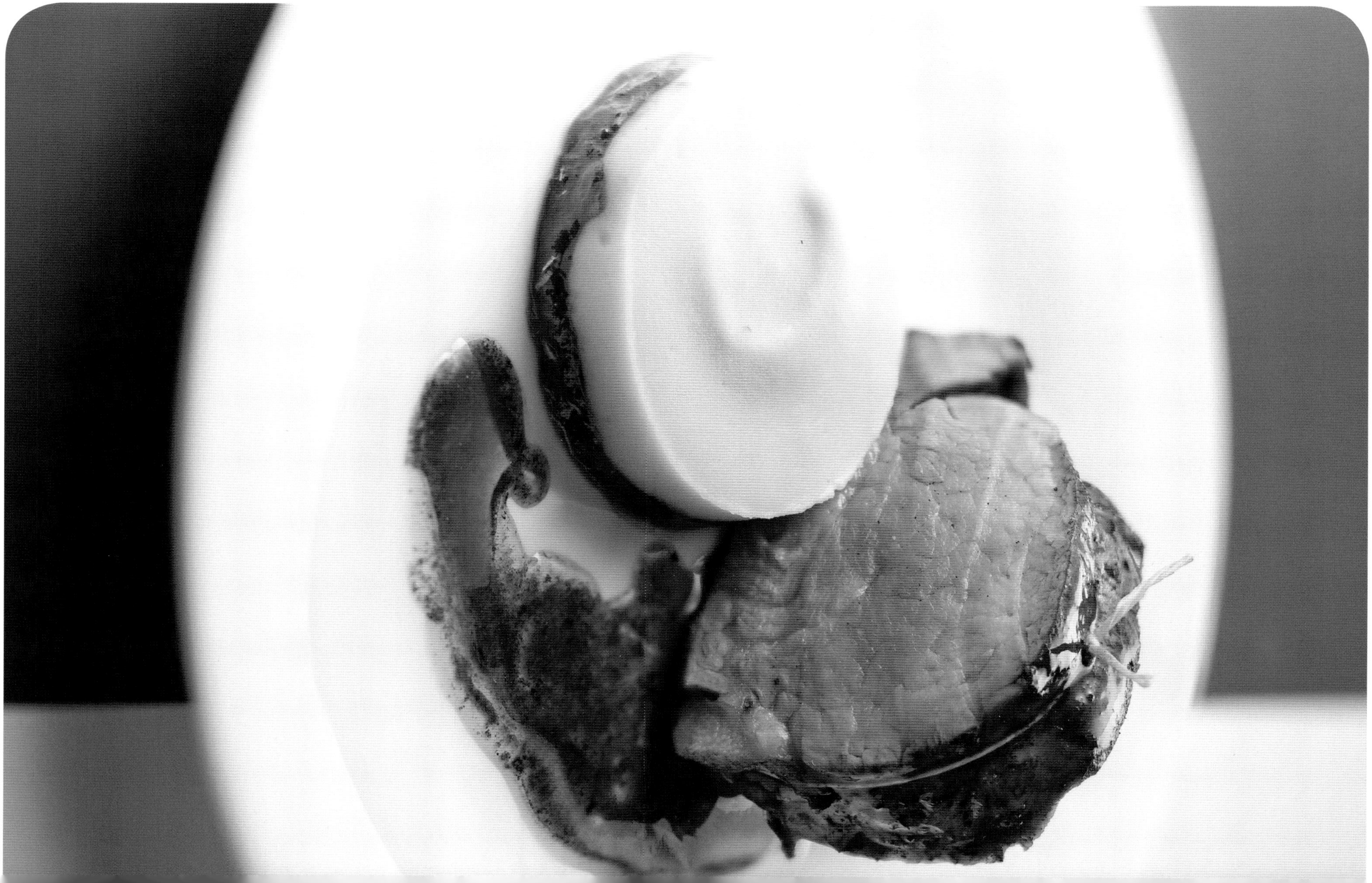

}

Poached egg with snail foam, galangal and artichokes

Snail foam? Yes, it is possible and, what's more, it is very subtle and sophisticated, especially with a hint of galangal (which you will find in Asian groceries). Everything in this dish can be prepared in advance.

The poached eggs

4 extra-fresh eggs
distilled white vinegar

The snail foam

150 ml/5 fl oz single (pouring) cream
130 ml/4¼ fl oz milk
150 ml/5 fl oz snail juices
½ teaspoon agar-agar
2 slices of fresh galangal or ginger

The artichokes and snails

2 raw artichoke hearts
olive oil
juice of ½ lemon
200 ml/7 fl oz white wine
500 ml/18 fl oz vegetable stock
   (see step-by-step method on p. 126)
1 tablespoon finely shredded
   coriander (cilantro)
2 dozen canned snails,
   with their juices
20 g/¾ oz salted butter
1 garlic clove
½ shallot
fine salt

Equipment

siphon

1 ~ The poached eggs

Crack each egg into a separate small bowl. Add the vinegar to a saucepan of water, then bring to the boil. Lower the heat so that the water just simmers, then stir it rapidly with a spoon to create a whirlpool effect. Hold each egg bowl near the surface of the simmering water, then gently slide in the egg: it will start to set immediately. Leave to cook, without letting the water boil, for 3 minutes. Remove the eggs with a slotted spoon, then immerse in a bowl of iced water. Leave to cool for 2–3 minutes, no longer. Drain the eggs and, using scissors, trim the rough edges to make lovely round poached eggs, being careful not to break the yolks. (See step-by-step method on p. 64.)

2 ~ The snail foam

In a lidded saucepan, mix together the cream, milk, snail juices and agar-agar. Bring to the boil, then immediately remove from the heat and add the chopped galangal. Cover and leave to infuse, off the heat, for 1 hour. Strain through a sieve, then pour into a siphon and insert 2 gas cartridges. Keep to one side. (You can also make the foam without a siphon, by frothing the mixture with a stick blender.)

3 ~ The artichokes and the snails

Cut the artichoke hearts into slices 1 mm/⅟₁₆ in thick, then cook in a lidded sauté pan or frying pan with a splash of olive oil, a little lemon juice, the white wine and the vegetable stock. Season with a little salt, cover and leave to cook for a few minutes, then stir in the chopped coriander. Put to one side. In another frying pan, sauté the snails with the butter and chopped garlic and shallot. Season.

4 ~ Serving

Arrange the artichoke slices in bowls, put the snails and poached eggs on top and finish with some snail foam.

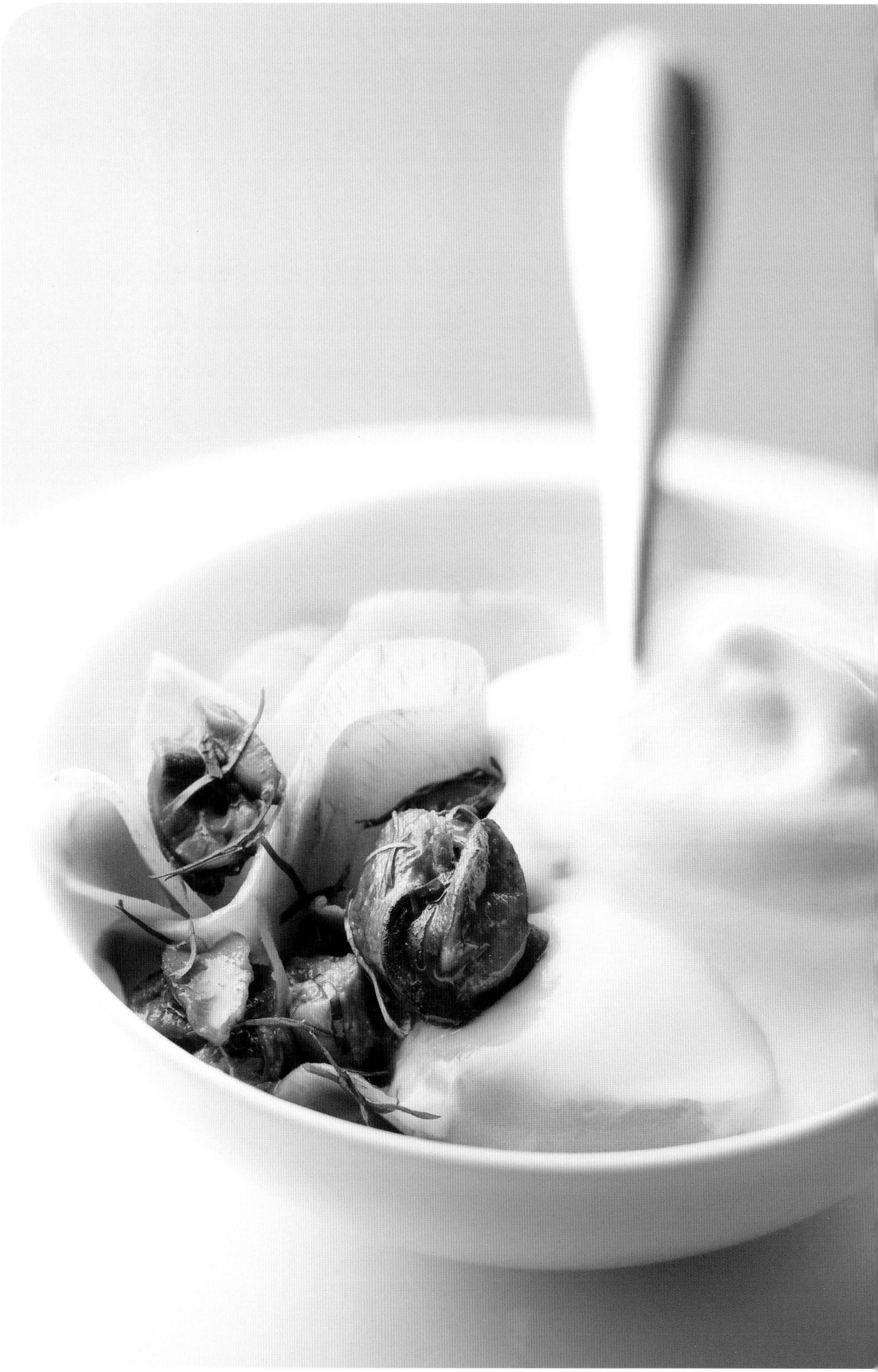

PATISSERIE

....

Patisserie is pure and utter pleasure.
Or rather it should be! Which is why, in this
chapter, I have included a combination of very
simple recipes, classics (brioche, lemon tart,
macaroons) and challenges (white chocolate fondant,
chestnut cream), all of which you can learn to make
at home. You can serve them as dessert, or as a treat
to share with children (especially the brioche and
chocolate spread). And in the Paris-Valence recipe,
you'll see that I have even taken a few tentative steps
towards creating a healthier, lighter dessert – but one
that's still just as delicious and enjoyable.

....

Makes 2 brioches (each for 6)
Preparation time: 30 min
Resting time: 45 min + 24 h
Cooking time: 30 min

}

Grandmother's brioche with chocolate hazelnut spread

Rediscover just how good brioche and chocolate spread can taste by making them yourself at home and giving your children a real treat! Just remember to make the brioche dough the day before, and use a good, full-flavoured dark chocolate for the spread. You should be able to find hazelnut paste in organic shops.

The brioche

500 g/1 lb 2 oz plain (all-purpose) flour
1½ teaspoons fleur de sel
80 g/3 oz caster (superfine) sugar
12 g/½ oz fresh yeast
250 g/8½ oz lightly beaten egg (about 5–6 eggs) + 1 egg yolk to glaze
250 g/8½ oz butter

The chocolate hazelnut spread

250 ml/9 fl oz double (heavy) cream
35 g/1¼ oz caster (superfine) sugar
200 g/7 oz dark (bittersweet) chocolate
200 g/7 oz hazelnut paste (see alternative below right)
20 ml/¾ fl oz sunflower oil

1 ~ The brioche

The night before, put the flour, fleur de sel, sugar, yeast and half the egg into a food mixer. Knead with the dough hook for 5 minutes, then add the diced butter in two lots, mixing well. When the dough comes away from the sides of the bowl, add the rest of the eggs and mix again. As soon as the eggs have been incorporated, leave the dough to rise for 45 minutes at room temperature. Mix again, so that it collapses, then chill in the fridge for 24 hours. The next day, shape the dough into 2 sausages and place in loaf tins. Lightly beat the egg yolk, then brush over the brioches to glaze. Leave to rise at room temperature for 2 hours, then bake in an oven preheated to 150°C (300°F; gas mark 2) for 30 minutes. (See step-by-step method on p. 164).

2 ~ The chocolate hazelnut spread

Put the cream and sugar in a saucepan and bring to the boil. Meanwhile, break the chocolate into pieces and place in a heatproof bowl, along with the hazelnut paste. Pour over the boiling cream and mix together well, then incorporate the oil. When the spread is smooth, leave it to rest for 30 minutes. It can be eaten straightaway or stored in the fridge.

3 ~ Serving

Cut the brioche into slices and serve with the spread on the side.

Tip |Can't get hold of hazelnut paste? Here's how to make it at home. Roast 200 g/7 oz shelled hazelnuts in an oven preheated to 150°C (300°F; gas mark 2) for 15 minutes. Remove from the oven and leave to cool, then blend until you have a fine paste.

Good to know | Keep the spread refrigerated and take it out 30 minutes before you want to use it, to allow it to soften.

How to make brioche

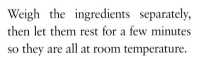

1

Weigh the ingredients separately, then let them rest for a few minutes so they are all at room temperature.

2

Put the flour, fleur de sel, sugar, yeast and half the egg into the bowl of an electric mixer.

3

Knead using the dough hook. Scrape the dough from the hook and the sides of the bowl, then knead for another 5 minutes.

4

Add the rest of the egg and knead again. Add the butter and knead until it is completely incorporated.

Put the dough into a large bowl, cover with cling film and chill for several hours in the fridge.

Shape the dough into one (or two) sausage(s) and put into loaf tin(s).

Brush the surface of the brioche with beaten egg yolk, then leave to rise for about 2 hours at room temperature.

Bake the brioche in the oven. Remove from the tin while still hot and leave to cool on a wire rack. Cut into slices to serve.

Makes 10
Preparation time: 20 min
Freezing time: 4 h
Cooking time: 6–7 min

}

White chocolate fondant with passionfruit and chocolate coulis

The famous dark chocolate fondant with a molten centre, invented by Michel Bras, can also be made with white chocolate. Surprise your guests by serving it with this easy and very different coulis.

The white chocolate fondant

140 g/5 oz white chocolate
125 g/4½ oz butter
80 g/3 oz caster (superfine) sugar
210 g/7½ oz beaten egg
   (about 4–5 eggs)
55 g/2 oz plain (all-purpose) flour
30 g/1 oz potato flour

The passionfruit and chocolate coulis

100 g/3½ oz passionfruit purée
25 g/1 oz caster (superfine) sugar
45 g/1½ oz dark (bittersweet)
   chocolate
45 g/1½ oz milk chocolate

Equipment

10 x 6–7 cm/2½–2¾ in pastry rings
   about 4 cm/1½ in high (or use
   a silicone muffin tray)

1 ~ The chocolate fondants

Break the chocolate into pieces and dice the butter, then put both into a saucepan. Put the saucepan in a bain-marie over a gentle heat to melt the butter and chocolate. Whisk the eggs and sugar together, then pour into the melted chocolate mixture. Fold in the flour and potato flour, mixing well, then fill the pastry rings (lined with baking parchment) or muffin tray with the mixture, about 70 g/2½ oz per fondant. Freeze for 4 hours. Preheat the oven to 180°C (350°F; gas mark 4) and bake the fondants for 6–7 minutes. Carefully remove the fondants from the rings or unmould from the tray.

2 ~ The passionfruit and chocolate coulis

Put the passionfruit purée and sugar in a saucepan and bring to the boil. Meanwhile, break the dark and milk chocolate into small pieces and place in a heatproof bowl. Pour the hot purée onto the dark and milk chocolate, then mix until smooth. Set aside at room temperature until needed.

3 ~ Plating up

Serve the fondants on plates with a little of the warm coulis alongside.

A tip on ingredients | *You should be able to find passionfruit purée ready-prepared in shops specializing in frozen food or online. Use very good-quality couverture white chocolate.*

For 4–6
Preparation time: 35 min
Resting time: 2 h
Cooking time: 5 min

Chestnut cream with pineapple and piña colada sorbet

Discover the delicate combination of chestnut and pineapple in this dessert, which is at once refreshing and melt-in-the-mouth. You need to make the chestnut cream in advance, but this will of course save you time on the day. Look for the coconut and pineapple purées in shops specializing in frozen food or online.

The chestnut cream

150 ml/5 fl oz milk
150 g/5½ oz chestnut purée
10 g/⅓ oz cornflour (cornstarch)
50 g/1¾ oz caster (superfine) sugar
1 egg yolk
2 g/0.07 oz gelatine leaf
95 g/3¼ oz butter

The piña colada sorbet

150 ml/5 fl oz milk
75 ml/2½ fl oz water
100 g/3½ oz caster (superfine) sugar
100 g/3½ oz coconut purée
280 g/10 oz pineapple purée
20 ml/¾ fl oz rum

The fruit

3 pineapples

Equipment

ice-cream maker

1 ~ The chestnut cream

Heat the milk with the chestnut purée and the cornflour. Meanwhile, mix the sugar and egg yolk together and soak the gelatine in cold water for 2–3 minutes. When the chestnut purée mixture comes to the boil, pour it onto the egg yolk mixture. Mix well, then pour back into the saucepan and simmer for 2–3 minutes. Remove from the heat and add the drained and squeezed-out gelatine, then leave the mixture to cool to 40°C/104°F – it will seem barely warm when you taste it. Dice the butter, then blend into the mixture using a stick blender. Pour into small glasses or cups and leave to set in the fridge for 2 hours.

2 ~ The piña colada sorbet

Make a syrup with the milk, water and sugar: put all three ingredients into a saucepan and bring to the boil, then remove from the heat immediately. Leave to cool, then pour this mixture onto the fruit purées and rum and mix well. Finally, pour the mixture into an ice-cream maker and follow the instructions. Once the sorbet is made, store it in the freezer.

3 ~ The fruit

Peel and trim the pineapples, then dice the flesh.

4 ~ Serving

Spoon some pineapple dice into each glass on top of the chestnut cream, then finish with a scoop of the sorbet.

Tip | *If you can't find chestnut purée, just blend some cooked chestnuts into the milk before heating it.*

Makes 15
Preparation time: 35 min
Resting time: 2 h
Cooking time: 20 min

Paris-Valence with red fruits

Try this – my very personal tribute to the famous Paris-Brest, which is usually made with praline. Here the cream used is lighter and laced with red fruits, adding a lovely sharpness.

The choux pastry

100 ml/3½ fl oz milk
100 ml/3½ fl oz water
4 g/⅛ oz salt
8 g/¼ oz caster (superfine) sugar
80 g/3 oz unsalted butter
120 g/4¼ oz sifted plain
  (all-purpose) flour
3 eggs
60 g/2¼ oz chopped almonds

The vanilla chantilly

500 ml/18 fl oz double or whipping
  (heavy) cream
50 g/1¾ oz caster (superfine) sugar
1 vanilla pod (bean)

The red fruits

100 g/3½ oz strawberries
100 g/3½ oz raspberries
50 g/1¾ oz blackcurrants
icing (confectioners') sugar,
  for dusting
a few roughly chopped unsalted
  pistachios

Equipment

piping bag

1 ~ The choux pastry

Preheat the oven to 165°C (320°F; gas mark 2–3). Put the milk, water, salt, sugar and butter in a saucepan and bring to the boil. Then, off the heat, pour in the sifted flour all in one go. Return to the heat for a minute, stirring all the time with a wooden spoon, to dry the mixture out. Pour the mixture into a large bowl then add the eggs one by one, mixing well to incorporate each one before adding the next. Transfer the dough to a piping bag and pipe rings 1 cm/½ in thick onto a lined baking sheet. Sprinkle with the chopped almonds, then bake in the oven for 20 minutes. Cool on wire racks.

2 ~ The vanilla chantilly

Using an electric whisk or food mixer, whip the cream with the sugar and the seeds from the vanilla pod until stiff.

3 ~ Plating up

Cut the choux rings in half and decorate one half with a mixture of the red fruits, followed by some of the chantilly. Place the other halves of the rings on top, dust with icing sugar, then scatter on the chopped pistachios. Place a few more red fruits in the middle of each Paris-Valence and serve immediately.

Tip | Put the cream and fruit onto the choux pastry at the very last minute before serving, otherwise the pastry may become a little soft.

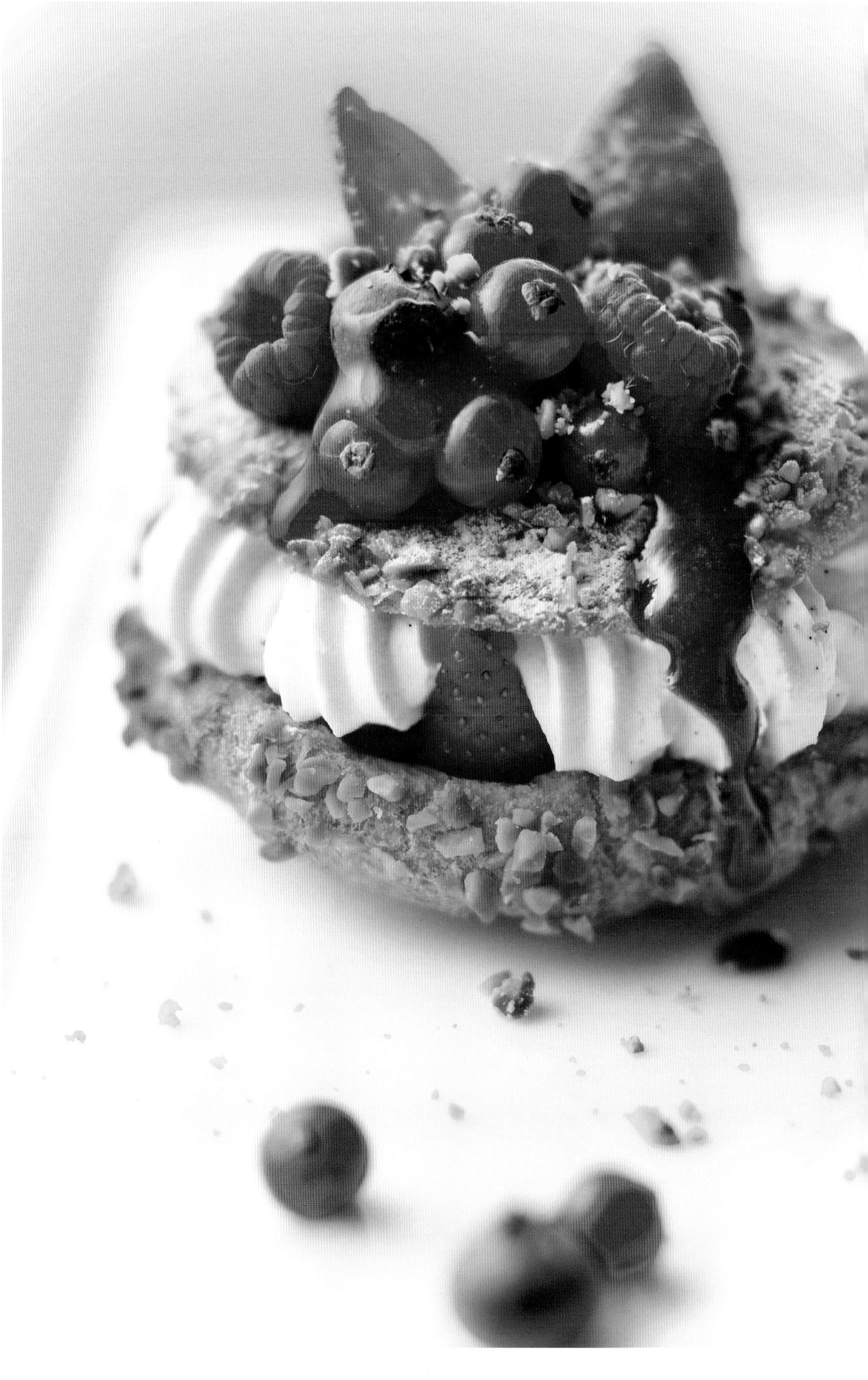

Makes 15
Preparation time: 35 min
Resting time: 40 min + 1 h
Cooking time: 10–12 min

Apricot macaroons

Despite popular opinion, macaroons aren't actually very difficult to make. You just need to be quite organized and methodically make the macaroon mixture and then the filling. Always use baking parchment to line the baking trays, as this will make it much easier to remove the macaroons once they're cooked.

The macaroon mixture

100 g/3½ oz egg white
(from about 3–4 eggs)
100 g/3½ oz caster (superfine) sugar
a pinch of powdered orange food
colouring (or a few drops of liquid
orange food colouring)
100 g/3½ oz icing (confectioners')
sugar
100 g/3½ oz ground almonds

The apricot compote

200 g/7 oz apricots
½ vanilla pod (bean)
a few drops of lemon juice
50 g/1¾ oz jam sugar

Equipment

piping bag

1 ~ The macaroon mixture

In a large bowl, whisk the egg whites with the caster sugar and colouring. Blend the icing sugar with the ground almonds, then sieve into the whisked egg whites. Fold in briefly, just until the mixture is soft and glossy, then fill a piping bag with the mixture and pipe rounds onto a lined baking sheet. Leave to rest for 1 hour at room temperature, until a crust forms on the surface, then bake in an oven preheated to 140°C (275°F; gas mark 1) for 10–12 minutes. Remove from the oven and leave to cool. (See step-by-step method on p. 174.)

2 ~ The apricot compote

Wash the apricots and remove their stones, then dice the fruit. Put the diced apricots in a saucepan with the vanilla pod, lemon juice and jam sugar. Cook over a gentle heat for about 20–30 minutes, stirring now and again. Remove from the heat and leave to cool completely (1 hour).

3 ~ Assembling the macaroons

Sandwich pairs of macaroons together with the cold aricot compote and serve immediately.

Variation | *Replace the apricots with strawberries, raspberries, mangoes or figs. Just remember to change the colouring to match!*

Tips | *If you use liquid food colouring, add it just before you finish whisking the egg whites. If you want to speed up the formation of the crust on the macaroons, put them in a very low oven (the lowest setting possible) for 30 minutes.*

Good to know | *If you use powdered food colouring, remove it from the packaging using the tip of a knife to prevent dying your fingers.*

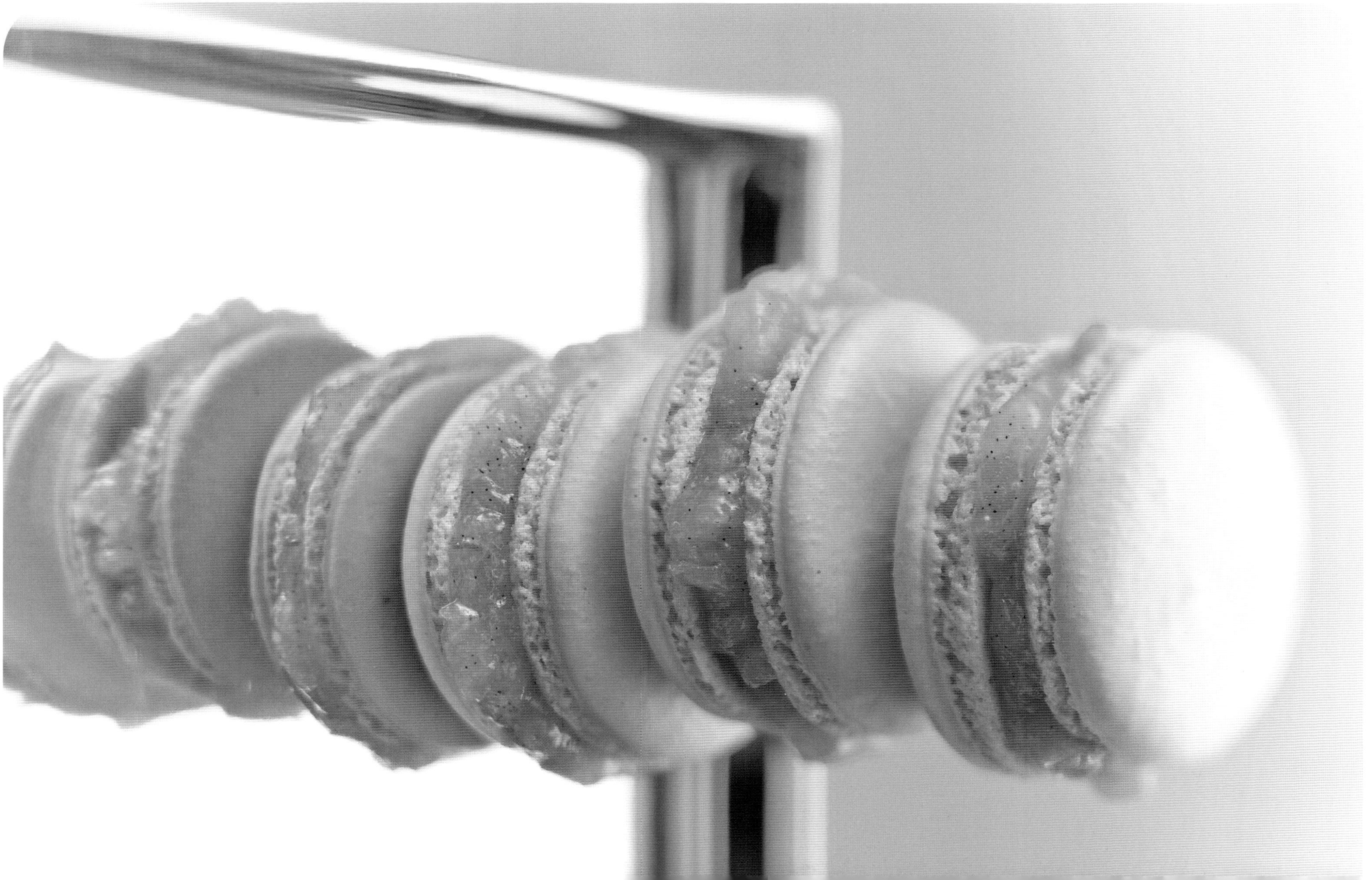

174 | How to make macaroons

1 - Mix the egg whites with the food colouring in a bowl.

2 - Blend the icing sugar and ground almonds until you have a very fine powder.

3 - Put the egg whites and food colouring into a mixer, then begin to whisk them. When they begin to form peaks, add the caster sugar.

4 - Sieve the blended icing sugar and ground almonds onto a sheet of baking parchment, to remove all the lumps.

5 - When the egg whites are very firm, and don't fall from the whisk when it is lifted, stop whisking.

6 - Add the sieved icing sugar and almond mixture to the egg whites and mix in.

7 - Stir the mixture gently with a spoon until it is soft and glossy.

8 - Fill a piping bag with the mixture. Hold the bag as shown in the photo.

9

9 - Squeeze the piping bag gently to pipe rounds onto a lined baking sheet. Leave some little space between them, as they will spread out as they cook. Finally, lightly tap the baking sheet to smooth out the mixture a little more.

10

10 - Leave the macaroons to rest for 1 hour at room temperature before cooking them. Their surface needs to dry out a little and form a crust. To check if they are ready, press gently with a finger; the mixture shouldn't stick to your finger.

11

11 - Bake the macaroons for 10–12 minutes at 140°C (275°F; gas mark 1). Remove from the oven and leave to cool, then remove from the baking sheet.

12

12 - Finish by filling the macaroons. Spoon a little filling onto a macaroon, then sandwich with another macaroon and gently press together.

Makes 1 tart (for 8)
Preparation time: 35 min
Resting time: 30 min
(the cream) + 2 h (the pastry
Cooking time: 15 min

}

Lemon tart
with Italian meringue

Everyone needs a recipe for lemon tart. I have made this one my own by tweaking the lemon cream, which is incredibly soft and melting. What are you waiting for... to your ovens!

The shortcrust pastry

180 g/6¼ oz plain (all-purpose) flour
65 g/2½ oz icing (confectioners') sugar
5 g/¼ oz vanilla sugar
75 g/2¾ oz butter
60 g/2¼ oz egg yolk (from about 3 eggs)

The lemon cream

125 ml/4 fl oz lemon juice
60 g/2¼ oz egg yolk (from about 3 eggs)
80 g/3 oz lightly beaten egg (about 2 eggs)
75 g/2¾ oz caster (superfine) sugar
75 g/2¾ oz butter

The Italian meringue

150 g/5½ oz caster (superfine) sugar
75 g/2¾ oz egg white (from about 3 eggs)
icing (confectioners') sugar

Equipment

cooking thermometer

1 ~ The shortcrust pastry

Rub the flour, sugars and butter together in a large bowl. When the mixture has a crumbly texture, mix in the egg yolks. Don't overmix it; the ingredients should be just combined. Leave the pastry to rest in the fridge for at least 2 hours. Preheat the oven to 150°C (300°F; gas mark 2). Roll the pastry out into a circle about 3 mm/⅛ in thick then ease it into a 28 cm/11 in tart tin, pressing it into the corners. Place a sheet of baking parchment on top of the pastry, cover with baking beans or 400 g/14 oz dried beans, then bake in the oven for 15 minutes. Remove from the oven and leave to cool, then remove the baking beans and parchment.

2 ~ The lemon cream

Put the lemon juice, egg yolk, beaten egg and sugar into a saucepan and bring to the boil. Simmer for a couple of minutes, then leave to cool to 30°C/86°F – the mixture should be warm to touch, no more. Using a stick blender, gradually mix the diced butter into the lemon mixture. Chill while making the meringue.

3 ~ The Italian meringue

Put the sugar into a saucepan with 50 ml/1¾ fl oz of water and heat to 121°C/250°F (check the temperature with a cooking thermometer). Whisk the egg whites to soft peaks, then, still whisking, slowly pour in the sugar syrup. Keep whisking for 5 minutes as the mixture cools.

4 ~ Finishing off

Preheat an overhead grill (broiler). Spread the lemon cream evenly over the base of the cooked tart shell, then top with the Italian meringue, shaping it as you wish. Sprinkle with icing sugar and grill for 2–3 minutes, or until the peaks of the meringue are golden brown. Leave to cool at room temperature for about 30 minutes before serving.

Variation | *Try replacing the lemon juice with juice from another citrus fruit: lime, pink grapefruit, orange, blood orange...*

Tip | *To create a more elegant tart, like the one in the photo, use a piping bag with a St Honoré nozzle to add the meringue to the tart.*

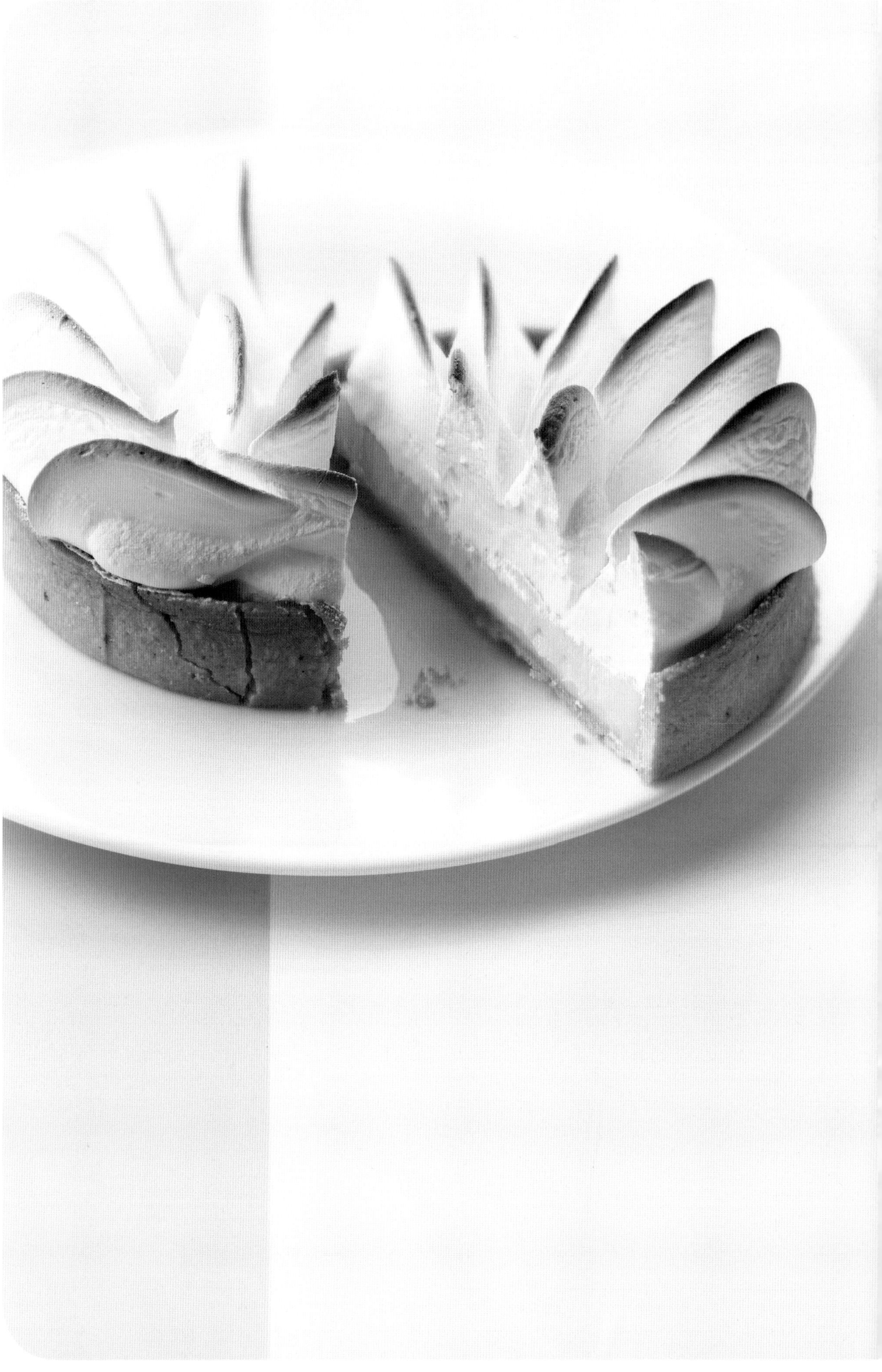

3

Classics

COLD DISHES AND STARTERS

Cold dishes, especially for a buffet,
are a traditional part of French hospitality:
guests should have something to snack on while
waiting for the more complicated hot dishes that
may need finishing off at the last minute.
They can also be used to showcase seasonal
ingredients or more demanding preparations,
such as terrines and eggs or fish set in jewel-
coloured jellies. These days cooking is changing,
because life is changing: in a world where simple
meals are a daily necessity, cold dishes come
into their own, just as they always have
at bistros and neighbourhood restaurants.

For 4
Preparation time: 45 min
Cooking time: 35 min
Resting time: 1 h 30 min

Soft-boiled egg in lemon jelly with foie gras royale

I really love eggs, as they work equally well in the most sophisticated dishes and the simplest. The foie gras royale (a crème brûlée mixture enriched with foie gras) is one of my signature preparations: cooking it very slowly intensifies the flavours and creates a texture that melds beautifully with the egg. Here I finish it with a lemon jelly, which adds a floral note and lifts the foie gras, making it taste fresher and lighter.

The soft-boiled eggs

splash of vinegar
2 extra-fresh eggs

The foie gras royale

100 g/3½ oz raw duck foie gras
40 ml/1½ fl oz crème fraîche
   (sour cream)
2 teaspoons milk
2 eggs
fine salt, freshly ground pepper

The lemon jelly

zest of 1 lemon
8 g/0.3 oz gelatine leaves
fine salt

Finishing off

fleur de sel
olive oil

Equipment

4 shallow dishes,
   about 8–10 cm/3¼–4 in across

1 ~ The soft-boiled eggs

Put the vinegar in a large pan of water and bring to the boil. Cook the eggs in the water for 6 minutes, then remove and cool in a large bowl of cold water for 5 minutes. Drain again and shell.

2 ~ The foie gras royale

Preheat the oven to 120°C (250°F; gas mark ¼–½). Dice the foie gras. Blend the foie gras, crème fraîche, milk and eggs with a little salt and pepper until smooth, then strain through a fine sieve and adjust the seasoning to taste. Pour into 4 shallow bowls, then place in a large baking dish. Fill the larger dish with enough water to come two-thirds of the way up the sides of the bowls, then cover with baking parchment. Bake in the oven for about 20 minutes, or until the centre trembles just slightly when removed from the oven. The cooking time will depend on the depth of the royale in the bowl. Leave to cool, then chill in the fridge for about 20 minutes.

3 ~ The lemon jelly

Simmer the lemon zest with 250 ml/9 fl oz of water in a small saucepan. Remove from the heat, cover and leave to infuse for about 10 minutes. Soak the gelatine leaves in cold water for 2 minutes. Add the drained and squeezed-out gelatine leaves to the warm lemon water. Stir to dissolve, then season with a little salt.

4 ~ Finishing off

Using a tablespoon, gently hollow out a space big enough to hold half an egg in the centre of each royale. Halve the eggs lengthways, then place a half in each hollow. Carefully pour the lemon jelly over the surface to completely cover the eggs and the royales. The jelly should still be liquid, but will slowly turn syrupy as the gelatine takes effect. Leave to cool and set for at least 1 hour. When ready to serve, garnish with a little fleur de sel and a few drops of olive oil. Serve chilled.

Tip | *It is important to use the right sort of foie gras: you need duck foie gras that is soft to the touch, even when cold, and uniformly coloured with no red spots.*

For 4
Preparation time: 40 min
Cooking time: 10 min
Resting time: about 30 min

}

Lobster 'bellevue' with saffron tomato jelly and rainbow tomatoes

'Bellevue' refers to a technique for lacquering seafood or meat with a jelly, which prevents the food from drying out and creates a beautiful showpiece. I also use this method to add more flavour and prevent discolouration. In this recipe I've married the dense yet subtle flesh of a lobster with the gentle acidity of ripe tomatoes and the perfume of saffron.

The saffron tomato jelly

3 ripe Roma tomatoes
½ teaspoon ground saffron
10 g/⅓ oz gelatine leaves
a few strands of saffron
fine salt

The lobster

2 x 600 g/1 lb 5 oz lobsters
coarse salt

The tomatoes

1 Green Zebra tomato
1 yellow tomato
1 beef (beefsteak) tomato
20 ml/¾ fl oz white balsamic vinegar
40 ml/1½ fl oz olive oil
fine salt

1 ~ The saffron tomato jelly

Wash the tomatoes, remove their stalks and quarter. Blend with 250 ml/9 fl oz of water until smooth, then pour into a saucepan and bring to the boil. Lower the heat and leave to simmer for about 30 minutes, then strain through a sieve lined with muslin (cheesecloth) or a clean tea towel. Leave to settle, then carefully pour off just the clear liquid. Taste the tomato water, and if the tomato flavour is not concentrated enough, bring to the boil again and reduce lightly, then taste again and season as necessary. Mix 500 ml/18 fl oz of this tomato water with the ground saffron, then strain into a clean saucepan. Soak the gelatine in iced water for 3 minutes. Heat the tomato water, without letting it boil, then stir in the drained and squeezed-out gelatine. Pour the jelly into a bowl and set aside.

2 ~ Cooking the lobster

Tie the lobsters as shown on p. 186; this ensures they cook more evenly. Cook them in a large saucepan filled with boiling salted water, then lift them out with a skimming spoon or tongs and drain. Remove the claws and cook them for another 2 minutes, then drain. Immerse the lobster tails and claws in iced water and leave to cool. Once completely cold, drain again, then remove all the shell. Slice the lobster tails into thick slices, remembering to remove the gut with the tip of a knife if necessary.

3 ~ Lacquering the lobster

Place a saffron strand on each slice of lobster (as in the photo) and then, using a tablespoon, cover the slice with the cold tomato jelly, which should still be liquid but syrupy. Place in the fridge and leave the jelly to set for 10 minutes, then remove from the fridge and add another layer of jelly to each slice. Keep chilled.

4 ~ The tomatoes, finishing off and plating up

Remove the stalks from the tomatoes, if necessary, then cut a cross in the top of each one. Peel the tomatoes (see step-by-step method on p. 22), then cut into very fine slices. Make a vinaigrette by whisking together the vinegar, oil and a little salt. Dress the tomato slices with the vinaigrette, then divide them between 4 plates, making sure each plate gets a mixture of colours. Place the lobster slices and claws on top and serve immediately.

How to cook a lobster

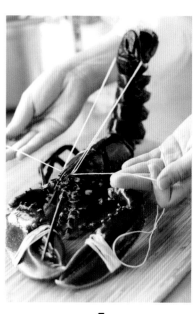

1

The lobster must be alive. It should feel heavy and dense (not hollow), and should react when touched or picked up.

2

Pass a length of kitchen string between the lobster's eyes (the piece of string should be at least twice the length of the lobster), so that you have an open loop.

3

Pull the strings down to the lobster's tail and wrap them under it, then run the strings back to the lobster's head.

4

Grab the two ends of the string, pull to tighten (the lobster's tail should lift), then tie a double knot to keep everything in place.

Remove the elastic bands from the lobster's claws, then immerse it in a large pan of boiling salted water.

Once cooked, drain the lobster and immerse it in a large bowl of water and ice cubes to stop the cooking process.

Remove the lobster tail from the rest of the body, break off the shell in pieces and carefully remove without damaging the meat.

Use the handle of a large knife to break the shell of the claws, then ease out the meat.

For 8
Preparation time: 1 h
Marinating time: 2 h
Resting time: 24 h
Cooking time: 1 h 10 min

Game terrine with red onion pickles

A traditional cold starter in France, game terrine used to be on the menu at the Auberge du Pin, my grandmother's restaurant set in the middle of the wild boar hunting grounds. The original version would be presented 'en croute', encased in hot-water pastry, but I prefer to serve it with crumbly Parmesan pastry rounds.

The game terrine

500 g/1 lb 2 oz game, such as
  wild boar, pheasant, venison, etc.
250 g/8½ oz pork neck
250 g/8½ oz pork back fat
500 ml/18 fl oz red wine
200 g/7 oz liver (chicken,
  calves' or game)
1 small shallot
20 ml/¾ fl oz Cognac
125 g/4½ oz cooked foie gras
groundnut (peanut) oil
20 g/¾ oz salt
2.5 g/0.09 oz pepper
2.5 g/0.09 oz caster sugar
1½ eggs
50 g/1¾ oz shelled pistachios
50 g/1¾ oz caul

The red onion pickles

1 red onion
100 ml/3½ fl oz white balsamic
  vinegar
50 g/1¾ oz caster (superfine) sugar

The Parmesan pastry

180 g/6¼ oz plain (all-purpose) flour
80 g/3 oz ground almonds
5 g/¼ oz salt
40 g/1½ oz grated Parmesan
160 g/5¾ oz soft butter
1 large egg
20 g/¾ oz capers
20 g/¾ oz cornichons

Equipment

mincer with a fine blade
terrine mould or loaf tin
cooking thermometer (optional)
10 cm/4 in round pastry cutter

1 ~ The game terrine

Roughly chop the game, pork neck and fat and place in a bowl with the red wine. Leave to marinate for about 2 hours. Sauté the liver with the finely chopped shallot in a little oil over a medium heat for 2–3 minutes, then add the Cognac and flambé. Remove from the heat and drain off the fat. Finely mince the game, pork neck and fat and sautéed livers into a large bowl. Add the diced foie gras, salt, pepper, sugar, eggs and chopped pistachios, then combine thoroughly. Line a loaf tin with the caul, leaving the excess to hang over the edges, fill with the terrine mixture, then cover with the excess caul. Press down on the surface with the palm of your hand. Preheat the oven to 160°C (320°F; gas mark 2–3). Cover the terrine with foil, then place in a deep roasting tin or baking dish. Pour in enough hot water to come about three-quarters of the way up the sides of the terrine, then bake for about 1 hour; if you have a cooking thermometer, insert it into the centre of the terrine to check the temperature – it should be 58°C/137°F. Remove the terrine from the oven and the water bath. Place a rectangular plate or dish on top of the terrine in its mould, then weigh down with something heavy (such as a can of food) to compress it as it cools. Chill in the fridge for at least 24 hours.

2 ~ The red onion pickles

Peel and trim the onion, then cut into thin segments. Bring the vinegar, sugar and 50 ml/1¾ fl oz of water to the boil in a saucepan, then add the onion. Simmer over a gentle heat for a few minutes, then remove from the heat and leave to cool.

3 ~ The Parmesan pastry

Preheat the oven to 180°C (350°F; gas mark 4). Combine the flour, almonds, salt and Parmesan in a bowl, then rub in the butter until the mixture is crumbly. Add the egg and bring the dough together, then mix in the drained and chopped capers and cornichons. Roll out the pastry quite thinly, then cut out four 10 cm/4 in circles. Place on a lightly floured baking tray and bake for 10 minutes, or until golden.

4 ~ Serving

Unmould the terrine and cut into even slices, then place on top of the pastry rounds. Top with some of the red onion pickles and serve immediately.

Tip | If you want to make other terrines, the amounts of egg and seasoning you'll need for 1 kg/2¼ lb mixture are: 1 egg, 15 g/½ oz salt, 2 g/0.07 oz pepper and 2 g/0.07 oz caster (superfine) sugar.

For 6
Preparation time: 1 h
Marinating time: 30 min
Cooking time: about 1 h
Resting time: 24 h
}

Duck foie gras terrine with rhubarb and tarragon compote

This foie gras and Rivesaltes terrine, a relative of the more traditional terrine, is a signature dish in my restaurant. I have pared back the spicing in order to preserve the magnificent flavour of the duck foie gras, then partnered the terrine with a rhubarb and tarragon compote, which adds a sharp yet sweet note that contrasts with the softness of the foie gras. The play of flavours is what makes this dish so special.

The duck foie gras terrine

1 lobe of fresh duck foie gras, about 500–600 g/1 lb 2 oz–1 lb 5 oz
9 g/0.3 oz salt (15 g/0.5 oz per 1 kg/2¼ lb foie gras)
1 g/0.03 oz pepper (2 g/0.07 oz per 1 kg/2¼ lb foie gras)
1 g/0.03 oz caster sugar (2 g/0.07 oz per 1 kg/2¼ lb foie gras)
50 ml/1¾ fl oz Rivesaltes

The rhubarb and tarragon compote

4 stalks red rhubarb
40 g/1½ oz caster (superfine) sugar
sprig of tarragon + a few extra leaves
fine salt

Finishing off

fleur de sel
freshly ground pepper
6 slices of good toast (sourdough or pain de campagne)

Equipment

terrine mould or loaf tin

1 ~ The duck foie gras terrine

Weigh the foie gras. Based on that, work out the exact weight of salt, pepper and sugar required and mix them together in a small bowl. Remove the nerves from the foie gras, then separate the large and small lobes. Place them on a work surface, cut-side facing up and, using a small knife, carefully remove all the veins. A word of warning: in the large lobe, there will be two groups of veins, one on the surface and one much more deeply buried; you need to remove the first and then dig out the second – you will need to cut through the foie to do this, but try to do as little damage as you can. Place the lobes on a sheet of baking parchment or in a dish and season with the salt-pepper-sugar mixture, then pour over the Rivesaltes. Cover with cling film and leave to marinate for at least 30 minutes. Preheat the oven to 120°C (250°F; gas mark ¼–½). Put the foie gras, uncut-side down, in a terrine mould or loaf tin, the press it down a little with your hand to remove any excess air. Cover the terrine with a lid or foil, then place in a deep roasting tin or baking dish. Pour in enough hot water to come about three-quarters of the way up the sides of the terrine, then bake for about 10 minutes for every 100 g/3½ oz foie gras. Remove the terrine from the oven and the water bath. Place a rectangular plate or dish on top of the terrine in its mould, then weigh down with something heavy (such as a can of food) to compress it as it cools. Chill in the fridge for at least 24 hours. (See step-by-step method on p. 192.)

2 ~ The rhubarb and tarragon compote

Wash and trim the rhubarb stalks, then cut into pieces. Put the rhubarb into a frying pan or saucepan with the sugar and cook over a gentle heat until very soft. Remove from the heat and add the tarragon sprig, then cover and leave to infuse for a few minutes. Adjust the seasoning with a little salt, then remove the tarragon sprig and leave to cool. When the compote is completely cold, add a few extra chopped tarragon leaves.

3 ~ Serving

Dip the bottom of the terrine mould or loaf tin in very hot water for 4–5 seconds, then unmould onto a board and slice evenly. Sprinkle a little fleur de sel and some freshly ground pepper on each slice. Place on plates with some toast and a little rhubarb compote, then serve immediately (the foie gras will discolour rapidly once sliced).

How to make a foie gras terrine

192

1

About 15–20 minutes before starting to cook, take the foie gras from the fridge and remove any packaging, so that it comes to room temperature.

2

Weigh the foie gras to work out the exact amount of seasoning required, then weigh out the seasonings.

3

Separate the two lobes of the foie gras with your hands and put them on a work surface. Make a cut about 1.5 cm/¾ in deep to reveal the veins, then use the tip of a knife to lift them out gently, being careful not to snap them.

4

Put the foie gras onto a piece of baking parchment. Mix together the salt, pepper and sugar and coat both sides of the foie gras with it. Then spoon over the alcohol and leave to marinate.

5

Put the foie gras into a terrine mould or loaf tin, uncut-side down, then press down on it gently – just to remove any excess air in the tin, especially in the corners.

6

Put the terrine into a water bath – the hot water should come almost to the top of the terrine. Cover the terrine and cook in the oven.

7

Remove the terrine from both the oven and the bain-marie. Place a rectangular plate or lid on the surface and press down a little to remove the excess fat.

8

Put a weight on top and leave it there while the terrine is chilling. This helps to make the terrine smooth, with a lovely texture.

For 4
Preparation time: 30 min
Cooking time: 15 min

} Mixed vegetables with smoked eel

This king of starters, which has become a bit unfashionable, is definitely worth resurrecting! It can be made with different vegetables every season, depending on what you like. Dressed with a smoked eel mayonnaise, which adds a lovely savoury note, this dish will reward you with a wonderful mixture of flavours, as long as you choose seasonal vegetables and cook them properly, preserving their taste and texture.

The vegetables

10 red radishes

1 black radish

2 carrots

¼ cauliflower

50 g/1¾ oz shelled petits pois

50 g/1¾ oz shelled broad (fava) beans

150 g/5½ oz trimmed green beans,
   cut into lengths

8 green asparagus spears,
   cut into lengths

splash of olive oil

1 garlic clove

sprig of thyme

100 ml/3½ fl oz vegetable stock
   (see step-by-step method on p. 126)

fine salt

Smoked eel mayonnaise

1 egg yolk

1 tablespoon mustard

250 ml/9 fl oz groundnut (peanut) oil

splash of sherry vinegar

15 g/½ oz smoked eel

fine salt, freshly ground pepper

1 ~ The vegetables

Trim the red radishes, then cut into quarters. Trim the black radish and peel, top and tail the carrots. Dice the black radish and the carrots. Break the cauliflower into florets. Cook all the green vegetables (petits pois, broad beans, green beans and asparagus) separately in boiling salted water for about 5 minutes, depending on the vegetable. Remove each of the vegetables, as they are cooked, with a slotted spoon and immerse in cold water to prevent them cooking any further and keep them crunchy. Drain in a colander. Warm a splash of olive oil in a frying pan over a medium heat, then add the carrots, black radish and cauliflower. Add the garlic and thyme and sauté for 1–2 minutes, then deglaze with the stock. Leave the vegetables to cook over a gentle heat for 5 minutes, or until tender, then drain and allow to cool.

2 ~ The smoked eel mayonnaise

Make a mayonnaise, following the recipe on p. 196. Add the diced smoked eel and season.

3 ~ Finishing off

In a large bowl, mix all the vegetables with a third of the mayonnaise (keep the rest, chilled, for another use). Check the seasoning and serve immediately.

Tip | *Here are some seasonal combinations I love:*
Spring: the selection of vegetables above;
Summer: mangetout (snow peas), petits pois, baby broad (fava) beans, different-coloured courgettes (zucchini), tomato;
Autumn: walnuts, carrots, pumpkin, bulb fennel, Jerusalem artichoke, apple;
Winter: beetroot (beet), romanesco, celeriac, turnip, carrot.

Cold sauces

Sauces are really important with cold starters. They bring out all the different facets and flavours of ingredients; they can soften something sharp, or refresh something in need of a lift. Use them to add an extra dimension to a dish – warmth, acidity or richness – and remember to make them your own, varying them as you see fit.

For 4
Preparation time: 5 min

}

1 egg yolk
1 tablespoon mustard
250 ml/9 fl oz groundnut (peanut) oil
splash of sherry vinegar
fine salt, freshly ground pepper

Mayonnaise

Mix the egg yolk with the mustard in a bowl. Using a hand whisk, whisk the mixture constantly while slowly pouring in the oil until the mixture comes together. Season with salt and pepper, then stir in the vinegar.

A lighter version | Stir 25 ml/1 fl oz of water into the finished mayonnaise – this makes the mayonnaise softer and a lighter colour.

When to use it | This is great with cold poached fish, such as salmon, cod or hake.

For 4
Preparation time: 5 min

}

1 egg yolk
1 tablespoon mustard
250 ml/9 fl oz groundnut (peanut) oil
splash of sherry vinegar
1 tablespoon diced capers
1 tablespoon sliced cornichons
1 tablespoon finely chopped parsley
1 tablespoon finely chopped tarragon
1 tablespoon finely chopped coriander
  (cilantro)
fine salt, freshly ground pepper

Sauce gribiche

Mix the egg yolk with the mustard in a bowl. Using a hand whisk, whisk the mixture constantly while slowly pouring in the oil until the mixture comes together. Season with salt and pepper, then stir in the vinegar. Add the capers, cornichons and herbs. Season again, if necessary, then mix well.

When to use it | Sauce gribiche is wonderful served with game terrines or calf's head.

}

For 4
Preparation time: 15 min

1 egg yolk
1 tablespoon mustard
250 ml/9 fl oz groundnut (peanut) oil
splash of sherry vinegar
1 tablespoon diced capers
1 tablespoon finely diced cornichons
1 tablespoon finely chopped parsley
1 tablespoon finely chopped tarragon
1 tablespoon chopped onion
fine salt, freshly ground pepper

Tartare sauce

Mix the egg yolk with the mustard in a bowl. Using a hand whisk, whisk the mixture constantly while slowly pouring in the oil until the mixture comes together. Season with salt and pepper, then mix in the vinegar. Add the capers, cornichons, herbs and onion. Season again if necessary then mix everything in well.

When to use it | *Tartare sauce is perfect with both cold meats (roast beef, pork or chicken) and grilled ones.*

}

For 4
Preparation time: 20 min

1 tomato
¼ red (bell) pepper
¼ green (bell) pepper
¼ yellow (bell) pepper
½ onion
½ bulb fennel
50 ml/1¾ fl oz white balsamic vinegar
100 ml/3½ fl oz olive oil
chopped coriander (cilantro)
fine salt

Vegetable sauce vierge

Dice all the vegetables. Mix them together, then stir in the vinegar, olive oil, coriander and a little salt.

When to use it | *This light sauce goes beautifully with fish like red mullet.*

1991

For 4
Preparation time: 45 min
Cooking time: 40 min
Resting time: 2 h

}

Jellied ham and parsley terrine

This is another classic that I have resurrected on the menu at Bistrot 7. Starting with a really good-quality cooked ham hock, from the butcher, I make a terrine that is set in a mushroom jelly and sharpened with a note of acidity. I particularly love the textural contrast between the slightly chewy ham and the jelly, which starts off firm then melts in the mouth, releasing notes of mushroom, caper and cornichon. Of course, you could vary this in lots of different ways, for example by using herbs or red onion pickles.

The mushroom jelly

400 g/14 oz button mushrooms
1 onion
25 g/1 oz salted butter
splash of olive oil
2 egg whites
10 g/⅓ oz gelatine leaves
fine salt

The jellied ham with parsley

1 shallot
50 ml/1¾ fl oz olive oil
400 g/14 oz ham in one piece,
   fat and rind removed
10 g/⅓ oz cornichons
1 tablespoon finely chopped
   flat-leaf parsley
1 tablespoon finely chopped tarragon
10 g/⅓ oz capers
250 ml/9 fl oz mushroom jelly
fine salt, freshly ground pepper

Equipment

1 terrine mould or 4 ramekins

1 ~ The mushroom jelly

First, make a mushroom stock. Trim the mushrooms. Finely chop the onion, then cook gently in the butter and olive oil for about 3–4 minutes. Cut half of the mushrooms into slices, add to the onion and cook for 5 minutes. Pour in 750 ml/ 25 fl oz of water, then cook for another 30 minutes. Strain through a sieve into a clean saucepan, then season lightly with salt and leave to cool. Clarify the stock as follows: chop the remaining mushrooms and mix them with the egg whites, then add to the stock in the saucepan. Bring to the boil, then lower the heat and leave to cook over a very gentle heat for about 10 minutes. Strain through a sieve or colander lined with muslin (cheesecloth) or a clean tea towel. (See step-by-step method on p. 138.) Soak the gelatine in iced water for a few minutes to soften it. Mix 250 ml/9 fl oz of the hot mushroom stock with the drained and squeezed-out gelatine. Check the seasoning and adjust as required, then set aside.

2 ~ The jellied ham with parsley

Finely chop the shallot, then cook, stirring, in a saucepan with the olive oil over a gentle heat for 3–4 minutes, without letting it colour. Drain the shallot and put it to one side. Dice the ham and the cornichons. Mix together the shallot, ham, cornichons, herbs and capers, then place in a terrine mould or divide between 4 ramekins. Cover with the almost-cold mushroom jelly and leave to set in the fridge for about 2 hours.

3 ~ Serving

Unmould the terrine and serve with a sauce gribiche (see p. 196). Croutons of bread are also lovely with this.

FAMILY FAVOURITES

Eating as a family is not only how we develop
our tastes and our love of cooking, but also
how we learn about sharing and conversation.
Eating together is a tradition well worth preserving:
it helps to create a sense of the joy of sharing food,
which hopefully stays with us throughout our lives.
Family meals, whether everyday ones or for special
occasions, demand a certain type of dish, and often
it is all about giving children food that is healthy,
nourishing and balanced. Traditional favourites,
such as calves' liver, chicory with ham and veal
paupiettes, achieve this in a subtle way. I've used
some more modern cooking techniques in these
recipes, to lighten both flavour and texture,
and to make them more suitable for daily
cooking and eating.

For 4
Preparation time: min
Cooking time: 40 min
Resting time: 1 h

Creamy chicory with ham

Here is a well-known family favourite, indeed a French classic, that I hated when I was a child! In this version, I have played with the textures, changed the way the dish looks and left out the grilled cheese. The result is a dish that is lighter, yet just as delicious. Comté cheese royale is layered with diced chicory and ham, and a chicory emulsion, for a subtle sweet-sour and light-as-air effect. The béchamel has gone, replaced by the richness of the royale and the frothy finish of the emulsion.

The cheese royale

250 ml/9 fl oz whole milk
80 g/3 oz grated Comté cheese
4 eggs
fine salt

The chicory emulsion

2 large heads chicory (endive)
splash of olive oil
juice of ½ lemon
100 ml/3½ fl oz whole milk
100 ml/3½ fl oz cream
100 g/3½ oz cooked mashed potato
fine salt

The garnish

1 head of chicory (endive)
splash of olive oil
splash of lemon juice
50 g/1¾ oz ham
fine salt

Equipment

4 x 150 ml/5 fl oz glasses or
   'Le Parfait' jars (as in the photo)
siphon
cooking thermometer (optional)

1 ~ The cheese royale

Preheat the oven to 120°C (250°F; gas mark ¼–½). Warm the milk in a saucepan, then add the grated Comté. Let the cheese melt, stirring it in well, then strain the sauce through a fine sieve. Leave to cool completely, then lightly whisk in the eggs and season with a little salt. Pour into 4 glasses or jars, then place in a bain-marie. Cover with baking parchment and cook in the oven for about 20 minutes: the royale should be quite firm, with the merest of trembles. Remove from the oven and the bain-marie, leave to rest for a moment, then chill in the fridge for 1 hour.

2 ~ The chicory emulsion

Wash and finely slice the chicory. Heat the olive oil in a frying pan over a gentle heat, then add the chicory and cook for 5 minutes, without letting it colour. Season with a little salt, then add the lemon juice to stop the chicory discolouring. Pour in the milk and cream and simmer for 5 minutes. Blend the mixture with the mashed potato until completely smooth, then strain through a fine sieve. Check and adjust the seasoning as necessary, then pour into a siphon and insert 2 gas canisters. Keep warm in a warm bain-marie (up to 60°C/140°F, no hotter – check the temperature with a cooking thermometer, if you have one).

3 ~ The garnish

Wash and finely slice the chicory. Sauté half of it in a frying pan with the olive oil for about 5 minutes, then add the lemon juice, followed by the diced ham. Remove from the heat, then gently stir in the remaining raw chicory. Check and adjust the seasoning as necessary.

4 ~ Finishing off and serving

Reheat the glasses or jars of cheese royale in a bain-marie for 5 minutes. Spoon the garnish on top, then finish with a little of the chicory emulsion. This is lovely served with croutons.

If you don't have a siphon | *Simply pour the chicory emulsion onto the garnish and royale.*

For 4
Preparation time: 50 min
Cooking time: 40 min
}

Veal paupiettes with mushrooms

The combination of veal and sage may be reminiscent of Italian cooking, but it is also common in the south of France. Here, I have re-invented the classic paupiette recipe by adding aromatic sage leaves to the stuffing, to accentuate the taste of the veal without masking it; lovage makes a good substitute in winter. Sautéed mushrooms and shallot complement these earthy flavours. Any leftover stuffing can be frozen and used to stuff aubergines (eggplant) or courgettes (zucchini).

The veal stuffing

300 g/10½ oz veal, such as shoulder
    or loin, fat removed
75 ml/2½ fl oz single (pouring) cream
2 teaspoons whole milk
120 g/4¼ oz egg white
    (from about 4 eggs)
100 g/3½ oz onion
100 g/3½ oz carrot
25 g/1 oz salted butter
splash of vegetable stock
    (see step-by-step method on p. 126)
100 g/3½ oz streaky bacon
small bunch of sage
fine salt, freshly ground pepper

The paupiettes

4 veal escalopes

The mushrooms

200 g/7 oz mousseron mushrooms
200 g/7 oz girolle mushrooms
splash of olive oil
25 g/1 oz butter
1 shallot
1 tablespoon finely chopped parsley
fine salt, freshly ground pepper

Finishing off

splash of groundnut (peanut) oil
knob of butter
150 ml/5 fl oz vegetable stock
    (see step-by-step method on p. 126)
a few sage leaves for decoration

1 ~ The veal stuffing

Blend the veal, cream, milk and egg white together, then sieve to remove any sinew or nerves. To check the seasoning, cook a little of the stuffing in a frying pan over a gentle heat, then taste and adjust the seasoning as necessary. Finely dice the onion and carrot, then cook over a gentle heat with the butter and vegetable stock until tender. Transfer to a bowl and leave to cool slightly. Cut the bacon into small pieces and add to the bowl, along with the veal mixture and the finely chopped sage. Mix well, then check the seasoning again.

2 ~ The paupiettes

Put the escalopes on a work surface. Flatten them gently, using a rolling pin or meat hammer, then place 50 g/1¾ oz of the veal stuffing on each one. Roll up the escalopes to enclose the stuffing, then wrap in cling film and squeeze lightly to remove any excess air. Bring a saucepan of water to the boil and immerse the paupiettes, then immediately remove the pan from the heat. Leave the paupiettes to poach in the hot water for 25 minutes, then drain. (See step-by-step method on p. 208.)

3 ~ The mushrooms

While the paupiettes are poaching, prepare the mushrooms. Clean them of any grit or debris, then cook in a frying pan with the olive oil and a pinch of salt over a gentle heat for about 3 minutes, stirring from time to time. Remove the pan from the heat and drain the mushrooms. In the same pan, melt the butter over a medium heat and add the finely chopped shallot. Leave to cook for a minute, then return the mushrooms to the pan and cook for another 3 minutes, stirring all the time. Finally, add the finely chopped parsley and adjust the seasoning as necessary.

4 ~ Finishing off and plating up

A few minutes before serving, remove the cling film from the paupiettes and brown them in a frying pan with a little oil and butter over a medium heat. Remove the paupiettes from the pan and keep warm. Pour the vegetable stock into the pan to deglaze, then bring to the boil and simmer until reduced to a jus. Divide the paupiettes and mushrooms between the plates, dress with a little of the jus and scatter over a few sage leaves.

How to make veal paupiettes

1

Get the escalopes from a butcher, and ask for large, very thin ones. Have the stuffing ready.

2

With a rolling pin or meat hammer, lightly flatten the escalopes. You could also ask the butcher to do this.

3

Put a large tablespoon of stuffing onto each flattened-out escalope, then roll up to make paupiettes.

4

Using your hands, close up the ends of the paupiette to make sure the stuffing is properly enclosed.

5

Using kitchen string, tie the paupiette lengthways then widthways, as if tying a roast. Don't pull the string too tight; it should just hold the paupiette's shape.

6

Wrap the paupiettes in cling film, squeezing out any air. Knot or tie the ends of the cling film securely.

7

Bring a saucepan of water to the boil. Immerse the paupiettes, then immediately remove the pan from the heat and leave the paupiettes to poach in the hot water.

8

At the last minute, just before serving, remove the cling film and string from the paupiettes. Melt a knob of butter in a frying pan and gently cook the paupiettes, turning them often, until they are golden all over.

For 6
Preparation time: 45 min
Cooking time: 10–15 min

}

Calves' liver soufflé from my childhood, with tomato coulis

When I was a child, this was the only dish that would persuade me to eat calves' liver, especially as my grandfather used to serve it in silver timbales with a tomato coulis alongside. Rich in iron and incredibly healthy, this is a great family meal. The liver, blended with a béchamel enriched with egg yolks and lightened with beaten egg white, becomes a melting cloud, its flavour lifted by the tomato.

The tomato coulis

4 tomatoes
3 spring onions (scallions)
knob of butter
1 garlic clove
sprig of thyme
pinch of fine salt

The béchamel sauce

40 g/1½ oz salted butter
40 g/1½ oz plain (all-purpose) flour
400 ml/14 fl oz whole milk

The soufflés

50 g/1¾ oz clarified butter (see p. 16)
1 shallot
250 g/8½ oz calves' liver
15 g/½ oz butter
5 egg yolks
2 tablespoons finely chopped parsley
6 egg whites
fine salt, freshly ground pepper

Equipment

piping bag
6 individual soufflé dishes,
    about 6 cm/2½ in across

1 ~ The tomato coulis

Prepare the tomatoes as shown on p. 22, cutting them into dice. Cut the spring onions into dice, then soften in a little butter over a gentle heat. Add the tomatoes, along with the garlic and thyme, and leave to cook for 10 minutes. Remove the thyme, then blend the tomato mixture to a smooth coulis, adding a little water if it is too thick. Season with salt and set aside.

2 ~ The béchamel sauce

In a saucepan, melt the butter over a gentle heat, then sift in the flour. Cook the roux for 2 minutes, stirring constantly, then slowly whisk in the cold milk little by little. Bring the sauce to the boil, stirring constantly until it thickens. Take off the heat and leave to one side.

3 ~ The soufflé

Using a pastry brush, coat the inside of the soufflé dishes with the clarified butter. Chill the dishes for 5 minutes, then repeat the process twice. Finely chop the shallot. Season the liver, then quickly sear in a frying pan with the butter and shallot. Remove the liver from the heat and cut into small pieces, then blend to a purée and sieve to remove any sinew or nerves. Transfer the liver purée to a blender, along with the béchamel, egg yolks and finely chopped parsley. Blend until smooth, then taste and adjust the seasoning. Preheat the oven to 200°C (400°F; gas mark 6). Whisk the egg whites with a pinch of salt to soft peaks. As soon as they are ready, fold them into the liver-béchamel mixture. (See step-by-step method on p. 212.)

4 ~ Cooking the soufflé

Fill a piping bag with the soufflé mixture and fill the soufflé dishes to 1 cm/½ in below the rim. Cook in the oven for 10–15 minutes, depending on the size of the dishes. Serve with the reheated tomato coulis.

Tip | Clarified butter is used in this recipe to grease the dishes. This is butter that has been heated and cooled, so that the milk solids can be removed; it can then be used at higher temperatures without burning.

How to make a soufflé

1

Melt the butter in a saucepan, then add the flour. Cook this roux for about 3–4 minutes, stirring all the time with a wooden spoon.

2

Slowly add the cold milk to the roux, whisking constantly.

3

Whisking constantly, bring the béchamel to the boil, then simmer for a minute to thicken.

4

Heat the butter in a frying pan. Add the finely chopped shallot and cook gently, without letting it colour, then add the seasoned liver and sear briefly. Remove the liver from the heat and cut into small pieces, then purée and sieve.

  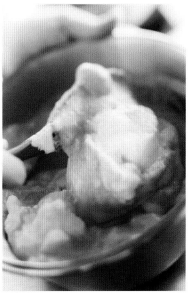 

5

Put the liver, béchamel, egg yolks and finely chopped parsley into a blender and blend until smooth. Meanwhile, whisk the egg whites to soft peaks.

6

You want a smooth, fine texture.

7

With a spatula or metal spoon, gently fold the egg whites into the liver-béchamel mixture.

8

Using a piping bag, fill the soufflé moulds with the mixture, then bake.

For 4
Preparation time: 20 min
Cooking time: about 10 min
}

Eggs Florentine with Beaufort cheese

Soft eggs with wilted spinach is a classic combination, but adding nutmeg and Beaufort cheese creates something even more seductive: the freshness of the spinach, the warmth of the nutmeg, the floral aroma of the cheese and the softness of the egg. It is important to just lightly cook the eggs, so their runny yolks mingle with the spinach.

The eggs

4 extra-fresh eggs
splash of vinegar

The béchamel sauce

40 g/1½ oz salted butter
40 g/1½ oz plain (all-purpose) flour
400 ml/14 fl oz whole milk
freshly grated nutmeg
fine salt

The spinach

400 g/14 oz fresh spinach
1 garlic clove
20 g/¾ oz salted butter
splash of olive oil
fine salt

Finishing off

40 g/1½ oz grated Beaufort cheese

Equipment

4 ramekins

1 ~ The eggs

Soft-boil the eggs: add a splash of vinegar to a saucepan of water, then bring to the boil. Cook the eggs in the boiling water for 6 minutes. Remove from the pan with a slotted spoon, immerse in a large bowl of iced water, then remove the shells.

2 ~ The béchamel sauce

Melt the butter, then stir in the flour and cook for 2 minutes until the mixture begins to froth. Gradually whisk in the cold milk, then cook over a low heat, stirring constantly, until the sauce thickens. Take off the heat and add a little nutmeg and salt.

3 ~ The spinach

Trim and thoroughly wash the spinach in several changes of water, then drain. Peel the garlic, flatten it with the blade of a knife, then place in a frying pan with the butter and oil over a gentle heat. Add the spinach, season with salt, and cook for 3–4 minutes. Remove from the heat and leave to cool, then remove the garlic clove.

4 ~ Finishing off and serving

Preheat an overhead grill (broiler). Divide the spinach between the ramekins, add an egg to each one, then cover with the béchamel and finish with the grated Beaufort. Grill for 5 minutes, then serve immediately.

Tip | *Wilting the spinach in a frying pan, without any extra water, prevents it from losing any of its flavour.*

For 6
Preparation time: 20 min
Cooking time: 25 min
Resting time: 2 h

}

Crème caramel with muscovado sugar

Muscovado sugar, a dark unrefined sugar with a hint of liquorice, makes crème caramel even better. This mixture is a sweet version of the 'royale' from previous recipes. It is important to get the cooking time just right: the cooked custard should still have a slight wobble — this way, it will keep its soft, luscious texture once it is chilled.

The muscovado caramel

100 g/3½ oz caster (superfine) sugar
100 g/3½ oz muscovado (brown) sugar

The crème caramel

½ vanilla pod (bean)
500 ml/18 fl oz whole milk
2 eggs
2 egg yolks
100 g/3½ oz caster (superfine) sugar

Equipment

6 moulds or ramekins
sugar thermometer

1 ~ The muscovado caramel

Put the ramekins or moulds on a work surface near the cooker. Place both sugars and 75 ml/2½ fl oz of water in a saucepan and bring to the boil, then lower the heat to medium and cook until the caramel reaches 160°C/320°F on a sugar thermometer. Remove the pan from the heat and pour the caramel into the ramekins, dividing it evenly between them, then leave to cool.

2 ~ The crème caramel

Split the half-vanilla pod in two lengthways and scrape out the seeds. Pour the milk into a saucepan, add the vanilla seeds and pod, then bring to the boil. Meanwhile, in a large bowl, lightly whisk the whole eggs, yolks and sugar together, then gradually whisk in the hot vanilla-infused milk. Remove the vanilla pod from the custard mixture.

3 ~ Cooking the crème caramels

Preheat the oven to 160°C (320°F; gas mark 2–3). Using a small ladle or a jug, fill the ramekins with the custard mixture, then place in a large roasting dish or tin. Pour enough hot water into the tin to come at least two-thirds of the way up the sides of the ramekins, then bake for 15–20 minutes. The crème caramels are done when the custard is just set, with a slight tremble. Remove from the bain-marie and leave to cool, then chill in the fridge for at least 2 hours.

Tip | *These crèmes caramels can be made in advance and left in the fridge until ready to serve. They are irresistible when served really cold.*

217

THE GREAT CLASSICS
OF FRENCH CUISINE

In the Middle Ages French cooking started out with a focus on acidic flavours, Eastern spices (ginger and nutmeg were considered to 'balance the imbalances in an ingredient') and light, fat-free sauces. Then, during the Renaissance, cooks strove to soften flavours, adding several fundamental elements of traditional French cuisine: butter and sugar started to appear, and meals were dictated by days for eating meat and days of abstinence. Gradually, the focus shifted to the natural flavour of ingredients, which in turn affected cooking techniques and the way dishes were prepared and seasoned. Here, then, are recipes from different periods of history that showcase the creativity and expertise of the chefs of yesteryear.

For 4
Resting time: overnight
Preparation time: 45 min
Cooking time: 50 min

}

Vol-au-vent

A classic vol-au-vent is a great way for any chef to show off their technical abilities. The result will be a flaky puff-pastry shell filled with sweetbreads and a fresh lemony sauce. Beware, this is not a light dish!

The puff pastry

1 block of puff pastry
  (see step-by-step method on p. 236)
1 egg, lightly beaten

The sweetbreads and filling

splash of vinegar
250 g/8½ oz calves' sweetbreads
100 g/3½ oz pearl or small onions
20 g/¾ oz butter + a little extra
150 ml/5 fl oz vegetable stock
  (see step-by-step method on p. 126)
200 g/7 oz white button mushrooms
splash of olive oil
fine salt

**The chicken cream sauce
with lemon**

20 g/¾ oz butter
20 g/¾ oz plain (all-purpose) flour
250 ml/9 fl oz reduced chicken stock
  (simmer 400 ml/14 fl oz of stock –
  see step-by-step method on p. 246 –
  to reduce to 250 ml/9 fl oz)
25 ml/1 fl oz double (heavy) cream
juice of ½ lemon + zest of 1 lemon
fleur de sel

Equipment

2 fluted round pastry cutters, about
  12 cm/4½ in and 10 cm/4 in across

1 ~ The puff pastry

Preheat the oven to 180°C (350°F; gas mark 4). Roll out the pastry and, using the 12 cm/4½ in pastry cutter, cut out 4 circles. Then, using the 10 cm/4 in cutter, cut out 4 smaller circles. Brush the 4 large circles with the beaten egg and press the smaller circles on top. Brush again with the beaten egg. Bake for 15–20 minutes, then remove from the oven and put to one side. Carefully cut off the lids of the vol-au-vents, to reveal the space for the filling.

2 ~ The sweetbreads and filling

Put the vinegar in a saucepan of water and bring to the boil. Once the water boils, poach the sweetbreads in it for 2 minutes, then drain and refresh in iced water. Put the cold sweetbreads on a plate and put another plate on top, then place a weight on top and chill overnight. The next day, using your fingers, carefully remove the membrane that covers the sweetbreads and cut them into small pieces (see step-by-step method on p. 222) and set aside. Peel the onions, then cook in the butter over a gentle heat for 2–3 minutes. Add the vegetable stock and cook for another 10 minutes, or until the onions are very soft, then put to one side. Clean and finely slice the mushrooms, then sauté in a frying pan with a splash of olive oil for 4–5 minutes. Season with salt and put to one side.

3 ~ The chicken cream sauce with lemon

Melt the butter in a saucepan, stir in the flour, then cook for 2 minutes, stirring all the time. Add the chicken stock and bring to the boil, then add the cream, lemon juice and zest. Taste and season as necessary, then strain the sauce through a fine sieve. Keep warm, either in a bain-marie or over a low heat, without letting it boil.

4 ~ Finishing off and plating up

Melt an extra knob of butter in a frying pan and sauté the sweetbreads for 5 minutes. Add the drained onions, the mushrooms and the sauce. Bring to a simmer but don't let it boil. Put the vol-au-vents on 4 plates and then, using a spoon, fill them with the sweetbreads, onions, mushrooms and sauce. Cover with the lids and serve immediately before the pastry goes soggy.

Tip | *You can cut out the puff pastry circles in advance and freeze them. Then, when you want to serve them, you only have to bake the pastry and make the filling.*

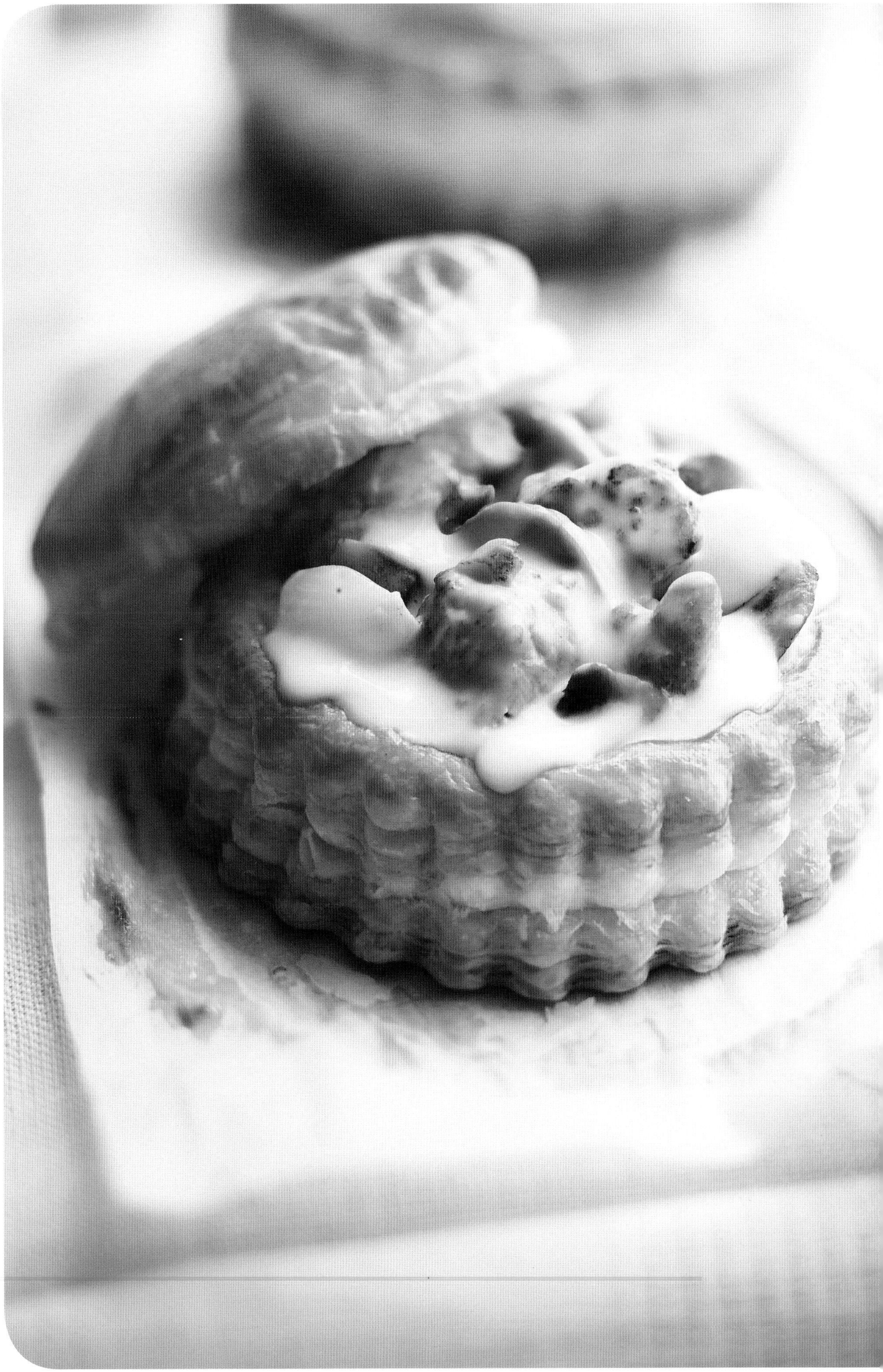

How to prepare sweetbreads

1

Put the sweetbreads in a large bowl, cover with cold water and leave under running water for about 20 minutes.

2

Pour a little distilled white vinegar into a large saucepan of water and bring to the boil.

3

Drain the sweetbreads and immerse in the hot water. Bring to the boil again, then poach the sweetbreads for 2 minutes.

  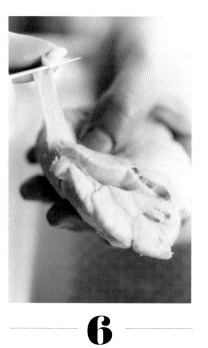 

4

Remove the sweetbreads with a slotted spoon, then immerse in a bowl of cold water and ice cubes to immediately stop them cooking.

5

Put the sweetbreads into a drainer with a tray underneath (or into a colander set over a bowl), then put weights on top to press them. Leave in the fridge overnight.

6

Using a small knife, trim the sweetbreads to remove the membrane that covers them.

7

Cut the sweetbreads into whatever size pieces are required, then cook straightaway or chill until needed.

For 4
Preparation time: 25 min
Cooking time: 8 min

}

Green asparagus with mint hollandaise sauce

I have my father to thank both for my love of asparagus and for this recipe. The mint adds a sharp note that sets off the asparagus flavour and the softness of the hollandaise. There are two very important techniques in this recipe: how to make a sabayon and how to cook asparagus.

The asparagus

20 green asparagus spears
splash of olive oil
150 ml/5 fl oz vegetable stock
  (see step-by-step method on p. 126)
2 sprigs of mint

The hollandaise sauce

100 g/3½ oz butter
2 egg yolks
2 tablespoons asparagus-cooking
  liquid
juice of ½ lemon
1 tablespoon finely chopped mint
fine salt

Finishing off

splash of olive oil
fleur de sel
mint leaves

1 ~ The asparagus

Prepare the asparagus spears by bending the stems until they snap, then discarding the woody ends. Then, using a small knife, remove the 'scales' on the remaining stems so they are smooth. Put a saucepan over a high heat, add the olive oil and sauté the asparagus all over, without letting it colour too much. Add the vegetable stock and the mint leaves. Cook for another 3–4 minutes (the asparagus should still be slightly crunchy). Drain over a bowl, reserving the cooking liquid, then chill the asparagus in the fridge. Remove the mint from the cooking liquid.

2 ~ The hollandaise sauce

Melt the butter over a gentle heat, then remove from the heat. Using a spoon, skim the foam from the top, then pour off the yellow clarified butter and discard the white milk solids that will have separated out. In a saucepan, whisk together the egg yolks, the asparagus-cooking liquid and a pinch of salt. Place over the lowest heat possible and whisk rapidly for 3–4 minutes. As soon as the sabayon is good and foamy, remove from the heat and gradually mix in the warm clarified butter. Finally, stir in the lemon juice and the finely chopped mint. Check the seasoning.

3 ~ Finishing off and plating up

Preheat the oven to 150°C (300°F; gas mark 2). Put the asparagus in a baking dish, cover with damp kitchen paper (to prevent it drying out) and reheat in the oven for 2 minutes. Divide between 4 plates. Using a pastry brush, coat the asparagus spears with a little olive oil to make them glossy, then scatter over the fleur de sel and a few mint leaves. Serve immediately with the hollandaise sauce.

Tip | *To save time, make up a large batch of clarified butter, then divide it into small portions and freeze. You can defrost as much or as little as you need as and when. You can also use clarified butter to grease moulds and tins.*

For 4
Preparation time: 30 min
Cooking time: 25 min

}

Du Barry velouté with orange

For a long time, the French dish 'potage' was quite a distinguished and sophisticated dish. Unlike the more popular and simple 'soupe', a 'potage' tends to be heftier in flavour, texture and colour. The du Barry velouté in this recipe is pale, bittersweet and smooth. I have changed it a little, to make it more my own, so the texture is even finer, the colour a subtle contrast of white and orange and, while still bittersweet, it has the sharp acidity of orange and the freshness of coriander.

The velouté

1 small cauliflower (600 g/1 lb 5 oz)
1 onion
splash of olive oil
150 g/5½ oz potatoes
250 ml/9 fl oz vegetable stock
  (see step-by-step method on p. 126)
250 ml/9 fl oz milk
250 ml/9 fl oz cream
fine salt, freshly ground pepper

The orange

1 orange

Finishing off

a few coriander seeds
splash of olive oil

1 ~ The velouté

Boil a saucepan of salted water. Remove the stalk from the cauliflower and break into florets. Immerse the florets in the boiling water for 5–6 minutes, or until tender. Meanwhile, peel and finely chop the onion. In another saucepan, slowly cook the onion with the olive oil until it is soft and translucent. Add the peeled and sliced potatoes, along with the drained cauliflower, vegetable stock, milk and cream, and leave to cook for 20 minutes. Blend until smooth, then check and adjust the seasoning

2 ~ The orange

Zest the orange, then peel it. Separate out the segments, removing the pith in between. Cut each segment into 2 or 3 smaller pieces, then put to one side.

3 ~ Finishing off

Pour the hot velouté into bowls, then add some pieces of orange segment and a little zest. Finish with a scattering of coriander seeds and a few drops of olive oil.

Tip | Blanching helps to sweeten the cauliflower and make it more digestible, so don't be tempted to leave out this step. You could also add some fresh almonds to this soup, when they're in season.

For 4
Resting time: overnight
+ 10 min
Preparation time: 40 min
Cooking time: 50 min

Pot-au-feu with sharp horseradish cream

Traditionally, pot-au-feu is cooked for a long time to soften and tenderize the cheaper cuts of meat used in it. But if you make it in a pressure cooker, the tenderizing process is accelerated, saving you time. I like to cook the meat and vegetables separately, adding marrow bones for flavour (though you can leave them out if you want a lighter result), before serving the dish with a sharp horseradish sauce. Pot-au-feu is a dish that deserves to be made all the time, not just for a family Sunday lunch.

The beef

distilled white vinegar
4 marrow bones
200 g/7 oz blade steak
200 g/7 oz chuck steak
100 g/3½ oz boneless rib of beef
2 litres/3½ pints vegetable stock
(see step-by-step method on p. 126)
2 onions
2 carrots
1 bouquet garni
3 garlic cloves
3 cloves
3 peppercorns
1½ teaspoons coarse salt

The vegetables

4 baby carrots
4 baby leeks
4 baby turnips
2 stalks celery
4 potatoes

The horseradish cream

150 g/5½ oz fromage blanc (quark)
½ teaspoon grated horseradish
1 tablespoon finely chopped chives
1 tablespoon finely chopped parsley
fine salt, freshly ground pepper

Finishing off

fleur de sel
roughly crushed black pepper

1 ~ The beef

Fill a large bowl with cold water, add a little white vinegar then immerse the marrow bones in it and leave them to soak overnight in the fridge. The next day, cut all the meat into pieces, put into a pressure cooker and cover with vegetable stock. Bring to a simmer and then skim off any foam from the surface. Add the trimmed and peeled onions and carrots, the bouquet garni, the crushed garlic, cloves, peppercorns and salt. Follow the manufacturer's instructions for bringing the cooker up to pressure, then cook for 45 minutes on the 'vegetables' setting. Leave the pressure cooker to rest for 10 minutes, off the heat, before carefully opening.

2 ~ The vegetables

Drain the soaked marrow bones and remove the marrow from the bones. Poach the marrow for 3 minutes in some of the beef-cooking liquid (from the pressure cooker), then keep to one side. Peel and trim the vegetables as required, leaving a little of the leaves on the carrots and turnips (as in the photo). Cook the vegetables in boiling salted water until tender, then refresh in cold water and drain.

3 ~ The horseradish cream

Meanwhile, mix the fromage blanc with the grated horseradish, chives and finely chopped parsley. Season with salt and pepper.

4 ~ Finishing off and serving

Skim the fat from the beef-cooking liquid, then strain through a fine sieve. Divide the meats and vegetables between 4 bowls or plates or dishes, and add a little marrow and broth to each one. Season with fleur de sel and roughly crushed black pepper. Serve hot with the horseradish cream.

For 4
Preparation time: 25 min
Cooking time: 7 min
}

Breaded whiting with maître d'hôtel butter and fried vegetables

It may not look like much, but fried whiting is well worth a second glance. I've updated this classic recipe so the fish is breaded with flour, egg and breadcrumbs, then pan-fried and served with fried vegetables and a maître d'hôtel butter. You can also make this with pollock or cod.

The whiting

4 whiting fillets
2 eggs + 1 tablespoon oil
100 g/3½ oz plain (all-purpose) flour
200 g/7 oz breadcrumbs
2 large knobs of butter for frying
2 tablespoons oil for frying
fine salt

The maître d'hôtel butter

100 g/3½ oz soft butter
1 tablespoon finely chopped parsley
juice and zest of 1 lemon
fleur de sel

The fried vegetables

2 carrots
1 potato
2 courgettes (zucchini)
2 litres/3½ pints groundnut
  (peanut) oil for deep-frying
¼ bunch of parsley
fine salt

Equipment

small pastry cutter or glass
cooking thermometer (optional)

1 ~ The whiting

Using small tongs or tweezers, remove any bones from the whiting fillets (or get the fishmonger to do it), then season with a little salt. Put the ingredients for the coating in three separate shallow bowls: flour in one; the eggs beaten with the oil and a little salt in a second; and the breadcrumbs in a third. Dip both sides of each fillet in the flour, egg and breadcrumbs to coat them completely. Keep to one side.

2 ~ The maître d'hôtel butter

Beat the butter to soften and reduce it to a paste. Finely chop the parsley, then mix into the butter, along with the lemon juice and zest and a pinch of fleur de sel. Place the butter between two pieces of baking parchment, then use a rolling pin to roll it out to a thickness of about 2 cm/¾ in. Chill until firm, then cut out 4 small circles using a pastry cutter or small glass.

3 ~ The fried vegetables

Peel and trim the carrots and potato, and top and tail the courgettes. Cut all the vegetables into very fine julienne strips. Heat the oil in a deep-fryer or large saucepan (the temperature of the oil should be 180°C/350°F – check with a cooking thermometer, if you have one), then fry the vegetables and the parsley leaves separately for about 1–2 minutes, or until crisp. Remove from the oil with a slotted spoon, drain on kitchen paper and season with salt.

4 ~ Finishing off and plating up

Heat the butter and oil in a frying pan over a medium heat, then cook the breaded whiting for 5–6 minutes, basting the fish with the foaming butter and oil, and turning them once halfway through. Once cooked, remove and drain briefly on kitchen paper. Place the whiting on plates, then serve with a slice of maître d'hôtel butter and the fried vegetables.

For 6
Preparation time: 25 min
Cooking time: about 90 min
Resting time: 30 min

}

Tarte tatin with tonka bean

I have updated the Tatin sisters' legacy by making this tart with a tonka bean, which makes the flavour bigger and warmer. The success of a tarte tatin lies in cooking the apples really slowly until they are properly caramelized, to bring out their flavour, and using a light, fine puff pastry.

The puff pastry

200 g/7 oz puff pastry
   (see step-by-step method on p. 236)

The caramelized apples with tonka bean

80 g/3 oz butter
1 kg/2¼ lb apples
juice of 1 lemon
100 g/3½ oz caster (superfine) sugar
1 tonka bean

Equipment

22 cm/8½ in diameter tatin tin
   or flameproof pie dish

1 ~ The puff pastry

Follow the method on p. 236 for making puff pastry.

2 ~ The caramelized apples with tonka bean

Melt the butter in the tatin tin over a medium heat, then remove from the heat while you prepare the apples. Peel, halve, core and de-pip the apples, then sit the apple halves snugly in the tatin tin, without leaving any gaps. Sprinkle the lemon juice over the apple, followed by the sugar. Grate the tonka bean and sprinkle it over the top too, making sure it is distributed as evenly as possible. Put the tin over a gentle heat and cook for about 50 minutes–1 hour, turning it regularly to ensure that the apples caramelize evenly all over. Remove from the heat. (See step-by-step method on p. 234.)

3 ~ Cooking and finishing off

Preheat the oven to 200°C (400°F; gas mark 6). While the oven heats up, roll out the puff pastry to a circle big enough to cover the tatin tin. When the apples are caramelized, cover them completely with the puff pastry, then bake for 15–20 minutes. The tatin is ready when the pastry is a light golden colour, no darker. Leave to cool for about 30 minutes. To unmould the tatin easily, heat the base of the tin for a couple of moments to soften the caramel. Place a plate over the pastry and, holding it firmly, carefully invert the pan, so that the tatin is apple-side up on the plate. Serve immediately.

Variation | *If you can't find a tonka bean, use a little cinnamon.*

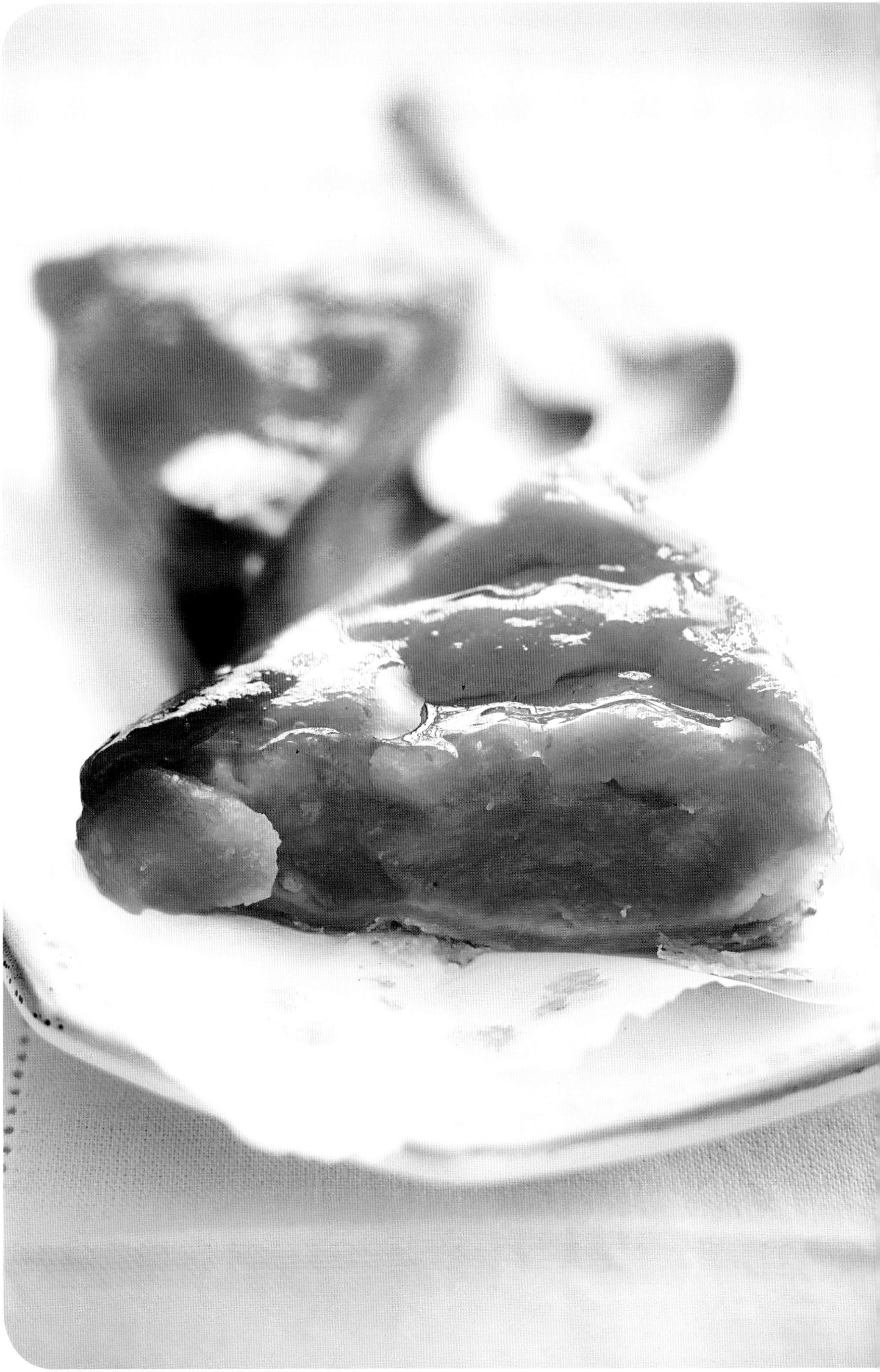

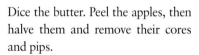

Dice the butter. Peel the apples, then halve them and remove their cores and pips.

Heat the tatin tin over a medium heat, add the butter and stir until it has melted.

Tuck the apple halves snugly into the tin, so that the base is covered and all the apples cook evenly.

Pour the lemon juice over the apples, making sure it is evenly distributed.

5

Scatter over the sugar and grated tonka bean as evenly as possible, then cook the apples over a gentle heat, turning the tin regularly. Watch that the caramel doesn't burn or catch.

6

Once the apples are cooked, remove from the heat and lay the circle of puff pastry over the top to cover the apples completely. Bake for about 15–20 minutes.

7

Remove the tarte tatin from the oven and leave to cool in the tin. To unmould, heat the base of the tin for a few minutes, then carefully turn out onto a plate.

How to make puff pastry

250 g/8½ oz butter
300 g/10½ oz plain (all-purpose) flour
5 g/¼ oz salt
150 ml/5 fl oz water

1

Weigh all the ingredients. Cut the butter into large dice, then leave at room temperature for 15 minutes.

2

Put the flour, salt, butter and water into an electric mixer.

3

Using the dough hook, mix the ingredients to a rough dough: the butter shouldn't be completely mixed in; it should still be visible.

4

Transfer the dough to a floured work surface, then shape into a ball and flour lightly.

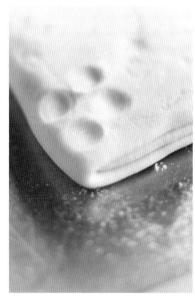

5

Roll out the pastry into a long strip about 1 cm/½ in thick.

6

Fold the strip of pastry over onto itself in thirds.

7

Give the pastry a quarter-turn and roll it out again to a strip 1 cm/½ in thick. Chill for 15 minutes, then fold the strip over onto itself in thirds again. Repeat this process twice more, remembering to chill the pastry in the fridge each time.

8

Every time you fold the pastry, give it a quarter-turn; make a mark on the pastry, so you know where you turned it the previous time.

For 6
Preparation time: 40 min
Cooking time: 1 h 30 min

}

Vacherin with vanilla ice cream and strawberry sorbet

This magnificent dessert, which would have once graced royal banquets and the grandest tables of the nineteenth century, is still just as impressive. In this recipe for individual vacherins, you will learn several useful techniques: how to make French meringue, ice cream and sorbet, as well as how to use piping bags to create a beautiful marbled effect.

The French meringue

100 g/3½ oz egg white
(from about 3–4 eggs)
100 g/3½ oz caster (superfine) sugar
100 g/3½ oz icing (confectioners')
sugar, sifted + a little extra
20 g/¾ oz flaked (slivered) almonds

The vanilla ice cream

1 vanilla pod (bean)
500 ml/18 fl oz whole milk
100 g/3½ oz caster (superfine) sugar
6 egg yolks

The strawberry sorbet

160 g/5¾ oz caster (superfine) sugar
1 tablespoon lemon juice
500 g/1 lb 2 oz strawberries

Finishing off

a few strawberries
a few raspberries

Equipment

ice-cream maker
3 piping bags
fluted piping nozzle
cooking thermometer (optional)

1 ~ The French meringue

Preheat the oven to 100°C (212°F; gas mark ¼ or just below). Put the egg white into a food mixer and whisk. When it begins to foam and thicken, add half the caster sugar and keep whisking, adding the rest of the sugar little by little. Once the whites have been beaten to stiff peaks, gradually fold in the icing sugar with a spatula. Fill a piping bag with the meringue and pipe balls about the size of a clementine onto a baking tray covered with baking parchment. Sprinkle with flaked almonds and a little extra icing sugar. Bake for 1 hour, then remove from the oven. Turn the hot meringues over and, with a small spoon, gently hollow them out, trying not to shatter them. Replace them on the baking tray and cook for another 30 minutes, then remove from the oven and set aside somewhere dry. (See step-by-step method on p. 240.)

2 ~ The vanilla ice cream

Split the vanilla pod open lengthways, then put in a saucepan with the milk and heat gently. In a large bowl, whisk the sugar and egg yolks with a hand whisk. Mix in a little of the hot milk, then tip this mixture back into the pan of hot milk and cook over a gentle heat, stirring all the time, until the custard is thick enough to coat the back of a spoon (about 82°C/180°F on a cooking thermometer). Sieve into a bowl, then cool it down quickly by sitting the bowl over a larger bowl of cold water and ice. Remove the vanilla pod, then churn in an ice-cream maker according to the manufacturer's instructions.

3 ~ The strawberry sorbet

Put the sugar, lemon juice and 80 ml/2½ fl oz of water in a saucepan and bring to the boil, then leave to cool. Wash and hull the strawberries, then blend to a purée and pour into the cold syrup. Transfer the mixture to an ice-cream maker and churn according to the manufacturer's instructions.

4 ~ Finishing off and serving

Fill one piping bag with vanilla ice cream and a second with strawberry sorbet, then put these two bags into a third bag fitted with a fluted nozzle. Squeeze over the meringue hollows to pipe out a marbled whirl of ice cream. Serve in cold bowls and decorate with a few strawberries and raspberries.

Variation | *Use different fruits, such as apricots or peaches, depending on the season. For a simpler presentation, just use a scoop to fill the meringues with the ice cream and sorbet instead.*

How to make French meringue

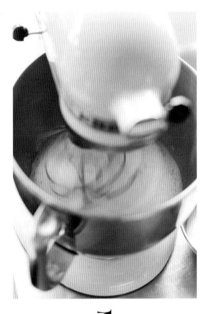

1

In an electric mixer, beat the egg white on a medium speed.

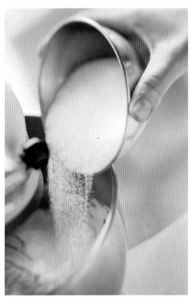
2

When the egg white starts to thicken, add the caster sugar and continue to whisk.

3

When the meringue forms stiff peaks and sticks to the whisk when it is lifted, as in the photo, stop whisking.

4

Add the sifted icing sugar and mix in with a spatula, then transfer the meringue into a piping bag.

5

Squeeze the piping bag gently to make small round meringues on a lined baking tray. Scatter over some flaked almonds and some more icing sugar.

6

Put the baking tray on top of another one before putting it in the oven. By doubling up the trays, the bottom of the meringues will cook more slowly, which makes it easier to hollow them out. Bake in the oven.

7

Remove the meringues from the oven. Turn the hot meringues over and, with a small spoon, gently hollow them out. Replace them on the baking tray and bake again as instructed in the recipe.

BISTROT CLASSICS

Since the Middle Ages, street food and restaurant
food have had very distinct culinary repertoires.
The restaurant, to 'restore health', was known
as the 'house of health' in the seventeenth century,
while the nineteenth-century bouillon restaurants
and the twentieth-century bistrot are indicative
of the French love of eating out in public places.
Yet all share the same essential culinary traditions –
from the gourmet cuisine of Auguste Escoffier
at the Ritz, through the daily menus at the Bouillon
Duval, which offer similar dishes to the more up-
market places at lower prices, to the regional recipes
at the famous Nationale 7. This chapter includes
lots of typical bistrot dishes, such as mackerel
escabeche, blanquette of veal and sole bonne femme,
all simplified as much as possible, so that they
can become part of your repertoire too!

For 4
Preparation time: 40 min
Cooking time: 40 min

}

Spring navarin of lamb

This dish, combining seasonal vegetables and lamb, is the epitome of spring. Using a pressure cooker makes it much faster to cook, but no less delicious. By reducing the cooking time, the meat remains meltingly soft; the vegetables, cooked separately, are done perfectly; and tarragon accentuates the freshness even more.

The navarin of lamb

1 carrot
1 stalk celery
1 onion
1 x 10 cm/4 in piece of leek
1 tomato
sprig of tarragon
splash of groundnut (peanut) oil
20 g/¾ oz butter
500 g/1 lb 2 oz diced lamb shoulder
50 ml/1¾ fl oz white wine
750 ml/25 fl oz chicken stock
 (see step-by-step method on p. 246)
fine salt, black peppercorns

The spring vegetables

8 baby carrots
8 baby leeks
8 spring onions (scallions)
100 g/3½ oz shelled petits pois
20 g/¾ oz butter
fine salt

Finishing off

finely chopped tarragon

1 ~ The navarin of lamb

Trim the carrot and celery. Peel the onion. Thoroughly wash the leek, tomato and tarragon. Dice all the vegetables and the tomato. Heat the oil and butter in a pressure cooker over a high heat, then add the lamb and brown all over until well coloured. Carefully tilt the pressure cooker and pour off the fat from the lamb, then add the vegetables, tomato, tarragon and a few peppercorns. Add the white wine and simmer to reduce by three-quarters, then add the chicken stock. Close and seal the pressure cooker and follow the manufacturer's instructions for bringing it up to pressure. Once pressurized, cook on the 'vegetables' setting for 25 minutes, then remove from the heat and let the pressure drop slowly. It is important not to remove the lid too quickly or the rapid drop in pressure may damage the texture of the meat. Remove the meat using a slotted spoon and put it to one side. Keep the cooking liquid.

2 ~ The spring vegetables

Wash and trim the carrots, leeks and spring onions. Cook each vegetable separately in boiling salted water for about 5 minutes, then refresh in iced water to preserve their texture and colour. Drain. A few minutes before serving, put all the vegetables in a frying pan, along with a little of the meat cooking liquid and a little butter. Bring to the boil, season with a little salt and cook for 3–4 minutes, letting the cooking liquid thicken slightly to coat the vegetables.

3 ~ The sauce

Strain the lamb cooking juices through a fine sieve into a large saucepan and bring to the boil. Leave to reduce and concentrate to your desired consistency, then check and adjust the seasoning.

4 ~ Finishing off

Add the meat and vegetables to the sauce and reheat very gently without allowing it to boil, stirring to make sure everything heats through evenly. Scatter over some finely chopped tarragon and serve immediately.

How to make chicken stock

1 small carrot
1 onion
1 small leek

1 kg/2¼ lb chicken wings
a few cloves
1 teaspoon coriander seeds

1

Prepare the ingredients. Peel and trim the carrot and onion; wash and trim the leek.

2

Cut each chicken wing into 4 pieces, then dice the carrot, onion and leek.

3

Put the chicken into a saucepan, cover with cold water and bring to the boil.

4

Using a small ladle or spoon, skim the greyish scum from the surface of the stock every so often. You may need to do this a few times.

5

Drain the chicken in a sieve or chinois, discarding the liquid.

6

Put the chicken into a clean saucepan with the vegetables and spices and cover with cold water.

7

Bring to the boil, then lower the heat so the stock is just simmering. Leave to cook for 40 minutes.

8

Strain the stock, then leave to cool.

For 4
Preparation time: 40 min
Resting time: 2 h
Cooking time: 25 min

}

Mackerel escabeche

Escabeche is a highly flavoured marinade: the aniseed of fennel, the freshness of coriander, the sweet acidity of white balsamic vinegar, the sharpness of lemon, the dry fruitiness of white wine, and the scent of thyme and bay... This intense reduction of natural flavours, which can be infinitely varied, will make the mackerel fillets (try to find quite small ones) shine brilliantly.

1 carrot
¼ bulb fennel
1 onion
1 garlic clove
250 ml/9 fl oz white wine
250 ml /9 fl oz water
10 coriander seeds
pinch of roughly crushed peppercorns
pinch of coarse salt
juice of 1 lemon
sprig of thyme
1 small bay leaf
75 ml/2½ fl oz olive oil
75 ml/2½ fl oz white balsamic vinegar
4 mackerel fillets
fine salt

Equipment

small tongs or tweezers

1 ~ The vegetables

Peel and trim the carrot, then cut into rounds. Wash and finely slice the fennel. Peel and finely chop the onion. Peel and halve the garlic clove, removing any green shoot from its centre.

2 ~ The escabeche

Mix together all the ingredients except the fish and fine salt in a wide saucepan. Bring to the boil, then lower the heat and leave to cook over a very gentle heat for 20 minutes.

3 ~ The mackerel

While the escabeche is cooking, rinse the mackerel fillets thoroughly under cold running water. Using small tongs or tweezers, remove the bones from the fish (see step-by-step method on p. 250), then chill. When the escabeche is ready, strain it through a fine sieve into a clean saucepan, reserving the vegetables and flavourings. Season the mackerel fillets with a little salt and put them into a non-metallic dish. Bring the escabeche back to a simmer, then pour over the fish. Add the reserved vegetables and flavourings, cover with cling film and leave to cool. Once cool, chill in the fridge for 2 hours.

4 ~ Finishing off and plating up

When the mackerel and escabeche are well chilled, stir the juices a little then serve.

Tip | If you can, prepare this the night before you want to serve it: the longer the mackerel marinates in the escabeche with the vegetables, the better it will be.

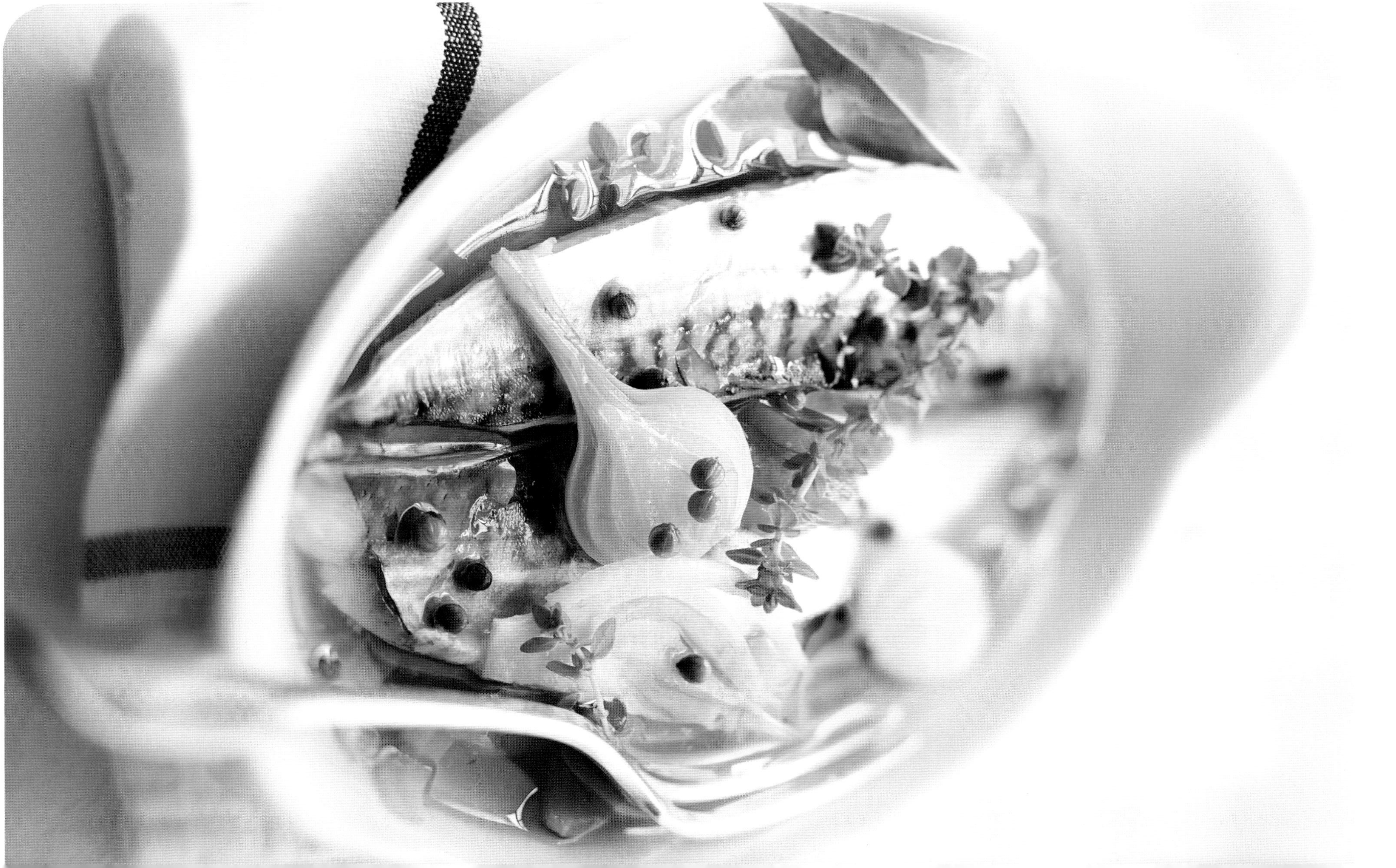

How to fillet a fish

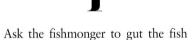

1

Ask the fishmonger to gut the fish and descale it, if necessary.

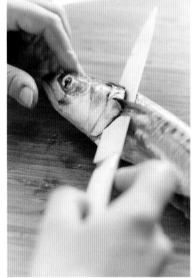

2

Using a fine-bladed, flexible knife, make an incision just behind the lateral fin of the fish, as shown.

3

Cut down the side of the fish, using the bones of the spine to guide you. By doing this, you won't leave any flesh on the bones.

4

Lift the fillet completely away from the bone, then turn the fish over and do the same on the other side.

Put the fillet skin-side down on the work surface. Cut away the edge of the fish that was next to the guts.

6

Using a pair of tweezers or small tongs, remove the bones. Grab each one firmly and lift out gently to avoid them breaking.

7

Gently run your fingers over the fish to check that all the bones have been removed. The fillets are now ready to use.

Blanquette of veal revisited

Unlike the traditional blanquette, this one doesn't contain any fat, but it is still rich and creamy, albeit lifted by a little sharpness. The sauce is a mixture of stock, agar-agar, egg white, a little mustard and lemon, all aerated with a siphon to produce a delicate and airy texture, giving this classic a whole new modern twist.

The blanquette

600 g/1 lb 5 oz veal for blanquette, such as shoulder or fillet

1.5 litres/2½ pints vegetable stock (see step-by-step method on p. 126)

1 bouquet garni

1 clove

pinch of coarse salt

The sauce

½ teaspoon agar-agar

½ teaspoon strong mustard

splash of lemon juice

1 egg white

fine salt

The vegetables

2 carrots

4 baby leeks

8 baby turnips

12 white button mushrooms

4 spring onions (scallions)

splash of olive oil

coarse salt

fine salt, freshly ground pepper

Equipment

siphon (optional)

cooking thermometer (optional)

1 ~ The blanquette

Cut the meat into pieces roughly 5 cm/2 in across, then put into a saucepan and cover with cold water. Bring to the boil, then remove from the heat and drain off the cooking liquid. Add the stock, bouquet garni, clove and salt to the veal. Bring to the boil again, then lower the heat to a rolling boil and cook for an hour, making sure that the meat is always covered in liquid. Strain the cooking liquid through a fine sieve and reserve. Place the meat in a bowl with some of its cooking juices to prevent it drying out. (See step-by-step method on p. 254.)

2 ~ The sauce

Measure out 250 ml/9 fl oz of the blanquette-cooking juices and pour into a pan with the agar-agar. Bring to the boil, then remove from the heat and leave the liquid to cool before adding the mustard, lemon juice and egg white. Season lightly with salt. Pour into a siphon, then seal and insert a gas cartridge. Place the siphon in a bain-marie or bowl of warm water (the temperature should be 50°C/120°F – check with a cooking thermometer, if you have one). (See step-by-step method on p. 254.)

3 ~ The vegetables

Peel and trim the carrots, then cut into slices on an angle. Thoroughly wash and trim the leeks. Peel and trim the turnips. Wipe the mushrooms clean and remove their stalks. Cook all the vegetables except the mushrooms separately in boiling salted water, for about 5–6 minutes. Drain, then immerse in cold water to preserve their colour. Drain again. Before serving, cook the mushrooms in a little olive oil over a gentle heat for 5 minutes. Add the other vegetables and cook for 3 minutes, then pour in 150 ml/5 fl oz of the blanquette-cooking juices and cook for another 3–4 minutes. Remove from the heat, check the seasoning and keep warm.

4 ~ Finishing off and plating up

Drain the meat, then divide between 4 plates. Divide the vegetables evenly between the plates, then finish with the sauce from the siphon. Serve immediately.

Making the sauce without a siphon | Melt 40 g/1½ oz butter in a saucepan over a gentle heat, stir in 40 g/1½ oz plain (all-purpose) flour and cook for 2–3 minutes, still stirring. Slowly add 500 ml/18 fl oz of the blanquette-cooking juices, stirring contantly, then bring to the boil. Leave to cook for another 2–3 minutes before finishing with 50 ml/1¾ fl oz cream. Season lightly with salt.

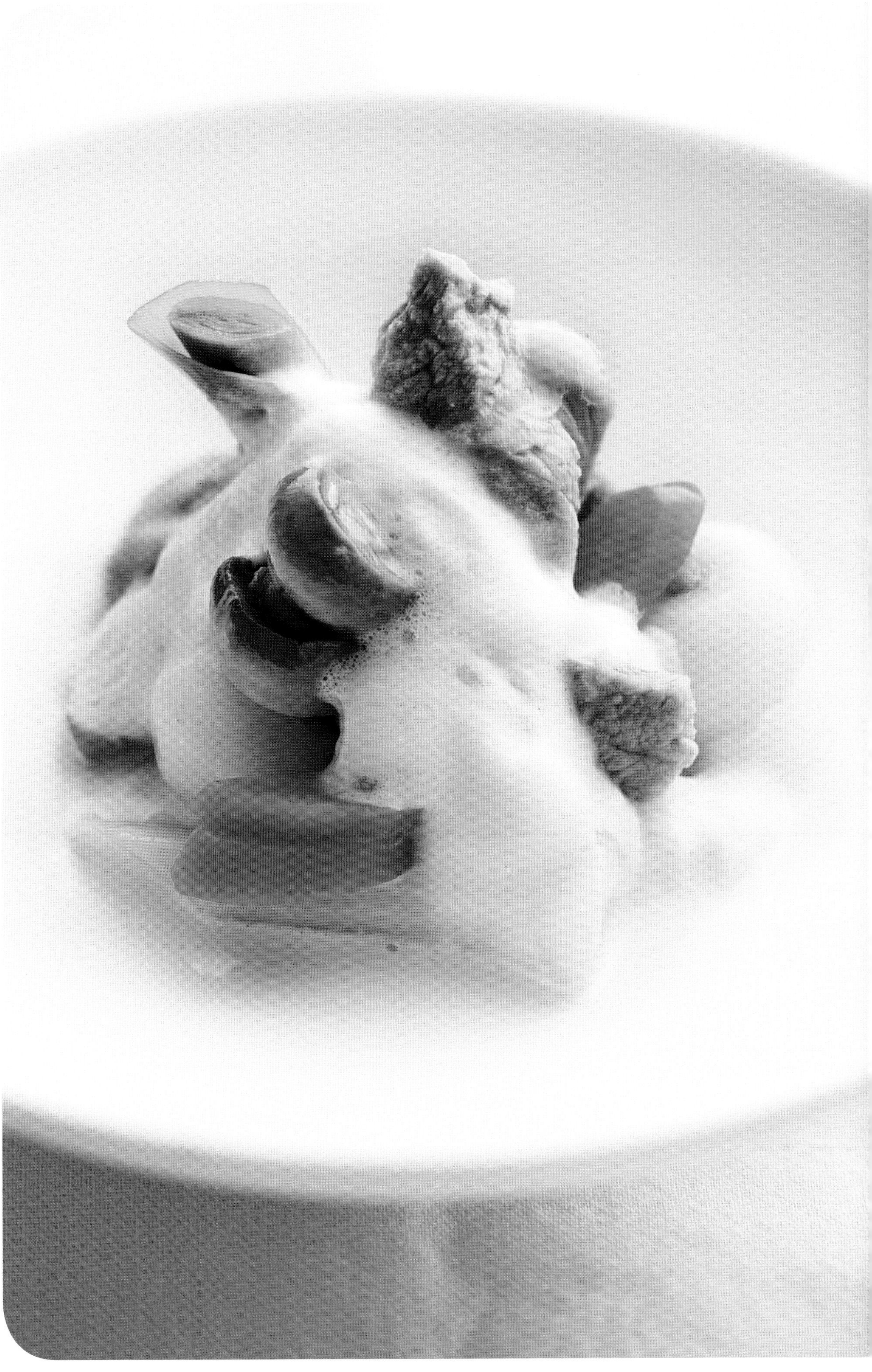

How to make blanquette of veal

1

Put the meat in a saucepan of cold water, then bring to the boil and skim off the scum that rises to the surface.

2

Drain the meat in a sieve and discard the cooking water.

3

Put the blanched meat and the vegetable stock into a saucepan, then bring to the boil and leave to cook over a gentle heat until the meat is tender.

4

Strain the cooking juices through a fine sieve, then put the meat aside.

Heat the blanquette-cooking juices with the agar-agar over a high heat, stir well and bring to the boil.

Remove from the heat and leave to cool. Add the lemon juice, then check the seasoning and add some fine salt as necessary. Whisk in the egg white.

Pour the agar-agar mixture into a siphon, then seal and insert a gas cartridge.

Do a test: press the siphon lever and check the texture – it should be light and frothy. Keep the siphon warm in a bain-marie until ready to serve.

For 4
Preparation time: 45 min
Cooking time: 50 min

}

Sole bonne femme and crushed potatoes with snails

These days sole has become too expensive for most restaurants, but once upon a time this used to be a classic bistrot dish, one that was found on every menu. Poached in white wine, flavoured with shallots, mushrooms and a little cream, bonne femme is a much lighter way of cooking sole than meunière. The crushed potatoes with snails add a touch of sophistication, and the combination of their earthy flavour with fish is lovely. You can also use other fish for this recipe, such as brill.

The sole

15 ml/½ fl oz white wine
150 ml/5 fl oz vegetable stock
   (see step-by-step method on p. 126)
splash of olive oil
8 small sole fillets
fine salt

The sauce

2 shallots
400 g/14 oz white button mushrooms
50 g/1¾ oz butter
50 ml/1¾ fl oz crème fraîche
   (sour cream)
fine salt

The crushed potatoes with snails

400 g/14 oz Charlotte potatoes
12 snails
a few sprigs of parsley
50 g/1¾ oz butter
2 teaspoons vegetable stock
   (see step-by-step method on p. 126)
coarse salt, fine salt, freshly
   ground pepper

Equipment

5 cm/2 in round pastry cutter

1 ~ The sole

Put the white wine, vegetable stock and olive oil in a frying pan and bring to a simmer. Season the sole with salt, then immerse in the simmering liquid and poach for 5 minutes, turning them halfway through the cooking time. Drain, reserving the cooking liquid, then keep the fish warm (between two shallow plates, for example).

2 ~ The sauce

Peel and trim the shallots and mushrooms, then slice them both finely. Melt the butter in a small saucepan, add the shallots and cook over a gentle heat for 1 minute, stirring all the time, then add the mushrooms. Leave to cook for about 4–5 minutes until most of the liquid has evaporated. Add 100 ml/3½ fl oz of the reserved sole-cooking liquid, bring to the boil and reduce again, this time by half. Add the cream and reduce again until the mixture is thick enough to coat the back of a spoon. Take off the heat and season lightly with salt, then put to one side.

3 ~ The crushed potatoes with snails

Preheat the oven to 180°C (350°F; gas mark 4). Wash the potatoes, if necessary, then put them in a large baking dish on a bed of coarse salt. Bake for about 45 minutes, or until tender. Meanwhile, chop the snails and the parsley. Remove the potatoes from the oven and peel them, then crush with a fork. Put the potatoes in a saucepan over a gentle heat and mix in the butter and snails, then add the parsley and vegetable stock. Season to taste with salt and pepper.

4 ~ Finishing up and plating up

Gently reheat the fish fillets in the sauce. Don't let it boil, or the texture of the fish will be spoiled. Using a pastry cutter, shape the crushed potatoes into rounds on the plates. Add the sole and the sauce and serve immediately.

For 4
Preparation time: 45 min
Resting time: 1 h 30 min
Cooking time: 1 h 50 min

Pike quenelles with Nantua sauce

My grandfather always loved making us pike quenelles. Based on a panade (choux pastry dough), these quenelles are smothered with Nantua sauce, a classic in our restaurant that combines crayfish butter with béchamel sauce and mushroom cream, then the whole lot is grilled until golden and bubbling.

The panade

60 g/2¼ oz plain (all-purpose) flour
125 ml/4 fl oz milk
pinch of freshly grated nutmeg
1 egg
fine salt, freshly ground pepper

The quenelles

225 g/8 oz skinless pike fillets,
    pin-boned
100 g/3½ oz soft butter
2 eggs
25 ml/1 fl oz cream
fine salt

Nantua sauce

340 g/11 oz butter
1 kg/2¼ lb crayfish heads (order
    these from your fishmonger)
150 g/5½ oz white button mushrooms
juice of a lemon
250 ml/9 fl oz cream
40 g/1½ oz plain (all-purpose) flour
500 ml/18 fl oz milk
fine salt

1 ~ The panade

Put the flour into a saucepan, then gradually mix in the cold milk (this helps to avoid lumps). Season with salt and pepper and add the nutmeg. Beat the egg, then mix that in too. Cook over a high heat, stirring constantly, for 25 minutes. Remove from the heat and leave to cool.

2 ~ The quenelles

Blend the pike flesh very finely. Season with salt, then push through a sieve into a bowl, using the back of a spoon to press it through the mesh. Add 150 g/5½ oz of the cold panade to the sieved pike, along with the butter, eggs and cream. Mix with a spatula, then check the seasoning and add some salt if necessary. Leave to rest in the fridge for 30 minutes. Using a tablespoon, scoop the mixture into 'quenelle' shapes (as in the photo). Bring a saucepan of water to the boil, then lower the heat to a simmer. Slip the quenelles into the simmering water and cook gently for 10 minutes. Be careful not to let the water boil. Lift out with a slotted spoon and drain on a clean tea towel.

3 ~ The Nantua sauce

Melt a knob of butter in a saucepan over a medium heat, then add the crayfish heads and cook until they are well caramelized, stirring all the time (don't let them catch on the pan). Add 300 g/10½ oz of the butter and reduce the heat to low, then leave to infuse for 1 hour, or until the butter is a rich red. Remove from the heat. Using a ladle, skim off the clear butter from the surface and strain through a fine sieve. Meanwhile, put the cleaned and finely chopped mushrooms into a saucepan with the lemon juice and cook for 4 minutes over a low heat, then add the cream and leave to cook gently for 15 minutes before straining through a fine sieve. Next, make a béchamel sauce: melt the remaining butter in a saucepan, then add the flour and cook for 2–3 minutes over a gentle heat, stirring all the time. Gradually stir in the milk, bring to the boil and simmer for 2–3 minutes, then take off the heat. Stir in the mushroom cream and 100 g/3½ oz of the crayfish butter. Check the seasoning.

4 ~ Finishing off and plating up

Preheat an overhead grill (broiler). Put the drained quenelles in a heatproof dish and cover with the Nantua sauce. Grill for 5 minutes, or until browned and bubbling, then serve very hot.

For 4
Preparation time: 30 min
Cooking time: 45 min

}

My pommes dauphine

Though these potato puffs might seem like a cheffy invention, they actually date from the nineteenth century and are typical of the sort of side dishes found on bistrot menus. A perfect combination of choux pastry and nutmeg-scented mashed potatoes formed into balls and then quick-fried, they are loved by children. If you like, you can freeze the balls and then cook them when you need them, but you'll need to add 3 more minutes to the cooking time.

500 g/1 lb 2 oz potatoes

The choux pastry

250 ml/9 fl oz water
65 g/2½ oz butter
125 g/4½ oz plain (all-purpose) flour
4 egg yolks, lightly beaten
pinch of freshly grated nutmeg
2 litres/3½ pints groundnut (peanut)
   oil for deep-frying
fine salt, freshly ground pepper

1 ~ The potatoes

Cook the potatoes, unpeeled, in boiling water. Once cooked, peel and then mash them in a potato ricer or mouli. Put the potato flesh in a bowl and keep to one side. (See step-by-step method on p. 262.)

2 ~ The choux pastry

Bring the water to the boil in a saucepan, then add the butter and a pinch of fine salt. When the butter has melted, with the pan still on the heat, add the flour all in one go and mix well with a spatula. Cook for about 10 minutes over a medium heat, stirring constantly, until the mixture is dry and starting to come away from the sides of the pan. Remove from the heat and tip into a large bowl, then slowly work in the beaten egg yolks. Add the potato flesh and the nutmeg, season with salt and pepper, and mix well. With lightly floured hands, form the mixture into balls. Put them on a lightly floured work surface.

3 ~ Cooking and plating up

Heat the groundnut oil in a large saucepan or deep-fryer, then immerse the balls in the hot oil and fry until they are a lovely golden colour. Remove with a slotted spoon, drain on kitchen paper and season with a little fine salt. Transfer to a dish and serve immediately.

How to make pommes dauphine

1

Cook the potatoes, unpeeled, in boiling water. Once cooked, peel the potatoes and then reduce to a pulp in a potato ricer or mouli and put to one side.

2

Bring the water to the boil in a saucepan, then add the butter and salt.

3

With the pan still on the heat, add the flour all in one go.

4

Again, still on the heat, mix in the flour with a spatula and keep stirring the mixture to dry it out.

5

Transfer the mixture to a large bowl. Add the beaten egg yolks and the potato flesh, season and mix well.

6

Lightly flour your hands and shape the pommes dauphine by rolling small amounts of the mixture in your hands to make balls. Put them on a lightly floured work surface.

7

Carefully put the pommes dauphine into the basket of a deep-fryer, then immerse in the hot oil until cooked through and golden all over.

8

Remove the pommes dauphine from the oil with a slotted spoon and drain on kitchen paper. Season lightly with salt and serve very hot.

Makes 10
Preparation time: 1 h
Resting time: 4 h 30 min
Cooking time: 30 min

}

Rum baba with chestnut sauce and vanilla whipped cream

What could be more retro and delicious than a rum baba? I like the combination of amber rum and earthy chestnut with the warmth of vanilla in this version. If you want to make one large baba, bake it in a bundt tin.

The baba dough

200 g/7 oz plain (all-purpose) flour
1 teaspoon salt
3 teaspoons caster (superfine) sugar
100 ml/3½ fl oz milk
10 g/0.35 oz fresh yeast
2 eggs
50 g/1¾ oz unsalted butter

The baba syrup

500 g/1 lb 2 oz caster (superfine) sugar
1 vanilla pod (bean)
200 ml/7 fl oz dark rum

The chestnut sauce

2 g/0.07 oz gelatine
50 g/1¾ oz caster (superfine) sugar
1 egg yolk
150 ml/5 fl oz milk
150 g/5½ oz chestnut purée
1 tablespoon cornflour (cornstarch)
80 g/3 oz butter

The vanilla whipped cream

1 vanilla pod (bean)
300 ml/10 fl oz very cold double or whipping (heavy) cream

Finishing off

splash of rum

Equipment

individual baba moulds
cooking thermometer (optional)

1 ~ The baba dough

Put the flour, salt and sugar in the bowl of an electric mixer. Warm the milk in a saucepan (if you have a thermometer, check that the temperature doesn't go above 30°C/86°F), then add the yeast and stir until dissolved. Pour onto the flour in the mixer bowl, add an egg and mix together slowly. As soon as the mixture is smooth, add the second egg and mix in, then stop the machine. Pour the melted butter all over the dough and leave at room temperature, without mixing or stirring, until the butter has soaked into the dough. Beat the mixture again until the butter is incorporated. Fill the baba moulds with the dough, then leave at room temperature to rise until doubled in size. Preheat the oven to 170°C (325°F; gas mark 3). Bake for 20–25 minutes, or until risen and golden. Remove the babas from the oven, unmould onto a wire rack and leave to cool.

2 ~ The baba syrup

Put the sugar and vanilla pod in a saucepan with 800 ml/27 fl oz of water. Bring to the boil and simmer for a few seconds. Remove from the heat and leave to cool, then pour in the rum. Immerse the cooled babas in the syrup and leave to soak for 2 hours, then drain on a wire rack with a baking tray underneath (to catch the drips).

3 ~ The chestnut sauce

Soak the gelatine in cold water for 2–3 minutes. In a large bowl, mix together the sugar and the egg yolk. Put the milk, chestnut purée and cornflour into a saucepan and bring to the boil, whisking all the time, then pour into the bowl with the sugar and egg yolk and mix together. Pour the mixture back into the saucepan and cook over a gentle heat, stirring constantly, until it thickens. Remove from the heat and add the drained and squeezed-out gelatine, stirring to dissolve, then leave to cool to 40°C/104°F (check the temperature with a cooking thermometer, if you have one). Mix in the diced butter, then pour the sauce into individual bowls and chill in the fridge for 2 hours.

4 ~ The vanilla whipped cream

Split open the vanilla pod lengthways, then scrape out the seeds. Put the cream into a bowl or electric mixer with the vanilla seeds and whip until thick.

5 ~ Finishing off and serving

Spoon a little vanilla cream onto the chestnut sauce and put a baba on top, then drizzle over a little rum. Serve immediately.

MY CLASSIC RECIPES

These are my favourite recipes, a winning
combination of both classics and new ideas.
Some are signature dishes, like the baby vegetable
tart with Parmesan cream, or the mint-marinated
langoustines with petits pois cream and minted
liquorice spring onions. But every one plays on the
different registers of flavour I love: the acid notes
of citrus or vinegar, sweet–sour mixtures enhanced
with warmth, textures that evolve – and, at the heart
of everything, the search for subtlety and a wish
to make the most of ingredients. I hope these recipes
will bring you as much pleasure in your kitchen
as they bring me in mine.

For 4
Preparation time: 45 min
Cooking time: 35 min

Mint-marinated langoustines with petits pois cream and minted liquorice spring onions

This recipe plays with contrasting textures and flavours to create a dish that highlights the vibrant green of peas, the softness of langoustines and the freshness of mint and liquorice.

The langoustines

12 langoustines
250 ml/9 fl oz grapeseed oil
½ bunch of mint
splash of olive oil
fine salt
fleur de sel

The spring onion compote

200 g/7 oz spring onions (scallions)
splash of olive oil
40 g/1½ oz salted butter
100 ml/3½ fl oz vegetable stock
  (see step-by-step method on p. 126)

The petits pois cream

250 g/8½ oz shelled petits pois
coarse salt
fine salt

The liquorice powder

5 g/¼ oz cachous (liquorice sweets)
  or 'Fisherman's Friend' aniseed
  lozenges

Equipment

wooden skewers
4 x 7 cm/2¾ in round pastry cutters

1 ~ The langoustines

Remove the langoustine tails, then shell them, except for the last section of the tail (as in the photo). Along the back of the langoustine, embedded in the flesh, you will see a thin black line: the gut. Remove this by lightly scoring the flesh with a knife, then lifting it out. Mix together the grapeseed oil and finely chopped mint, then immerse the langoustines in this flavoured oil. Chill.

2 ~ The spring onion compote

Peel the spring onions, then slice them finely. Heat a frying pan, add a little olive oil and the butter, then add the spring onions and let them cook very gently. Add the vegetable stock little by little, to help them cook down. The spring onions should be soft after about 30 minutes of slow cooking.

3 ~ The petits pois cream

Fill a saucepan with cold water and add a pinch of coarse salt. Bring to the boil, then add the petits pois and cook until tender. Refresh in cold water and drain. Blend until smooth, then season with a little fine salt and put to one side.

4 ~ The liquorice powder

Preheat the oven to 180°C (350°F; gas mark 4). Bake the cachous or lozenges in the oven. As soon as they swell, remove them from the oven and crush to a powder, then sieve to remove any coarse pieces.

5 ~ Finishing off and plating up

Heat the petits pois cream in a saucepan – it should be a very fine purée, almost liquid. In another saucepan, reheat the spring onion compote. Put a little olive oil into a non-stick frying pan. While it is heating, remove the langoustines from the mint oil, thread them onto the skewers in threes and season with fine salt. Place a pastry cutter on each plate. Spoon a layer of spring onion compote inside, then top with a layer of petits pois cream and keep the plates warm. Next, add the langoustines to the hot frying pan and cook for about 3–4 minutes in total, or until coloured on both sides (don't overcook them; they should stay translucent in the middle). Remove the pastry cutters from the plates. Take the langoustines off the skewers and arrange three on each stack of spring onion compote and petits pois cream. Season with fleur de sel, scatter over the liquorice powder and serve immediately.

For 4
Preparation time: 1 h
Cooking time: 40 min

} Shoulder of kid goat with sorrel and fondant potatoes

I love the contrasts in this dish: the sharpness of sorrel rolled in tender goat meat that melts in the mouth, plus the rich jus, all of which reminds me of family meals when I was a child. With a few fondant potatoes, covered in the sauce, this is a delight.

The shoulder of kid goat

¼ bunch of sorrel
1 deboned shoulder of kid goat, about 750 g/1 lb 10 oz
splash of groundnut (peanut) oil
25 g/1 oz butter
700 ml/24 fl oz vegetable stock (see step-by-step method on p. 126)
1 garlic clove
sprig of thyme
1 small bay leaf
zest of 1 orange
fine salt, freshly ground pepper

The potatoes

300 g/10½ oz new potatoes
500 g/1 lb 2 oz salted butter
1 crushed garlic clove
sprig of thyme
1 small bay leaf

Finishing off

1 tablespoon finely chopped sorrel
zest of 1 orange
fine salt, freshly ground pepper

1 ~ The shoulder of kid goat

Carefully wash and dry the sorrel leaves, then generously season the inside of the kid goat shoulder with salt and pepper. Lay the sorrel leaves nice and flat over the meat, then roll the shoulder up into a sausage shape and tie it, like a joint, with kitchen string. Heat the oil and butter in a pressure cooker, add the meat and brown all over, making sure it doesn't burn. Carefully tilt the pressure cooker to pour off the oil from the meat, then add the vegetable stock, garlic, thyme, bay and orange zest. Following the manufacturer's instructions, bring the cooker up to pressure and cook for 40 minutes. Remove from the heat and let the pressure drop slowly. Take out the meat, then strain the cooking juices through a sieve. Check and adjust the seasoning as necessary.

2 ~ The confit new potatoes

Wash and lightly scrub the potatoes to remove their thin skins. Melt the butter in a saucepan, then add the garlic, thyme and bay. Immerse the potatoes in the butter (they should be completely covered) and leave to cook at a simmer for about 10–15 minutes – they should be meltingly soft. Remove them from the pan with a slotted spoon.

3 ~ Finishing off

A few minutes before serving, put a little of the goat-cooking juices with the drained potatoes in a frying pan. Cook until the juices are thick enough to coat the potatoes, stirring gently throughout. Add the finely chopped sorrel, then check and adjust the seasoning as necessary. Slice the goat, then warm a little oil in a frying pan over a high heat and sear the goat slices on each side. Put some potatoes and a couple of slices of goat on each plate, sprinkle with the orange zest and pour over a little of the hot cooking juices. Serve immediately.

Tip | In the autumn or winter, try this recipe with shoulder of lamb.

For 4 Resting time: 24 h
Preparation time: 1 h
Cooking time: 5 min

John Dory with cucumber pickle and purée and an aniseed sauce

This combination of delicate, flaky John Dory with puréed and pickled cucumber and an aniseed beurre monté is one of my favourite recipes. It's a subtle dish that can also be made with other white fish or green asparagus.

The cucumber purée

1 cucumber
1 teaspoon aniseed
fine salt

The marinated cucumber

1 cucumber
90 ml/3 fl oz white balsamic vinegar
80 g/3 oz caster (superfine) sugar

The aniseed beurre monté

200 g/7 oz soft unsalted butter
4 teaspoons aniseed
50 ml/1¾ fl oz vegetable stock
  (see step-by-step method on p. 126)
50 ml/1¾ fl oz double (heavy) cream

The John Dory

500 g/1 lb 2 oz salted butter
2 teaspoons aniseed
4 John Dory fillets

Finishing off

aniseed
fleur de sel

Equipment

cooking thermometer
4 cm/1½ in round pastry cutter

1 ~ The cucumber purée

Peel the cucumber. Cut it in half lengthways, remove the seeds then slice. Cook in boiling salted water for 2 minutes. Drain, immerse in cold water, drain again then blend until smooth. Add the aniseed (allow 1¾ teaspoons aniseed for every 1 kg/2¼ lb purée), mix together, put in a sieve over a bowl, cover with a clean tea towel and leave in the fridge overnight. The next day, push the purée through a fine sieve, check the seasoning then chill again.

2 ~ The marinated cucumber

Peel the cucumber, then cut it into diagonal slices about 1 cm/½ in thick. Put the vinegar and sugar into a saucepan, bring to the boil, then leave to cool. Put the cucumber and cold vinegar-sugar marinade into a bowl, leave to marinate for half a day then drain.

3 ~ The aniseed beurre monté

Mix the butter with 3 teaspoons of the aniseed and leave to infuse in the fridge. Meanwhile, put the rest of the aniseed in a saucepan with the vegetable stock. Bring to the boil and reduce for 5 minutes, then add the cream and simmer until reduced by half. Remove from the heat, then add the aniseed butter and blend thoroughly. Taste and adjust the seasoning if required. Leave to infuse for a few minutes, then strain through a fine sieve.

4 ~ The John Dory

Melt the butter in a frying pan over a gentle heat, add the aniseed and leave to infuse for 15 minutes, keeping the butter's temperature close to 60–65°C/140–149°F. A few minutes before serving, immerse the fish in the hot butter and cook over a gentle heat for about 5–6 minutes, or until a thermometer inserted into the centre reads 50°C/120°F. Lift the fish out carefully, letting the hot butter drain back into the pan.

5 ~ Finishing off and plating up

Put the pastry cutter on a plate and fill with cucumber purée, then remove the cutter. Place some pickled cucumber slices alongside, then add the fish and a ramekin of aniseed beurre monté to the plate. Sprinkle with fleur de sel and aniseed, then serve immediately.

For 4
Preparation time: 1 h
Resting time: overnight
Cooking time: 15 min

Roast scallops with spaghettini and rum emulsion

This combination of scallops poached in butter and served with homemade spaghettini in a rum sauce contrasts the firmness of seafood with the softness of the foam.

The spaghettini

250 g/8½ oz plain (all-purpose) or 'oo' flour
25 g/1 oz durum wheat semolina
1 teaspoon fine salt
5 egg yolks
25 ml/1 fl oz extra virgin olive oil
25 ml/1 fl oz water
1 teaspoon distilled white vinegar

The rum reduction

200 ml/7 fl oz double (heavy) cream
20 ml/¾ fl oz rum
fine salt

The rum emulsion

1 shallot
knob of butter
100 ml/3½ fl oz rum
80 ml/2½ fl oz vegetable stock (see step-by-step method on p. 126)
400 ml/14 fl oz whole milk

The scallops

12 whole scallops (with coral)
300 g/10½ oz salted butter
fine salt

Equipment

pasta machine
cooking thermometer

1 ~ The spaghettini

Combine the flour, semolina and salt in a large bowl or an electric mixer. Add the beaten egg yolks, then mix the oil, water and vinegar together and add those too. Beat until a dough forms, then shape into two balls. Wrap in cling film and chill overnight in the fridge. The next day, roll out the dough very thinly with a rolling pin (you should be able to see through it) or a pasta machine. Cut into spaghettini and then into 5 cm/2 in lengths. Dust the spaghettini with flour, then spread out on a baking tray or large plate, cover with cling film and chill in the fridge. Cook the pasta just before serving, for 2 minutes in boiling salted water. Drain, refresh in cold water and drain again.

2 ~ The rum reduction

Boil the cream in a saucepan until it is thick enough to coat the back of a spoon. Season with salt, then stir in the rum. Put to one side.

3 ~ The rum emulsion

Peel and finely slice the shallot. Melt the butter in a frying pan, add the shallot and soften, then add the scallop corals and any other trimmings. They will give out a liquid: let it reduce by half. Add the rum and bring to the boil, then reduce by half. Next, add the vegetable stock and reduce by half. Finally, pour in the milk and heat through, then strain the sauce through a fine sieve. Just before serving, froth the warm emulsion with a stick blender to create a light foam.

4 ~ Finishing off and plating up

Lightly season the scallops with salt. Melt the butter over a gentle heat in a saucepan. Add the scallops, bring the temperature of the butter up to a steady 60°C/140°F and cook for 5 minutes, turning the scallops every so often. Meanwhile, gently reheat the spaghettini and rum emulsion together in a saucepan; don't let them boil. Divide the spaghettini between the plates, then add the scallops (lifted out of the butter with a slotted spoon, and quickly drained on kitchen paper). Dress with the foamy rum emulsion and eat straight away.

Tip| The spaghettini recipe above can be used to make lots of different homemade pasta, such as tagliatelle, spaghetti and linguine.

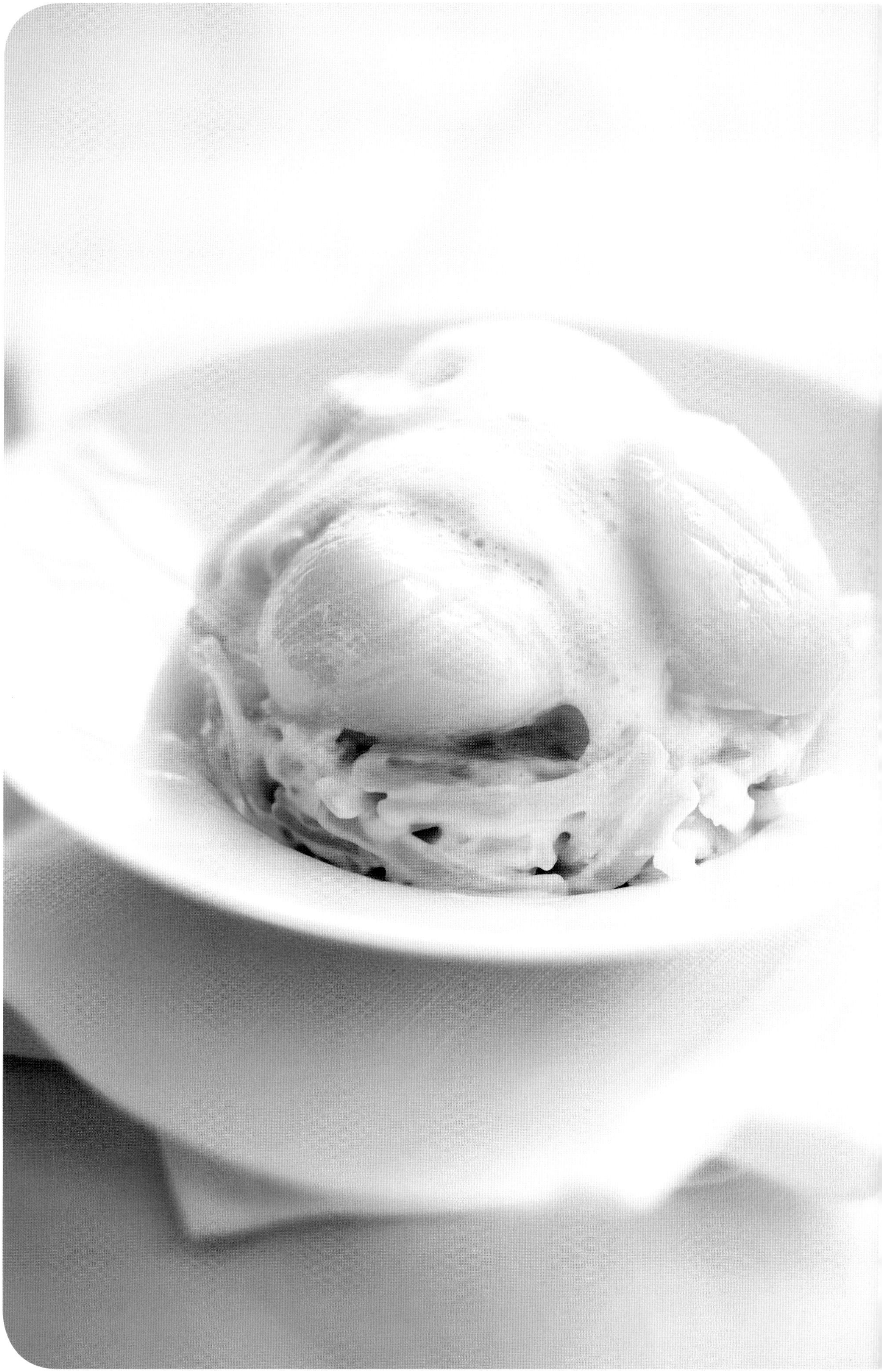

For 4
Preparation time: 45 min
Freezing time: 15 min
Cooking time: 20 min

Vegetable tart with young Parmesan cream

This tart, which I created in 2009, is one of my signature dishes. Here, made with spring vegetables, it is a riot of colour and full of fresh greenery, but you can adapt it by using other seasonal vegetables. In the summer, try it with a fresh young sheep's or goat's cheese instead of Parmesan.

The Parmesan cream

100 g/3½ oz young Parmesan
200 ml/7 fl oz whole milk
fine salt

The shortcrust pastry

100 g/3½ oz butter
50 g/1¾ oz ground almonds
100 g/3½ oz plain (all-purpose) flour
½ teaspoon fine salt
1 teaspoon lavender flowers
1 whole egg + 1 egg yolk to glaze

The vegetables

4 spring onions (scallions)
splash of olive oil + extra for
  finishing off
100 ml/3½ fl oz vegetable stock
  + extra for finishing off
  (see step-by-step method on p. 126)
50 g/1¾ oz baby broad (fava) beans
50 g/1¾ oz petits pois
8 green asparagus spears
100 g/3½ oz mangetout (snow peas)
a few cauliflower florets
¼ bunch of radishes
1 garlic clove, peeled, left whole
  and squashed
sprig of thyme
splash of aged sherry vinegar
fine salt

Equipment

5–7 cm/2–2¾ in round pastry-cutter

1 ~ The Parmesan cream

Finely grate the Parmesan, then put it in a saucepan with the milk. Heat gently to melt the cheese, then remove from the heat and blend. Strain through a fine sieve, then season with a little salt if necessary and keep to one side at room temperature.

2 ~ The shortcrust pastry

Put all the ingredients except the egg in an electric mixer and mix to form a crumbly dough. Add the whole egg and mix again until the dough comes together in a ball. On a work surface, roll out the dough to a thickness of 2.5 mm/⅒ in, wrap in cling film and freeze for 15 minutes. Preheat the oven to 150°C (300°F; gas mark 2). Using the pastry cutter, cut out 4 circles, brush with egg yolk, then bake for 15 minutes. Remove from the oven and leave to cool.

3 ~ The vegetables

Peel and trim the spring onions, then cut in half. Sauté them in olive oil for 2 minutes, then add the vegetable stock and cook slowly until the onions are meltingly soft. Meanwhile, cook the baby broad beans, petits pois, asparagus and mangetout separately in boiling salted water, one after the other, for about 2–3 minutes. Refresh in cold water, then drain. Cook the cauliflower florets very briefly in boiling water. Slice the radishes very finely, using a mandoline if possible, then chill in iced water for about 10 minutes to firm them up, then drain.

4 ~ Finishing off and garnish

Just before serving, heat a little olive oil in a frying pan and sauté all the vegetables (except the radish) with the garlic and thyme for 2–3 minutes. Stir in the vinegar and a little extra vegetable stock and leave to cook for a minute. Tip the vegetables into a colander to drain, removing the garlic and thyme, then put them into a large bowl and season to taste with a little salt. Put a shortcrust pastry disc onto each plate, decorate with a mixture of the vegetables and some radish slices, then season with salt and a few drops of olive oil. Dress with the Parmesan cream and serve immediately.

Tip | Use a very young Parmesan; it will melt more easily.

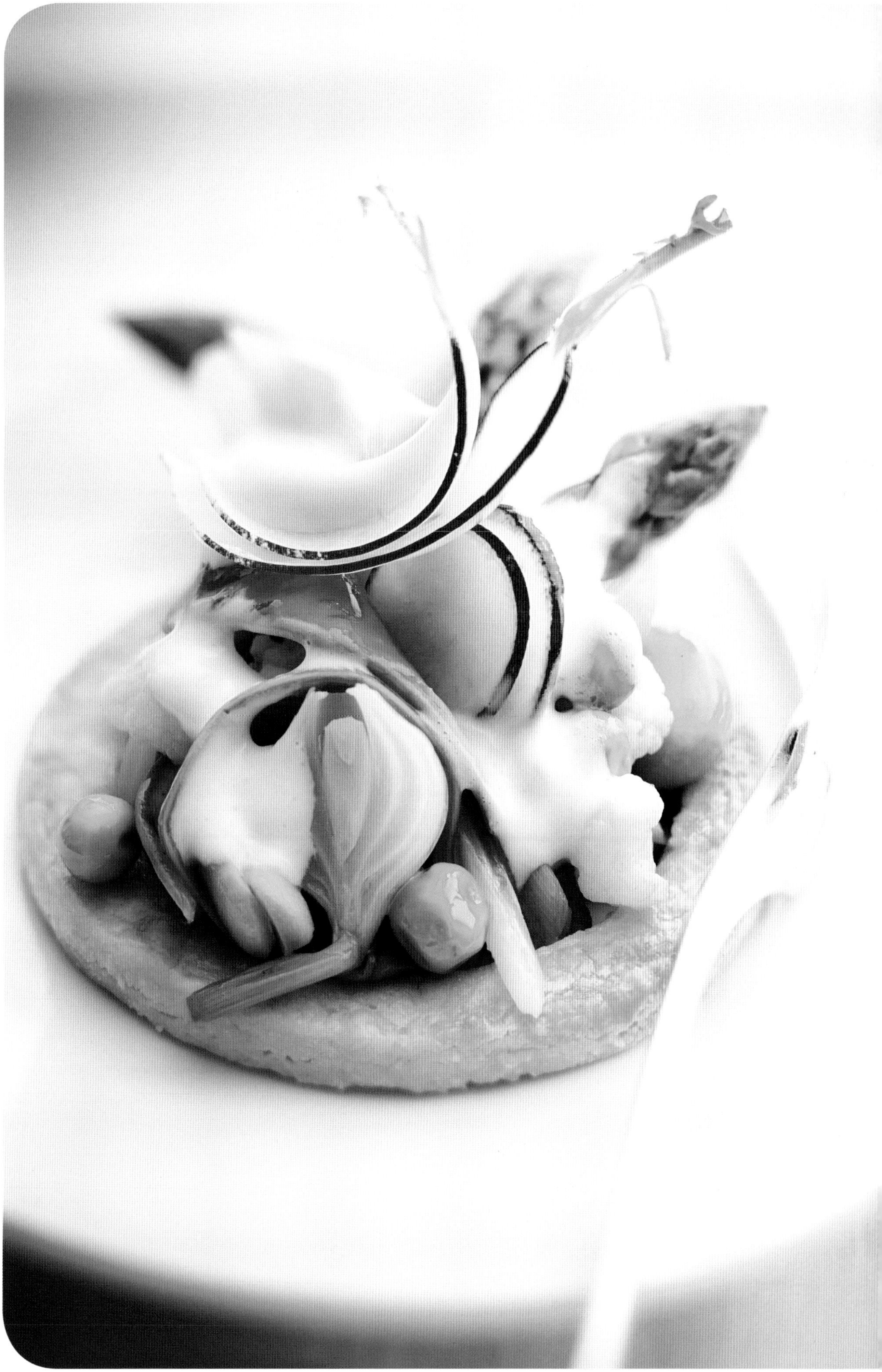

For 6
Preparation time: 30 min
Freezing time: 6 h
Cooking time: 5–10 min

Iced Grand Marnier soufflé

My father reinvented this classic many years ago and, although it may seem a bit old-fashioned these days, I urge you to let yourself be tempted to try it at home. Once your friends have tasted it, they'll want you to make it again and again. It's a great family favourite, and easy to make.

90 ml/3 fl oz orange juice
70 g/2½ oz caster (superfine) sugar
zest of 1 orange + a little extra for
  decoration
75 g/2¾ oz egg yolk (from about
  3 eggs)
100 ml/3½ fl oz double (heavy) cream
50 ml/1¾ fl oz Grand Marnier
icing (confectioners') sugar

Equipment

cooking thermometer
individual soufflé dishes

1 ~ Making the iced soufflé

Put the orange juice, sugar and orange zest into a saucepan and bring to the boil. Place a thermometer in the syrup and, when the temperature reaches 105°C/220°F, remove the pan from the heat. Meanwhile, put the egg yolks into an electric mixer and whisk rapidly, then pour in the boiling syrup and continue to whisk until the mixture is completely cold. Whip the cream to soft peaks, then fold gently into the mixture, along with the Grand Marnier.

2 ~ Preparing the soufflé dishes

Cut out 6 strips of baking parchment, each long enough to wrap around the outside of a soufflé dish twice and high enough to extend 2–3 cm/1 in above its rim. Wrap a strip twice around the outside of each dish and tie in place with kitchen string or an elastic band.

3 ~ Freezing the soufflés

Pour the mixture into the prepared dishes and leave to set in the freezer for at least 6 hours.

4 ~ Serving the soufflés

Remove the baking parchment, then sprinkle the soufflés with icing sugar and decorate with a curl of orange zest. Serve immediately.

Variations | *Try using another liqueur, such as limoncello, one flavoured with mandarin or other citrus fruit, or a pear brandy.*

For 8
Preparation time: 45 min
Cooking time: 25 min
Resting time: 30 min

}

Chocolate-mint profiteroles

This is an irresistible combination of choux pastry, mint ice cream and a hot chocolate-mint sauce. Here I've served the profiteroles individually, but there is nothing to stop you building an incredible centrepiece with them.

The choux pastry

125 ml/4 fl oz milk
60 g/2¼ oz butter
1 teaspoon fine salt
1 teaspoon caster (superfine) sugar
70 g/2½ oz plain (all-purpose) flour
2 eggs

The mint ice cream

200 ml/7 fl oz whole milk
90 ml/3 fl oz double (heavy) cream
10 g/⅓ oz milk powder
2 sprigs of mint
70 g/2½ oz caster (superfine) sugar
1 egg yolk

The chocolate mint

150 ml/5 fl oz milk
50 g/1¾ oz caster (superfine) sugar
5 g/¼ oz mint leaves
135 g/4¾ oz dark (bittersweet)
  chocolate

Equipment

piping bag
cooking thermometer (optional)
ice-cream maker

1 ~ The choux pastry

Preheat the oven to 165°C (320°F; gas mark 2–3). Put the milk, butter, salt and sugar into a saucepan and bring to the boil, then, off the heat, add the flour all in one go. Return the pan to the heat and cook for 30 seconds, stirring constantly, to dry out the pastry. Transfer to a large bowl, then mix in the beaten eggs. Put the pastry into a piping bag and pipe small, choux-puff-sized rounds onto a baking sheet. Bake for 17 minutes, then remove from the oven and leave to cool.

2 ~ The mint ice cream

Heat the milk, cream and milk powder in a saucepan, then add the mint, cover and remove from the heat. Leave to infuse for 15 minutes, then strain through a fine sieve. Whisk the sugar and egg yolk together in a bowl, then pour on the mint-infused milk. Stir well, then transfer to a saucepan and heat gently, stirring constantly, until it thickens (around 82°C/180°F). Remove from the heat and strain again through a fine sieve, then pour into a bowl. Sit this bowl over a larger bowl of cold water and ice to speed up the cooling process. As soon as the mixture is good and cold, churn in an ice-cream maker according to the manufacturer's instructions.

3 ~ The chocolate-mint sauce

Heat the milk with the sugar in a saucepan. Remove from the heat and add the mint, then cover and leave to infuse for 15 minutes. Meawhile, grate the chocolate into a large bowl. Strain the mint-infused milk through a fine sieve onto the grated chocolate. Mix well, then keep warm, preferably in a bain-marie.

4 ~ Finishing off

Halve or open the choux puffs and use a spoon to fill them with mint ice cream, then close them up again. Put 4 profiteroles on each plate and pour over a little warm chocolate-mint sauce.

Variation | *Try making these with different chocolates, such as darker or stronger-flavoured ones.*

4

Homemade

THE APERITIF

The joy of an aperitif lies in the combination of lots of different people trying lots of flavours and tastes, with the food whetting not only the appetite but the conversation! You could make things to go specifically with a wine or fresh fruit juice, focus on vegetables and spices, cheeses and oils, or try something new like a spicy éclair or something sweet-sour. Food for this part of a meal should be easy to prepare and perfectly matched to both the next courses and what you're drinking. The methods for these dishes are easy to learn, for example how to make melba toast and a surprise sandwich loaf (or 'pain surprise') – try using them in other recipes too.

For 10
Preparation time: 25 min
Cooking time: 15 min
Resting time: 3 h

}

Peanut marshmallows

Served with champagne or dry white wine, these are perfect: the soft texture of marshmallows is a lovely reminder of childhood, the combination of flavours is a great talking point, and the contrast of textures is a surprise. As they'll keep in the fridge for up to three days, they're also great for a party. Try making different flavoured ones, by replacing the peanuts with the same amount of hazelnuts or pistachios.

The marshmallow

150 g/5½ oz caster (superfine) sugar
300 g/10½ oz egg white
(from about 10–12 eggs)
120 g/4¼ oz gelatine leaves
240 g/8½ oz peanut butter
10 g/⅓ oz Maldon salt

Finishing off

75 g/2¾ oz ground peanuts

Equipment

cooking thermometer
20 cm/8 in square baking tin
lined with baking parchment

1 ~ The marshmallow mixture

Put the sugar into a saucepan with 45 ml/1¾ fl oz of water. Bring to the boil, then put a thermometer into the syrup and keep cooking until the thermometer reads 121°C/250°F (about 4 minutes on a fast boil). During this time, whisk the egg whites until they are foamy and thick but not too firm. When the syrup reaches the correct temperature, pour it onto the egg whites and keep whisking. Soak the gelatine in cold water for 4–5 minutes, then drain it well. Put it in a microwaveable bowl (so plastic or ceramic, not metal), then heat it in the microwave until it melts into a liquid. Weigh the gelatine: it should weigh 600 g/1 lb 5 oz; if it doesn't, add enough water to make it up to this weight.

2 ~ Making the marshmallow

Mix the gelatine with the peanut butter, then add the Maldon salt. Pour this mixture onto the egg whites and syrup. Mix again, then pour into the lined baking tin to make a layer about 2 cm/¾ in thick. Leave to set and cool at room temperature for 3 hours. When the marshmallow is firm, remove it from the tin and cut it into neat 2 cm/¾ in cubes with a knife.

3 ~ Finishing off

Sprinkle the marshmallow cubes all over with ground peanuts.

Tip | *Keep the marshmallow wrapped in baking parchment until ready to serve. Only sprinkle a light coating of ground peanuts on the cubes, and at the very last moment, to prevent them drying out. Serve and eat the marshmallows quickly while they are still lovely and soft.*

Good to know | *Maldon salt, from Maldon in Essex, is an intensely white salt with flakes that resemble sequins. Its flavour is more iodine-y than Guérande fleur de sel. You can also use Halen Mon salt from Wales. You will find both these salts in good supermarkets and food shops.*

For 4
Preparation time: 45 min

} A surprise sandwich loaf

To make this very simple surprise sandwich loaf (or 'pain surprise'), you need to be quite precise. It's a lovely combination of healthy vegetables and the sort of flavoured butters I use all the time in my dishes. You can make different flavoured butters as you wish. Get the bread from a good baker, choose interesting flavours and textures for the fillings, and serve with a lovely chilled white wine, like a Sauvignon from the Loire. Easy to carry, this is also great for a picnic.

The loaf

1 large cob or cottage loaf

Smoked tea butter with crunchy radishes

50 g/1¾ oz salted butter
½ teaspoon smoked tea
  (such as lapsang souchong)
10 radishes
fine salt

Green Szechuan pepper butter with Parmesan

50 g/1¾ oz salted butter
½ teaspoon green Szechuan pepper
10 slivers of very young Parmesan

Saffron and tomato butter

50 g/1¾ oz salted butter
pinch of ground saffron
1 tomato
fine salt

Aniseed butter with cucumber

50 g/1¾ oz salted butter
½ teaspoon aniseed
1 cucumber
fine salt

Equipment

pestle and mortar

1 ~ The loaf

Cut and shape the loaf as shown on p. 290.

2 ~ Smoked tea butter and crunchy radishes

Beat the butter until it is very soft and malleable. In a small mortar, crush the smoked tea to a fine powder with a pestle, then mix into the softened butter. Wash and trim the radishes, then slice finely (preferably with a mandoline). Spread the bread with a thin layer of tea butter, then cover with a thin layer of radishes. Season with salt and cover with a second slice of bread, then cut into triangles.

3 ~ Green Szechuan pepper butter with Parmesan

Follow step 2 but, instead of tea, crush the pepper and mix that into the softened butter. Spread the bread with a thin layer of pepper butter, then put the Parmesan slivers on top. Cover with a second slice of bread, then cut into triangles.

4 ~ Saffron and tomato butter

Beat the butter until it is very soft, then simply mix in the saffron. Wash the tomato, remove the stalk, then slice thinly and season with salt. Spread the bread with a thin layer of saffron butter, then put the slices of tomato on top. Cover with a second slice of bread, then cut into triangles.

5 ~ Aniseed butter with cucumber

Follow step 2 but, instead of tea, crush the aniseed and mix that into the softened butter. Wash and peel the cucumber. Cut it in half lengthways, then remove all the seeds and slice very finely lengthways (as in the photo on p. 291). Spread the bread with a thin layer of aniseed butter, then put the slices of cucumber on top. Season with salt and cover with a second slice of bread, then cut into triangles.

6 ~ Finishing off

Fill the surprise sandwich loaf by putting the triangular sandwiches inside, alternating the different types in layers. Eat immediately.

How to make a surprise sandwich loaf ('pain surprise')

1

Using a large bread knife, cut down through the loaf of bread, 1 cm/ ½ in in from the edge. The aim is to hollow out the centre of the loaf in one piece, leaving a 'case'.

2

Be careful not to go through the bottom/sides of the loaf. Always keep at least 1 cm/½ in away from the edge.

3

Still keeping 1 cm/½ in away from the bottom, use a see-sawing motion across the bread to release the centre. Turn the bread and do this again.

4

Grab the top of the loaf and gently pull it to lift out the centre of the bread in one piece. Leave the 'case' to one side.

Slice through the top of the loaf, again about 1 cm/½ in deep, and put the crust to one side. Once the sandwiches are finished, the crust goes back on top of the loaf.

6

Cut the loaf into 1 cm/½ in slices.

7

Spread half the slices with the different flavoured butters, then add the toppings and cover with the remaining slices of bread.

8

Cut the sandwiches into triangles, then put them back into the bread 'case' and cover with the crust. Serve immediately or chill until needed.

For 4
Preparation time: 12 min
Cooking time: 10 min + 2 min

}

Melba toast with lardo di Colonnata and Comté cheese

The marriage of lardo and Comté is unusual and different but the result is pure, crunchy deliciousness. You need to buy a dense white loaf, nothing full of holes, to make it easy to cut very thin slices of bread. You could also try this with other combinations of fatty meats and cheese, like bacon with Gruyère. These Melba toasts are delicious with a white wine from the Languedoc.

100 g/3½ oz white bread
4 slices lardo di Colonnata (available in good Italian delicatessens and online)
8 slices Comté cheese, cut into 5 cm/2 in squares
Sarawak pepper

1 ~ Preparing the melba toast

Preheat the oven to 180°C (350°F; gas mark 4). Slice the bread as thinly as possible. Cover each slice with a piece of lardo and a slice of Comté, then top with another slice of bread, as if you were making a sandwich.

2 ~ Making the melba toast

Put the melba 'sandwiches' onto a baking sheet and cover with baking parchment, then put another baking sheet on top of the parchment. Bake for about 10 minutes. Remove from the oven, take off the second baking sheet and the parchment, then cut the toasts to the shape required. Leave them on the baking sheet.

3 ~ Finishing off

Preheat an overhead grill (broiler). At the very last minute, just before serving, put another slice of Comté on top of each melba toast and grill for 2 minutes, just long enough for the cheese to melt. Grind over some Sarawak pepper and serve hot.

Good to know | *Lardo di Colonnata is from Tuscany. Made from pork fat, it comes in a thick rectangular slab: the top is covered in salt, black pepper, rosemary and garlic, while the lower part is the pork rind. Lardo is pinkish-white, and tastes very fresh, almost sweet.*

For 4
Preparation time: 15 min
Cooking time: 45 min

}

Grilled aubergine caviar with turmeric

This classic dish of grilled aubergine and turmeric is delicious. Turmeric is renowned for its health-giving qualities, especially when combined with the piperine in pepper, which is reason enough to make the most of this easy, summery recipe at aperitif time. It is particularly delicious with a glass of rosé from the south of France.

1 kg/2¼ lb aubergines (eggplants)
100 ml/3½ fl oz olive oil
1 garlic clove
1 teaspoon ground turmeric
fine salt, freshly ground pepper

Equipment

cast-iron grill pan
small glasses (as in the photo;
    large shot glasses would be ideal)

1- Preparing the aubergines

Preheat the oven to 180°C (350°F; gas mark 4). Meanwhile, put a cast-iron grill pan over a high heat. Cut the aubergines in half lengthways, then season with salt and brush their skins with olive oil.

2- Cooking the aubergines

Grill the aubergine halves on both sides for a few minutes, then put them all in a large piece of foil, along with the peeled garlic clove, and wrap up tightly. Bake for 30 minutes.

3- Finishing off and serving

Remove the foil parcel from the oven and scoop the aubergine flesh out of the skins. Chop the flesh, then season with salt, turmeric and pepper and mix well. Serve in small glasses with some lightly toasted bread.

For 4
Preparation time: 40 min
Marinating time: 8 min
Cooking time: 3 min

}

Herb-salt marinated anchovies with Green Zebra tomatoes

Anchovies are great to snack on before dinner, and this way of preparing them will really wake up your tastebuds. Once you have learnt how to salt anchovies, you can vary the flavourings to make all sorts of recipes. Green Zebra tomatoes are a cultivated variety with distinctive green and yellow striped skin and tart flesh. A young Clairette de Die or other aromatic sparkling white wine makes a perfect foil for the strong flavours here.

The marinated anchovies

1 teaspoon Voatsiperifery pepper
½ garlic clove
sprig of basil
sprig of tarragon
1 teaspoon grated horseradish
100 g/3½ oz Guérande salt
zest of ½ lemon
12 fresh anchovy fillets
100 ml/3½ fl oz olive oil

The tomatoes

2 large Green Zebra tomatoes
100 g/3½ oz salted butter
½ teaspoon freshly grated nutmeg

Finishing off

fleur de sel

Equipment

pastry cutter

1 ~ The marinated anchovies

Blend all the ingredients except the anchovy fillets and olive oil until you have a beautiful green salt. Put half the green salt into a dish in an even layer, then place the anchovy fillets on top and cover with the rest of the salt. Leave to marinate for 8 minutes in the fridge. Remove the fillets from the salt and rinse under cold running water. Dry carefully, then place in a clean dish and cover with the olive oil.

2 ~ The tomatoes

Bring a pan of water to the boil. Cut a cross in the base of the tomatoes, then immerse in the boiling water for a few seconds. Remove and plunge into iced water before peeling back the skins (see step-by-step method on p. 22). Cut the tomatoes into slices 1 cm/½ in thick, then chill. Beat the butter until very soft, then mix in the nutmeg. Put the butter between two sheets of baking parchment and use a rolling pin to flatten it out to a thickness of 3 mm/⅛ in. Chill until firm.

3 ~ Cooking and finishing off

Preheat an overhead grill (broiler). Remove the butter from the fridge and peel off the top piece of parchment. Using a pastry cutter or the rim of a glass, cut out circles of butter the same size as the tomato slices. Put the tomato slices onto a baking tray, cover with a slice of butter and grill for 3 minutes (just long enough to warm the tomato and melt the butter). Lift the anchovies out of the oil, shaking off any excess, then place on top of the tomatoes. Dress with fleur de sel and eat immediately.

Tip | This salting technique can also be used with other fish, but the marinating time for each one will be different: for example, 20 minutes for mackerel fillet, 15 for sardines.

LUNCH WITH THE GIRLS

We want to keep in shape, eat healthily, treat ourselves, respect our bodies and the environment: actually, we want everything! And so do men! These salads will help: there are salads for every season, salads that you can adapt depending on what you want to eat and achieve, energy-giving salads full of grains and vitamins, and all of them are great for the skin and the figure. There are also some quick options for everyday meals. Remember that tasty salad doesn't have to be covered in lots of dressing; in fact, too much dressing can overwhelm. Try different oils, vinegars and spices to keep refreshing your ideas and tastebuds.

For 4
Preparation time: 25 min
Cooking time: 15 min

Beetroot salad with Arabica coffee salt

This salad, with its winning combination of sweet and bitter, is one I serve in my restaurant in Valence. Different types of beetroot, with varying colours and contrasting textures, some cooked and some raw, are layered together and then dressed with coffee salt. Once again you'll find my much-loved pressure cooker being used to make this. The result: a beautiful, colourful, easy and elegant dish.

The beetroot

12 red beetroot (beets)
1 white beetroot (beets)
2 golden beetroot (beets)
2 Chioggia beetroot (beets)
coarse salt

The vinaigrette

pinch of fine salt
1 tablespoon sherry vinegar
3 tablespoons olive oil

The coffee salt

5 Blue Mountain coffee beans
50 g/1¾ oz Maldon salt

Finishing off

1 Chioggia beetroot (beet)
1 golden beetroot (beet)

Equipment

coffee grinder
pestle and mortar

1 ~ The beetroot

Wash the beetroot in plenty of running water, then group the beetroot according to their size. Put the first group in the basket of a pressure cooker, fill the base with water and add some coarse salt, then follow the instructions to bring the cooker up to pressure. Cook small (up to 2 cm/¾ in diameter) beetroot for 5–6 minutes, medium beetroot (4–6 cm/1½–2½ in diameter) for 7–8 minutes and large beetroot (from 8–12 cm/3–4½ in diameter) for 9–15 minutes. At the end of each cooking time, take the pressure cooker off the heat and let the pressure drop, then remove the beetroot and peel and quarter them. Put to one side.

2 ~ The vinaigrette

Stir the salt into the sherry vinegar until it dissolves, then mix in the olive oil.

3 ~ The coffee salt

Grind the coffee beans in a coffee grinder, then tip into a mortar and crush them even more finely with the pestle. Mix with the Maldon salt, then keep to one side.

4 ~ Finishing off and plating up

Peel, trim and finely slice the raw beetroot. Put the slices in a bowl of iced water for 10 minutes to make them firm and crunchy, then drain in a sieve. Dress the cooked beetroot slices with vinaigrette and arrange on the plates, then add the slices of raw beetroot and scatter over the coffee salt.

For 4
Preparation time: 30 min
Chilling time: 2 h

}

Melon soup with aniseed and goat's cheese cream

This summery soup, which is incredibly light and very easy to make, demands that you choose your melons very carefully. I highly recommend nice, firm Charentais melons, if you can get them. But there are lots of other possible combinations: try it with watermelon, Voatsiperifery pepper, fresh almonds or orange flower water. Depending on what you find, this recipe can be endlessly reinvented.

The melon soup

2 melons, each about 1 kg/2¼ lb
200 ml/7 fl oz iced mineral water
1 tablespoon aniseed
fine salt

The goat's cheese cream

120 g/4¼ oz fresh goat's cheese
150 ml/5 fl oz very cold double (heavy) cream
8 g/¼ oz gelatine leaves
40 ml/1½ fl oz milk
fine salt

Serving

1 teaspoon aniseed

1 ~ The melon soup

Halve the melons and remove the seeds, then use a spoon to scoop out the flesh. Blend with the mineral water, aniseed and a pinch of fine salt. Strain through a fine sieve into a bowl, then cover with cling film and chill in the fridge until needed.

2 ~ The goat's cheese cream

Beat the goat's cheese with a spatula or wooden spoon until it is very smooth. In an electric mixer, or another large bowl, whip the cream. Soak the gelatine leaves in cold water for a few minutes to soften them. Warm the milk in a saucepan, then add the drained and squeezed-out gelatine and stir until it completely dissolves. Pour this mixture onto the goat's cheese and mix well. Fold in the whipped cream and check the seasoning, adding a little salt if necessary. Pour into 4 shallow dishes, then chill for 2 hours.

3 ~ Serving

When ready to serve, pour the cold melon soup on top of the goat's cheese cream, then scatter over a few aniseeds and serve.

For 4
Preparation time: 40 min
Infusing time: 20 min
Fermenting time (yogurt): 8 h
Cooking time: 10 min

Quinoa salad with minted yogurt

This salad is good all year round. Both comforting and healthy, it contains carbohydrates (quinoa here, but cracked wheat or spelt would be equally delicious), vegetables for crunch and dairy to bind everything together, so it is full of flavour. You'll also learn how to make natural yogurt, which can be used not only in this dish, but also as a base for sweet versions with fruit or as an ingredient in the many Turkish and Indian recipes that combine vegetables and yogurt.

The yogurt

500 ml/18 fl oz whole milk

3 sprigs of mint

75 g/2¾ oz (½ small pot) full-fat natural yogurt

2 tablespoons milk powder

The quinoa

knob of salted butter

80 g/3 oz quinoa

500 ml/18 fl oz vegetable stock (see step-by-step method on p. 126)

5 red radishes

½ black radish

½ cucumber

a few mint leaves

1 tablespoon white balsamic vinegar

3 tablespoons olive oil

fine salt

Finishing off

a few mint leaves

Equipment

cooking thermometer

4 small glasses (as in the photo opposite)

yogurt maker

1 - The yogurt

Heat the milk in a saucepan, then remove from the heat and add the clean mint leaves. Cover and leave to infuse for 20 minutes, then strain through a fine sieve and discard the mint. Bring the infused milk to the boil, then leave to cool to 42°C/108°F (this gives the yogurt a lovely acidity). Meanwhile, mix the natural yogurt with the milk powder and, when the hot milk reaches 42°C/108°F, stir it in and mix well. Pour into 4 of the containers in the yogurt maker and leave to ferment according to the manufacturer's instructions (usually for about 8 hours), then chill. (See step-by-step method on p. 340.)

2 - The quinoa

Melt the butter in a saucepan and stir in the quinoa, then just cover with vegetable stock. Bring to the boil, then lower the heat and cook until all the liquid is absorbed, around 10 minutes. Take off the heat and leave to cool completely, then chill. Trim and quarter the radishes. Peel and dice the cucumber and finely chop the mint. In a small bowl, stir a pinch of salt into the vinegar, then add the olive oil to make a vinaigrette.

3 - Finishing off

Gently mix together the quinoa, vegetables and chopped mint, then dress with the vinaigrette. Spoon the cold yogurt into the glasses, top with the quinoa-vegetable mixture and decorate with some mint leaves.

For 4
Preparation time: 45 min
Marinating time: 10 h

Gravadlax and celeriac remoulade with Meaux mustard

This winter salad, which is a lovely contrast of sweet and sharp, is served in my bistrot. The herbaceous flavour of celeriac, which I love, goes really well with gravadlax. This is a perfect dish, with a great combination of marvellous textures and sheer harmony of flavours, that could easily be served instead of smoked salmon at Christmas and New Year.

The gravadlax

1 tablespoon coriander seeds
1 teaspoon aniseed
1 teaspoon black peppercorns
50 g/1¾ oz coarse salt
20 g/¾ oz brown sugar
2 sprigs of dill
1 x 500 g/1 lb 2 oz piece of skinless salmon fillet, pin-boned

The celeriac remoulade

¼ head of celeriac
1 egg yolk
1 tablespoon Meaux mustard or other wholegrain mustard
250 ml/9 fl oz groundnut (peanut) oil
splash of sherry vinegar
fine salt

Finishing off

sprig of dill
20 g/¾ oz salmon roe

Equipment

pestle and mortar

1 ~ The gravadlax

Toast the coriander, aniseed and peppercorns in a dry frying pan over a gentle heat for a few minutes, stirring constantly, until they smell fragrant. Remove from the heat and leave to cool, then crush using a pestle and mortar. Mix the crushed spices with the coarse salt, brown sugar and finely chopped dill, then put to one side. Line a shallow dish with a large sheet of cling film, then tip in half of the spice mixture. Place the salmon fillet on top, cover with the remaining spice mixture, then wrap the cling film around the fish and leave to marinate in the fridge for 10 hours. At the end of the marinating time, rinse the salmon under cold running water, then pat dry with a clean tea towel and set aside somewhere cool. (See step-by-step method on p. 308.)

2 ~ The celeriac remoulade

Peel and trim the celeriac as necessary. Using a sharp knife or a mandoline, cut the celeriac into fine julienne strips, then immerse in iced water for 10 minutes to make them nice and crunchy. Meanwhile, in a large bowl, vigorously whisk the egg yolk with the mustard and a pinch of salt. Still whisking, slowly add the oil to make a mayonnaise. Add a splash of sherry vinegar and season lightly with salt. Drain the celeriac in a colander, then add to the mayonnaise and mix well.

3 ~ Finishing off and plating up

Cut the salmon into slices 5 mm/¼ in thick. Lay a few overlapping slices on each plate, then place a spoonful of celeriac remoulade alongside and scatter over the chopped dill and salmon roe.

308 | How to make gravadlax

1

Organize all the ingredients on a work surface. The salmon needs to be incredibly fresh.

2

Put the spices, coarse salt, sugar and dill in a large bowl.

3

Mix together the spices and other ingredients until you have a coarse mixture a bit like damp sand.

4

Line a shallow dish or tray with a piece of cling film, leaving plenty of overhang. Pour in half of the spice-salt mixture, spreading it out evenly, then put the salmon on top.

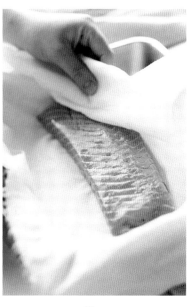

5

Coat the salmon with the rest of the spice-salt mixture. The fish should be completely covered with it.

6

Wrap the cling film tightly round the coated fish. Put into the fridge and leave to marinate.

7

Unwrap the salmon, then rinse it carefully under cold running water to remove all the salt and spices.

8

Using a clean, dry tea towel, pat the fish dry before slicing it.

For 4
Preparation time: 30 min
Infusing time: 10 min
Cooking time: 10 min
Chilling time: at least 2 h

Heritage tomatoes with buffalo mozzarella pannacotta

Tomato and mozzarella salad is an unmissable part of summer, and here I reinvent it completely: a creamy mozzarella pannacotta, served with a basil and tomato salad, and all portable enough to take on a picnic. I can't resist this combination, and every year I think of new variations.

The mozzarella pannacotta

200 ml/7 fl oz whole milk
150 ml/5 fl oz double (heavy) cream
½ bunch of basil
10 g/⅓ oz gelatine
170 g/6 oz buffalo mozzarella
splash of olive oil
pinch of salt

The heritage tomato salad

1 Green Zebra tomato
1 Black Russian tomato
1 Hawaiian Pineapple tomato
20 yellow and red cherry tomatoes
5 basil leaves
6 tablespoons olive oil
3 tablespoons white balsamic vinegar
pinch of salt

Equipment

4 small bowls or large shot glasses

1 - The mozzarella pannacotta

Put the milk, cream and basil in a saucepan and bring to the boil, then remove from the heat. Cover and leave to infuse for about 10 minutes. Meanwhile, soak the gelatine leaves in cold water to soften them. Chop the mozzarella and add it to the hot infusion, along with the drained and squeezed-out gelatine leaves. Remove the basil leaves (keeping them for later), then blend until smooth and strain through a fine sieve. Season the pannacottta with salt and stir in the olive oil, then pour into the bowls or glasses and chill in the fridge for at least 2 hours, or until set.

2 - The heritage tomato salad

Cut a cross in the base of the large tomatoes, then immerse in a saucepan of boiling water for a few seconds. Remove with a slotted spoon and immerse in a bowl of iced water. Peel, quarter and deseed the tomatoes, then cut into petals (see step-by-step method on p. 22) and place in a large bowl. Halve the cherry tomatoes, then add to the bowl. Finely chop the basil and add to the bowl, along with the olive oil and white balsamic vinegar. Season lightly with salt and toss gently.

3 - Serving

Arrange the tomato salad on top of the chilled pannacotta and serve.

For 4
Preparation time: 35 min
Cooking time: 20 min

}

Pumpkin soup with Blue Mountain coffee

Whipped cream with coffee slowly melts into this pumpkin soup, creating a voluptuous texture. The bitterness of the coffee offsets the sweetness of the pumpkin; orange zest would have a similar effect. This delicious soup is a great joy in the winter, and is very healthy since it is packed with vitamins, but it is also wonderful in the spring.

The pumpkin soup

500 g/1 lb 2 oz pumpkin
1 onion
splash of olive oil
20 g/¾ oz salted butter
200 ml/7 fl oz vegetable stock
   (see step-by-step method on p. 126)
150 ml/5 fl oz cream
pinch of fine salt

The whipped cream with coffee

1 tablespoon Blue Mountain
   coffee beans
150 ml/5 fl oz very cold double
   or whipping (heavy) cream
pinch of salt

Equipment

pestle and mortar
4 large glasses or small glass dishes

1 ~ The pumpkin soup

Trim, peel and deseed the pumpkin, then cut it into small pieces. Peel and finely slice the onion. Heat the oil and butter in a saucepan over a gentle heat, then add the pumpkin and onion and sweat for 5 minutes. Season with a pinch of salt, then add the vegetable stock and cream and bring to the boil. Leave to simmer for 15 minutes, then blend until smooth. Check and adjust the seasoning with a little salt, if needed. Keep the soup warm but don't allow it to boil.

2 ~ The whipped cream with coffee

Grind the coffee beans to a powder using a pestle and mortar, then sieve to remove any large pieces. Pour the cream into a bowl, then sit the bowl inside another, larger bowl filled with ice. Whip the cream, incorporating as much air as possible, until thick. Fold in the coffee powder and season with salt.

3 ~ Finishing off

Pour the hot pumpkin soup into the glasses, add a spoonful of the coffee whipped cream and serve immediately.

Tip | *Blue Mountain coffee is a rare 100% Arabica Jamaican coffee, that you can buy from specialist coffee suppliers. You can substitute another coffee, but it needs to be 100% Arabica, which is strong and bitter.*

THE PICNIC

What could be simpler and more lovely
than conjuring up easy finger food for a picnic?
And by packaging it up beautifully, the fun
is doubled. Part of the joy of a picnic is in the
pleasure of anticipation: thinking about ideas,
colours and flavours; what to nibble, what to
prepare in advance, what can be carried. Picnics
are real treats, a moment shared somewhere
beautiful, a pleasure to be had the world over.
In terms of recipes, terrines are a great idea, as are
jars and containers full of more intricate things.
And, for dessert, may I suggest shortbread biscuits
filled with jam…

For 4
Preparation time: 30 min
Cooking time: 20 min
Chilling time: 2 h

}

Salmon rillettes with tonka bean and green apple

What could be simpler for a picnic than rillettes on good bread? I add a little cream to lend richness to this perfectly balanced mixture of warm and sharp flavours. For the best texture and taste, you need to eat this when it is very fresh.

500 ml/18 fl oz vegetable stock
  (see step-by-step method on p. 126)
400 g/14 oz skinless salmon fillet,
  pin-boned
1 shallot
small knob of salted butter
splash of olive oil
splash of white wine
1 Granny Smith apple
juice of ½ lemon
100 ml/3½ fl oz crème fraîche
  (sour cream)
100 g/3½ oz whipped cream
1 tonka bean
slices of toast
fine salt

1 ~ Cooking the salmon

Bring the vegetable stock to the boil in a saucepan. Immerse the seasoned salmon in it and lower the heat so the stock just simmers. Cook the salmon for 15 minutes, without letting it boil, then remove and leave to cool completely before flaking the fish with a fork. Remove any remaining bones, then chill in the fridge.

2 ~ Preparing the flavourings

Peel and finely chop the shallot. Put the butter and oil in a saucepan over a gentle heat, then add the shallot and cook until soft and translucent, stirring every so often. Add the white wine and cook for 5 minutes, then remove from the heat and leave to cool. Meanwhile, wash, core and dice the apple, adding the lemon juice to stop it discolouring.

3 ~ Finishing off and serving

Mix the salmon with the shallot and white wine, the two creams and some grated tonka bean. Add the diced apple, check the seasoning and add some salt if necessary. Chill for at least 2 hours. (See step-by-step method on p. 318.) Serve well chilled with toast.

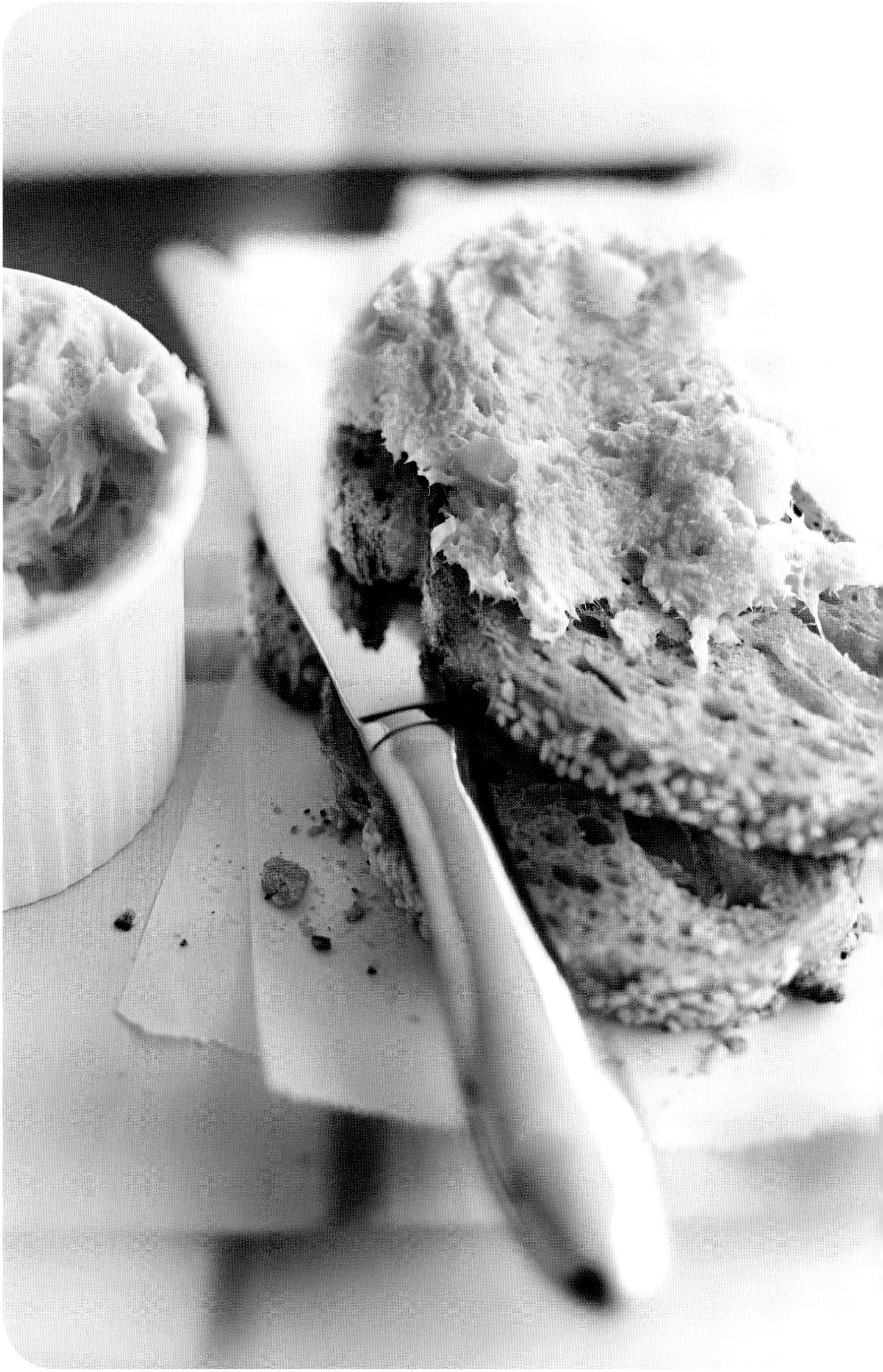

How to make salmon rillettes

1

Get all your ingredients ready. The salmon should be really fresh.

2

Immerse the salmon in the pan of simmering stock.

3

At the end of the cooking time, drain the salmon and leave it to cool, then flake it with a fork. Chill in the fridge.

4

Peel and finely chop the shallot, then cook it in a saucepan with a knob of butter and a splash of oil over a gentle heat.

5

Add the white wine, bring to the boil and then cook over a low heat until the shallot is meltingly soft. Take off the heat and leave to cool.

6

Wash, core and dice the apple. Squeeze over the lemon juice to prevent the apple from discolouring.

7

In a large bowl, mix the salmon with the diced apple, shallot and creams. Season with salt.

8

Make sure everything is thoroughly incorporated, then chill for 2 hours, or until ready to serve.

For 8
Preparation time: 45 min
Cooking time: 50 min

}

Monkfish terrine with prawns and saffron

Fish terrines are a delicious summer pleasure, easy to make and full of interesting flavours and textures. I use dried tomatoes, because the terrine doesn't need more moisture, and I often make this with other firm white fish, as well as different seafood. The secret to this recipe, which I got from a friend's mother, lies in cooking the seafood first, and separately. You can replace the saffron with pepper or turmeric, if you prefer.

The terrine

1 litre/1¾ pints vegetable stock
  (see step-by-step method on p. 126)
1.3 kg/3 lb skinless monkfish
  (angler fish) fillet
1 kg/2¼ lb large raw prawns (shrimp)
olive oil
50 ml/1¾ fl oz Noilly Prat
150 g/5½ oz sun-dried tomatoes
10 medium eggs
pinch of ground saffron
fine salt

The tomato mayonnaise

1 egg yolk
1 tablespoon mustard
pinch of fine salt
250 ml/9 fl oz groundnut (peanut) oil
splash of sherry vinegar
1 tablespoon tomato purée (paste)

Equipment

24 cm/9½ in terrine mould or loaf tin

1 - The monkfish

Bring the vegetable stock to the boil in a sauté pan, then immerse the monkfish. Return the stock to a simmer and cook the fish for 10 minutes; don't let the stock boil. Carefully remove the fish, then put in a dish and leave to cool. Once it is cold, cut the fish into pieces and set aside.

2 - The prawns and tomatoes

Shell the prawns. Heat some olive oil in a frying pan and sauté the prawns for 2–3 minutes, then add the Noilly Prat. Remove from the heat and leave to cool. Dice the sun-dried tomatoes and put them to one side too.

3 - The terrine

Preheat the oven to 200°C (400°F; gas mark 6). Beat the eggs in a bowl, then add a little salt, a pinch of saffron and the monkfish pieces. Remove some monkfish pieces from the egg and arrange in a layer in the base of the terrine mould. Add some diced tomato, then a layer of the cooked prawns, followed by some more tomato dice. Repeat these layers (monkfish, tomato, prawns, tomato) until everything is used up. Finally, pour in the egg, drizzling it over evenly, then cook in the oven in a bain-marie for 50 minutes. Remove the terrine from the oven and from the bain-marie, then leave to cool.

4 - The tomato mayonnaise

Mix the egg yolk with the mustard and a pinch of salt, then slowly add the oil, whisking all the time, to make a mayonnaise. Stir in a splash of sherry vinegar and the tomato purée.

5 - Serving

Turn out the cooled terrine and slice carefully using a very sharp, thin knife. Serve with the mayonnaise on the side.

For 4
Preparation time: 1 h
Salting time: 2 h
Cooking time: 35 min

Rabbit rillettes with chorizo and mint

Perfect for summer, these delicious rabbit rillettes are cooked in the pressure cooker for tenderness, and then the chorizo and mint are stirred through at the end, to add spice and freshness. Try them with some cherry tomatoes for extra sweetness. These rillettes are also great as a filling for ravioli, and can be sterilized in jars if you want to keep them for longer than three days in the fridge.

The flavoured salt

1 teaspoon Voatsiperifery pepper
1 teaspoon pink peppercorns
100 g/3½ oz coarse grey salt
1 garlic clove
sprig of thyme
1 bay leaf

The rabbit rillettes

2 rabbit legs
1 onion
large knob of butter
splash of olive oil
500 ml/18 fl oz vegetable stock
  (see step-by-step method on p. 126)
50 g/1¾ oz cooked foie gras
50 g/1¾ oz chorizo
sprig of mint
fine salt, freshly ground pepper

Equipment

pestle and mortar

1 ~ The flavoured salt

Using a pestle and mortar, crush the Voatsiperifery pepper and pink peppercorns, then mix with the coarse salt, the peeled and crushed garlic, the thyme leaves and the chopped bay leaf. Put to one side.

2 ~ Preparing the rabbit rillettes

Put the rabbit legs in a non-metallic dish and cover with the flavoured salt, then leave to marinate somewhere cool for 2 hours. Remove the legs from the salt, rinse under cold running water and dry with a clean tea towel. Peel and finely chop the onion.

3 ~ Cooking the rabbit rillettes

Heat the butter and oil in a pressure cooker over a medium heat. Add the chopped onion and cook, stirring, for 2–3 minutes, without letting it colour. Add the rabbit legs, turn up the heat, and brown them all over. Pour in the vegetable stock, then close the pressure cooker and follow the manufacturer's instructions for bringing it up to pressure. Once pressurized, cook for 30 minutes. When the time is up, remove from the heat and let the pressure drop before opening.

4 ~ Finishing off

Remove the meat from the pressure cooker, then strain the cooking juices through a sieve. Use a fork to shred the meat, removing all the bones and adding a little of the strained cooking juices to moisten. Stir in the diced foie gras, thinly sliced chorizo and finely chopped mint. Season with salt and pepper and chill. Serve chilled with wholemeal toast.

For 4
Preparation time: 30 min
Cooking time: 30 min
(piperade and spring onions) +
3 min (poached eggs)

}

Poached egg and piperade with cloves

Made in a jar so it's easy to carry, this piperade is full of colour, spiced with cloves and finished with a lovely runny poached egg. Don't forget to peel the peppers to make them more digestible, either with a peeler or by roasting them in the oven, depending on how much time you have. This is a perfect dish for a real-life 'déjeuner sur l'herbe'.

The poached eggs

4 really fresh eggs
splash of distilled white vinegar

The piperade

1 red (bell) pepper
1 green (bell) pepper
1 yellow (bell) pepper
3 cloves
100 ml/3½ fl oz olive oil
fine salt

The softened spring onions

2 bunches of spring onions (scallions)
splash of olive oil
knob of butter
1 clove
200 ml/7 fl oz vegetable stock
  (see step-by-step method on p. 126)
fine salt

Finishing off

fleur de sel

Equipment

4 ramekins

1 ~ The poached eggs

Break the eggs carefully into 4 ramekins. Put 1 litre/1¾ pints of water in a saucepan with the white vinegar and bring to the boil. Lower the heat until the water is just simmering, then stir it rapidly with a spoon to create a whirlpool effect. Lower the eggs very gently into the water and leave to cook for 2 minutes. Lift them out with a slotted spoon and immediately immerse in iced water to stop them cooking any more. Leave the eggs in the water for 2 minutes, then remove with a slotted spoon, drain on some kitchen paper and put to one side. (See step-by-step method on p. 64.)

2 ~ The piperade

Preheat the oven to 180°C (350°F; gas mark 4). Remove the stalks from the peppers and empty out the seeds (a spoon will help), then place them on a piece of foil big enough to wrap them completely. Season the peppers with salt, add the cloves and pour over a little olive oil, then close up the foil to make a parcel and bake for 20 minutes. Remove from the oven and leave to cool. Peel off the pepper skins, then cut the flesh into neat slices and mix in a large bowl. Check the seasoning and add a little salt if necessary, then set aside somewhere cool.

3 ~ The softened spring onions

Trim and finely slice the spring onions. Warm the olive oil and butter in a saucepan over a low heat, then add the onions, a little salt and the clove. When the onions are coloured all over, add the vegetable stock and cover the onions with a circle of baking parchment with a 2 cm/¾ in hole in the centre, making sure it touches the onions. Cook over a gentle heat for 10 minutes, then remove from the heat and take out the clove.

4 ~ Finishing off and serving

Divide the softened spring onions between 4 ramekins, then top with the piperade. Place a poached egg in the centre of each one, scatter with fleur de sel and serve warm or cold.

For 4
Preparation time: 25 min
Marinating time: 24 h
Chilling time: 2 h
Cooking time: 15 min

}

Raspberry shortbread biscuits

I used to eat these for breakfast when I was a child in Valence, and now they are a great excuse for me to share my way of making jam with you. Remember to check the set of your jam by dropping a little onto a cold plate – it should wrinkle when you push your finger through it. You can also flavour the shortbread with other spices, or with chocolate.

The raspberry jam

300 g/10½ oz raspberries

200 g/7 oz caster (superfine) sugar

The sweet shortbread

60 g/2¼ oz butter

150 g/5½ oz plain (all-purpose) flour

50 g/1¾ oz icing (confectioners') sugar

1 tablespoon vanilla sugar

2 egg yolks

Finishing off

icing (confectioners') sugar

Equipment

2 round pastry cutters,
   7 cm/2¾ in and 2.5 cm/1 in across

1 ~ The raspberry jam

Mix the raspberries and sugar together in a non-metallic bowl, then leave to marinate for 24 hours in the fridge. The next day, tip the mixture into a saucepan and cook over a fairly high heat to preserve the colour of the fruit. Boil for 4–5 minutes, stirring often to prevent the jam from sticking, then take off the heat and leave to set somewhere cool.

2 ~ The sweet shortbread dough

Dice the butter and place in a large bowl with the flour, icing sugar and vanilla sugar. Mix by hand until you have a crumbly dough, then add the egg yolks and mix to a smooth dough. Wrap in cling film and chill for 2 hours.

3 ~ The shortbread biscuits

Preheat the oven to 150°C (300°F; gas mark 2). Roll out the dough to a thickness of 2 mm/¹⁄₁₆ in, then use the larger pastry cutter to cut out circles. Put half of them onto a baking sheet lined with baking parchment. Using the smaller pastry cutter, cut holes in the middle of the other circles to make rings, and lay these on the lined baking sheet too. Bake for about 15 minutes, or until golden. Remove from the oven and leave to cool.

4 ~ Finishing off

Spread a thin layer of raspberry jam over each whole shortbread, then cover with a shortbread ring and press gently together. Dust with icing sugar and serve.

For 10
Preparation time: 15 min
Cooking time: 7 min
}

Chocolate financiers

Financiers are so difficult to resist but, when they are even softer than usual, like these ones, it's impossible! The secret is the mixture of flours and ground nuts which gives them their gorgeous texture. I love the combination of almonds and chocolate, but you could also replace the cocoa with tonka bean, vanilla or any other warm, comforting flavour that would suit teatime. Easy, quick and delicious!

125 g/4½ oz butter
150 g/5½ oz icing (confectioners') sugar
15 g/½ oz cocoa powder
15 g/½ oz cornflour (cornstarch)
40 g/1½ oz plain (all-purpose) flour
50 g/1¾ oz ground almonds
30 g/1 oz honey
125 g/4½ oz egg white
(from about 4–5 eggs)

Equipment

financier tins, or silicone or paper cake cases

1 ~ The brown butter

Put the butter in a saucepan over a gentle heat and cook until it is a light brown, hazelnut colour. Take off the heat, empty into a bowl and leave to one side. Preheat the oven to 180°C (350°F; gas mark 4).

2 ~ The financier mixture

Mix together the icing sugar, cocoa, cornflour, flour and ground almonds, then stir in the warm brown butter. Finally, mix in the honey and egg whites.

3 ~ Baking

Pour the mixture into the financier tins or cake cases and bake for 7 minutes. Remove from the oven, leave to cool for a minute or two, then remove from the tins/cases and eat while still warm.

THE AFTERNOON PICK-ME-UP

Like a French take on afternoon tea,
these treats offer the energy boost we all want
and need at 4pm, whether small or grown-up!
Perhaps a reward after school, or a snatched moment
of relaxation between two meetings, this simple
ritual is one that gives great pleasure. My focus
is on fruit, yogurt and pannacotta: you can make
fruits in syrup in the summer, yogurt at weekends,
and prepare your own spreads every month.
Try out different flavours and ideas, and make
this precious pause in the day count.

Makes 1 pogne (for 6)
Preparation time: 30 min
Resting time: 12 h + 2 h + 2 h
Cooking time: 25 min

Pogne de Romans

Another childhood favourite that's very dear to me, this brioche flavoured with orange flower water hails from the Drôme region of France. In the town of Romans-sur-Isère, where it originated, every family has their own version, but the recipe is always a closely guarded secret! Poolish is a pre-ferment or starter that uses yeast as a raising agent and is easy to make, if a bit time-consuming. This delicious brioche is best eaten very fresh.

The poolish

120 g/4¼ oz plain (all-purpose) flour
120 ml/3¾ fl oz cold water
4 g/⅛ oz fresh yeast

The pogne dough

8 g/¼ oz fresh yeast
400 g/14 oz plain (all-purpose) flour
80 g/3 oz caster (superfine) sugar
10 g/⅓ oz fine salt
2 eggs, beaten
35 ml/1½ fl oz milk
100 g/3½ oz cold butter
zest of ½ lemon
30 ml/1 fl oz orange flower water

Finishing off

1 beaten egg for glazing
granulated sugar (optional)

Equipment

electric mixer

1 ~ The poolish

The day before baking, whisk together all the poolish ingredients. Cover with cling film and leave to ferment in the fridge for 12 hours.

2 ~ The pogne dough

The next day, put the poolish into the bowl of an electric mixer fitted with the dough hook. Add, in the following order and without mixing in between, the crumbled yeast, flour, sugar and salt. Knead for 3 minutes, then gradually add the beaten eggs, followed by the milk. Keep kneading until the mixture comes away from the sides of the bowl. Add the diced butter and knead until the dough comes away from the sides of the bowl again. Finally, mix in the chopped lemon zest and the orange flower water. Cover the bowl with cling film and leave the dough to rest at room temperature for 2 hours.

3 ~ Shaping

Tip out the dough onto a lightly floured work surface and briefly knead again, this time by hand. Reshape the dough into a ball. Make a hole in the middle with your index finger, then stretch the dough evenly to make a ring. Place on a lined baking sheet again and leave to rest and rise for 2 hours. (See step-by-step method on p. 334.)

4 ~ Baking and finishing off

Preheat the oven to 180°C (350°F; gas mark 4). Brush the pogne with a little beaten egg, then slash the top with a knife and, if you like, sprinkle with granulated sugar. Bake for about 25 minutes, or until risen and golden brown. Remove from the oven, then leave to cool for a minute before serving in generous slices.

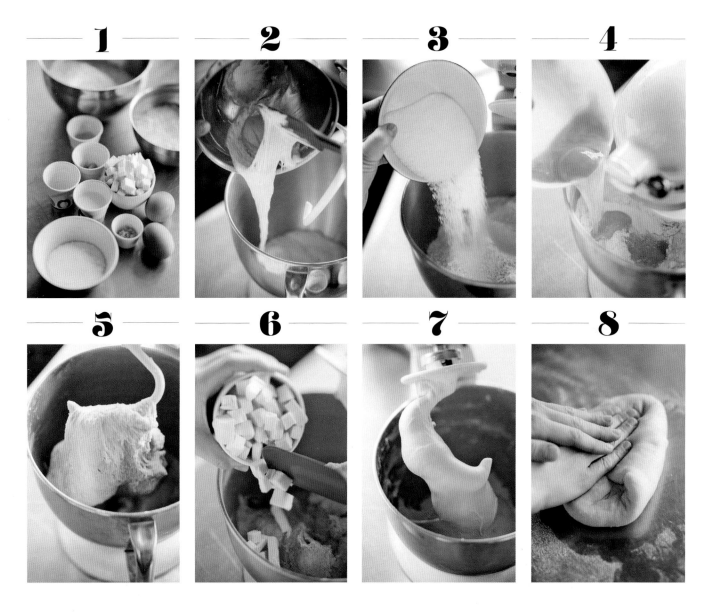

1 ~ Before starting, weigh out all the ingredients and put them into separate bowls. The butter should be very cold and diced.

2 ~ Put the poolish you made the night before (see recipe on p. 332) into the bowl of an electric mixer fitted with the dough hook.

3 ~ In order, add the yeast, flour, sugar and salt, then mix slowly with the dough hook.

4 ~ Gradually add the beaten eggs, then the milk.

5 ~ Knead the dough until it comes away from the sides of the bowl.

6 ~ Add the butter, lemon zest and orange flower water.

7 ~ Beat the dough again until it is smooth and everything is incorporated. Cover the bowl with cling film and leave the dough to rest at room temperature for 2 hours.

8 ~ Tip out the dough onto a floured work surface and knead it with your hands.

9 ~ Shape the dough into a neat ball.

10 ~ With your index finger, make a hole right through the middle of the dough.

11 ~ Use your finger to stretch the dough and shape it into a neat ring. Place on a lined baking tray and leave to rise for 2 hours.

12 ~ Brush the pogne with beaten egg to glaze.

13 ~ With a blade or knife, slash the surface of the pogne.

14 ~ Finally, sprinkle with a little granulated sugar, then bake in an oven preheated to 180°C (350°F; gas mark 4) for about 25 minutes.

For 4
Preparation time: 15 min
Cooking time: 12 min (pears)
+ 6–8 min (peaches)

}

Nathan's favourite fruits in syrup

This is a recipe to make in the summer, when soft fruits are in season, and then to enjoy in the winter. The fruit is preserved in sugar, but don't worry, the syrup is a light one. You need to choose really beautiful firm fruit that will hold up during the cooking process and look magnificent in a glass jar. Children love these!

The poached pears

2 vanilla pods (beans)
1 tonka bean
300 g/10½ oz caster (superfine) sugar
4 pears

The poached peaches

4 white peaches
300 g/10½ oz caster (superfine) sugar
5 green cardamom pods

Equipment

2 x 1 litre/1¾ pint 'Le Parfait'
  or other sealable jars

1 - The poached pears

Split the vanilla pods lengthways and scrape out the seeds from the inside. Put the seeds and the pods into a saucepan, along with the grated tonka bean, the sugar and 1.5 litres/2½ pints of water, then bring to the boil. Meanwhile, peel and core the pears and put them in a glass jar. Pour the hot syrup over the fruit, then seal the jar. Pour some water into the base of a pressure cooker, then put the jar in the basket. Bring the cooker up to pressure and cook for 12 minutes. At the end of this time, allow the pressure to drop, then open the cooker and put the jar to one side.

2 - The poached peaches

Bring a large saucepan of water to the boil, then immerse the peaches for about 10 seconds. Lift out with a slotted spoon and immediately immerse in iced water, then lift out again. Peel the peaches, then remove the stones. Cut the peaches into quarters, then put into a second glass jar. Pour 1.5 litres/2½ pints of water into another saucepan and add the sugar and crushed cardamom pods. Bring to the boil, then immediately pour over the peaches. Cook the peaches in the same way as the pears, but only for 6–8 minutes. At the end of this time, allow the pressure to drop, then open the cooker and put the jar to one side.

Tip | *When the jars have cooled down, check that the vacuum seal is working properly. To do this you just need to remove the metal closures; the rubber seal should still hold the lid in place.*

Variation | *Try using apricots in this recipe or flavouring the syrup with something other than tonka bean: cinnamon or aniseed work well.*

Makes 8
Preparation time: 40 min
Infusing time: overnight (for the
violet, aniseed and jasmine)
Fermenting time: 8 h
Chilling time: 3 h

}

Homemade yogurts: violet, orange flower, jasmine and aniseed

Making your own yogurt is very easy if you have a yogurt maker. You can use any milk, but raw is best. Two things will really help you succeed: heat the milk to between 42 and 45°C (108 and 113°F) to activate the culture, and add the flavourings when the milk is cold for the best flavour.

The violet milk

1 litre/1¾ pints whole milk
40 g/1½ oz clean violet flowers or
    a few drops of violet extract

The orange flower water milk

1 litre/1¾ pints whole milk
2 tablespoons orange flower water

The aniseed milk

1 litre/1¾ pints whole milk
20 g/¾ oz aniseed

The jasmine milk

1 litre/1¾ pints whole milk
30 g/1 oz clean jasmine flowers or
    a few drops of jasmine extract

The yogurt

1 litre/1¾ pints infused milk
150 g/5½ oz (1 small pot) full-fat
natural yogurt or 1 packet of
    yogurt cultures
30 g/1 oz milk powder

Equipment

pestle and mortar
cooking thermometer
8 clean, empty yogurt pots
yogurt maker

1- The violet infusion

Before making the yogurts, make the infused milk with your chosen flavouring. For the violet version, mix the violet flowers with the milk and leave it to infuse overnight in the fridge. Strain before using. If you are using violet extract, just add it to the hot milk and proceed with step 5 below.

2- The orange flower water infusion

Mix the milk and orange flower water together. There is no need to leave this milk to infuse overnight; you can use it to make yogurt immediately.

3- The aniseed infusion

Crush the aniseed in a pestle and mortar, then mix it with the milk. Leave it to infuse overnight in the fridge. Strain through a fine sieve before using.

4- The jasmine infusion

Wash the jasmine flowers and mix with the milk, then leave to infuse overnight in the fridge. Strain through a fine sieve before using. If you are using jasmine extract, just add it to the hot milk and proceed with step 5 below.

5- Making the yogurt

Put the infused milk into a saucepan and bring to the boil, then immediately take off the heat. Leave to cool to 44°C/111°F; you can speed this up by sitting the pan over a bowl of ice. Mix the yogurt or yogurt cultures with the milk powder, then whisk in the hot milk. Pour this mixture into the 8 yogurt pots, then leave to ferment in the yogurt maker for 8 hours. Once made, chill in the fridge for 3 hours before eating. (See step-by-step method on p. 340.)

How to make yogurt

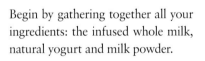

1

Begin by gathering together all your ingredients: the infused whole milk, natural yogurt and milk powder.

2

In a large bowl, whisk together the yogurt and the milk powder.

3

Meanwhile, bring the milk to the boil, then take off the heat immediately.

4

Cool the milk to 44°C/111°F by sitting the saucepan over a bowl of ice.

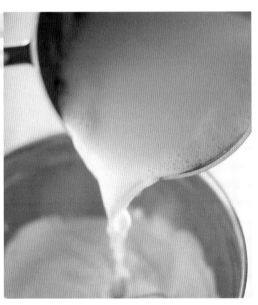

Pour the warm milk onto the milk powder and natural yogurt and whisk together.

6

Strain the mixture through a fine sieve if there are any lumps, then fill the yogurt pots almost to the brim.

Put the yogurt pots into the yogurt maker and leave to ferment for 8 hours, or as per the manufacturer's instructions. Store the yogurts, sealed with their lids, in the fridge.

For 4
Preparation time: 45 min
Cooking time: 40 min
Chilling time: 2 h
(pannacotta) + 1 h (crumble)

}

Almond pannacotta with raspberry confit and crumble

This is the sort of pudding you dream of. The play of texture, colour and flavour is something else: it is creamy yet fresh, the sharpness of the fruit cuts through the cream, and it works with lots of different fruits. The pannacotta can be varied as much as you like; I serve it in little glasses for breakfast in my Valence hotel. It is a perfect treat for when you're feeling a bit down, but is also good for celebrations!

The raspberry confit

250 g/8½ oz raspberries
20 g/¾ oz caster (superfine) sugar
½ vanilla pod (bean)

The almond pannacotta

6 g/0.2 oz gelatine leaves
50 g/1¾ oz marzipan
600 ml/20 fl oz double (heavy) cream
50 g/1¾ oz caster (superfine) sugar

The crumble

110 g/3¾ oz salted butter
50 g/1¾ oz brown sugar
150 g/5½ oz plain (all-purpose) flour
2 g/0.07 oz baking powder
25 g/1 oz cornflour (cornstarch)

Equipment

4 small glasses

1~ The raspberry confit

Put 200 g/7 oz of the raspberries in a saucepan with the sugar and the half vanilla pod and cook over a gentle heat for 20–30 minutes until lightly caramelized. Remove the vanilla, then blend in the saucepan with a stick blender and leave to cool completely. Cut the remaining raspberries in half, stir into the confit and leave to one side.

2~ The almond pannacotta

Soak the gelatine in iced water to soften it. Blend the marzipan with 500 ml/18 fl oz of the cream and the sugar. Strain through a fine sieve and then, in a small saucepan, bring a quarter of it to a simmer. Remove from the heat and stir in the drained and squeezed-out gelatine, followed by the rest of the marzipan mixture. Mix together well, then leave to cool. Meanwhile, whip the remaining cream, then fold this into the marzipan mixture. Pour into 4 small glasses and leave to set for at least 2 hours in the fridge.

3~ The crumble

Put all the crumble ingredients into the bowl of an electric mixer and mix until a dough forms. Put the dough into the fridge for 1 hour to firm. Meanwhile, preheat the oven to 180°C (350°F; gas mark 4). Using a grater, grate coarse pieces of the dough onto a baking sheet, then bake for 8–10 minutes. Remove from the oven and leave to cool before roughly chopping the crumble.

4~ Serving

When ready to serve, spoon some raspberry confit on top of each pannacotta, scatter over the crumble and then eat immediately.

Variation | *Try making this recipe with apricots or, later in the summer, with really ripe figs.*

ONE-COURSE DINNERS

Don't have the strength to make a three-course meal? Then just make one course, either with ingredients bought on the day or using food you have made in advance, preserved and stored. Protein, carbohydrates and vegetables are all there in the one dish, allowing you to cope with whatever life throws at you. In our busy lives, this is a great way of cooking and leaves you plenty of time to spend at the table, not in the kitchen. The method is simple, though you will need a pressure cooker and jars, and it allows you to keep ready-made dishes for between 8 and 15 days, which means you can always be ready for dinner with friends or family.

For 4
Preparation time: 35 min
Resting time: overnight
Cooking time: 40 min

Chard, sheep's cheese and ricotta ravioli

This has been a classic in the restaurant for a long time. It uses all of the chard, both the white and green parts, which is quite rare, and marries it with the creamy freshness of soft sheep's cheese and ricotta. The ravioli, here cooked first in a frying pan and then in vegetable stock, can be made in advance and frozen. This is also great served with grilled fish, such as red mullet.

The ravioli dough

500 g/1 lb 2 oz plain (all-purpose) or 'oo' flour
10 g/⅓ oz fine salt
16 egg yolks
splash of olive oil
1 teaspoon distilled white vinegar

The filling

5 shallots
olive oil
6 bunches of young chard
100 ml/3½ fl oz vegetable stock
   (see step-by-step method on p. 126)
¼ bunch of chives
¼ bunch of chervil
zest of 1 lemon
80 g/3 oz ricotta
80 g/3 oz fresh soft sheep's cheese
fine salt, freshly ground pepper

Cooking the ravioli

50 g/1¾ oz butter
200 ml/7 fl oz vegetable stock
   (see step-by-step method on p. 126)
fine salt

Equipment

food processor
pasta machine
3 cm/1¼ in round pastry cutter

1~ The ravioli dough

Switch on the food processor and then, in the following order, add the flour, salt, egg yolks one by one, olive oil and vinegar. Mix until it forms a dough, then shape into a ball, wrap in cling film and leave to rest in the fridge overnight.

2~ The filling

Peel and chop the shallots. Put them into a small saucepan with a splash of olive oil and cook over a gentle heat for 10 minutes, stirring often, then remove from the heat and set aside. Trim the chard, then dice the white parts. Put them in another saucepan with a little olive oil and cook over a gentle heat for about 2 minutes. Add the vegetable stock and cook for 5 minutes, then remove from the heat. Cut the green parts of the chard into thin strips, then immerse for a few seconds in boiling salted water. Drain and refresh under cold running water, then drain again. Finely chop the herbs. Chop the lemon zest. Mix together all these ingredients, along with the cheeses, then season with salt and pepper and put to one side.

3~ Making the ravioli

Roll out the pasta dough until it is 5 mm/¼ in thick, then use a pastry cutter to cut out 3 cm/1¼ in circles. Put a spoonful of the filling on top of half of the circles, then cover these with the remaining circles and press the edges together to seal, pressing out as much air as possible.

4~ Cooking the ravioli

Melt the butter in a frying pan over a medium heat, add the ravioli and cook for about 2 minutes, or until coloured on both sides. Pour in the vegetable stock, bring to the boil and cook for another 2–3 minutes, or until the sauce has reduced and is thick enough to coat the ravioli. (For extra richness and gloss, add a little more cold diced butter to the sauce.) Season lightly with salt, if necessary, and serve immediately. (See step-by-step method on p. 348.)

How to cook ravioli

1

You can use fresh or frozen ravioli for this. If using frozen, add 1–2 minutes to the cooking time.

2

Melt the butter in a non-stick frying pan. Add the uncooked ravioli.

3

Cook the ravioli in the foaming butter, turning them carefully.

4

Add the vegetable stock to the pan and bring to the boil.

5

Leave the ravioli to cook for 2–3 minutes, so that the liquid in the pan evaporates, concentrating the flavours.

6

When the cooking juices are reduced and concentrated, add the cold diced butter to the frying pan.

7

Gently stir the butter into the cooking juices, creating a rich, glossy sauce to coat the ravioli. Serve immediately.

For 4
Preparation time: 35 min
Marinating time: 2 h
Infusing time: 20 min
Cooking time: 40 min

Duck confit with lavender and spices

Part of a dish served at my bistrot in Valence, this recipe adds a floral note to duck, thanks to the lavender, without being too sweet. This is a lighter way to make confit, using vegetable stock rather than the traditional duck fat, and marinating the meat in salt to make it even juicier. You can eat the duck confit immediately or keep it in its jar in the fridge for up to 15 days.

The duck

1 teaspoon Voatsiperifery pepper
1 teaspoon Szechuan pepper
1 teaspoon coriander seeds
1 teaspoon pink peppercorns
1 tablespoon lavender flowers
200 g/7 oz coarse grey salt
4 duck legs, knuckle bones removed
  (ask the butcher to do this for you)
splash of groundnut (peanut) oil
40 g/1½ oz salted butter
8 sprigs of thyme
4 bay leaves

The lavender stock

400 ml/14 fl oz vegetable stock
  (see step-by-step method p. 126)
1 tablespoon lavender flowers

Equipment

pestle and mortar
4 vacuum-sealable glass jars,
  each big enough to hold a duck leg

1- Seasoning the duck

Crush the spices and lavender in the pestle and mortar, then mix with the coarse salt. Put half the salt and spices on a baking tray, then flatten the duck legs on top. Cover the meat with the rest of the spiced salt and leave to marinate in the fridge for 2 hours. Rinse off all the salt under running water, then dry the duck legs with kitchen paper.

2- The lavender stock

Heat the vegetable stock in a saucepan, add the lavender flowers and leave to infuse for 20 minutes. Strain through a fine sieve then put to one side.

3- Browning the duck

Put the groundnut oil and butter in a frying pan over a high heat, then add the duck legs and brown them all over. Leave to cool on a tray or large plate.

4- Cooking the confit

Put a duck leg in each jar, along with a couple of thyme sprigs and a bay leaf, then divide the lavender stock between the 4 jars to cover the meat. Close the jars and put them in the basket of a pressure cooker, then pour some water into the cooker and bring to the boil. Follow the manufacturer's instructions for bringing it up to pressure, then cook for 40 minutes. Let the pressure drop before removing the jars and leaving the confit to cool.

5- Serving

Reheat the jars of confit for a few minutes in a bain-marie, then open them carefully. Use a spoon to remove the fat from the surface, then serve either in the jars or on plates, with the cooking juices poured over the top.

Tip | When the jars of duck confit have cooled down, check that they are properly vacuum sealed before storing in the fridge: undo the metal clip and the rubber seal should still hold the lid in place.

For 4
Preparation time: 30 min
Cooking time: 2h 20 min

Black rice risotto with bouillabaisse jus

Black Venere rice, or riso nero venere, is grown in Italy's Po valley, and its deep colour looks beautiful on the plate. As it can be pre-cooked and finished off at the last minute, it's hard to go wrong with it for risotto. This is my classic recipe that you can adapt by using different flavours and ingredients.

The bouillabaisse jus

1 kg/2¼ lb small whole fish, such as rouget, rascasse, mullet, bream
250 g/8½ oz velvet crabs
50 ml/1¾ fl oz olive oil
50 ml/1¾ fl oz white wine
25 ml/1 fl oz pastis
pinch of ground saffron
pinch of ground star anise
pinch of ground bird's eye chilli
pinch of ground aniseed
1 small carrot
½ bulb fennel
1 small onion
1 stalk celery
2 garlic cloves
150 g/5½ oz butter
1 bouquet garni
1 tablespoon tomato purée (paste)

The risotto

1 onion
2 knobs of butter
500 ml/18 fl oz vegetable stock (see step-by-step method on p. 126)
300 g/10½ oz black Venere rice
50 ml/1¾ fl oz white wine
50 g/1¾ oz Parmesan
fine salt

1 ~ The bouillabaisse jus

Chop up the fish and crabs. Heat the olive oil in a large flameproof casserole, add the fish and crab and cook over a gentle heat for 5 minutes, then add the white wine, pastis and all the spices. Peel and trim the carrot, fennel, onion and celery as needed, then dice them. Peel the garlic. Put 50 g/1¾ oz of the butter into a sauté pan over a gentle heat. Add the diced vegetables, garlic and bouquet garni and cook until the vegetables have softened, then tip into the casserole. Pour in enough water to just cover, then stir in the tomato purée and leave to simmer for 2 hours. At the end of the cooking time, blend until smooth, then strain through a fine sieve.

2 ~ The risotto

Peel and finely chop the onion. Put a knob of butter in a saucepan, add the chopped onion and cook until translucent (don't let it colour). Meanwhile, gently heat the stock in another saucepan. When the onion is soft, stir in the rice, then pour in the white wine. Bring to the boil and allow to reduce, then stir in enough hot stock to cover the rice. Place a circle of baking parchment with a hole in the middle over the risotto and leave to cook gently until all the liquid has been absorbed, then add a little more stock. Continue to add small amounts of stock to the risotto, stirring it in, then replacing the paper and leaving the stock to be absorbed, until only a few spoonfuls of stock remain. Season the risotto lightly with fine salt. Stir in the grated Parmesan, the last of the vegetable stock and a large knob of butter. Check and adjust the seasoning as necessary, then take off the heat and leave to rest for a few minutes. (See step-by-step method on p. 354.)

3 ~ Finishing off and plating up

Reheat the bouillabaisse jus, then add the remaining butter, blending it in the pan using a stick blender. Serve the risotto with the hot, foamy jus poured over the top.

Tip | When they are in season, serve this risotto with baby squid, sautéed in a frying pan with a little olive oil, salt and pepper.

How to make risotto

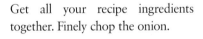

1

Get all your recipe ingredients together. Finely chop the onion.

2

Cook the chopped onion in a pan with a knob of butter for several minutes, stirring often.

3

Add the rice and continue to cook over a gentle heat, stirring all the time, so that every grain of rice is coated in hot butter and looks shiny.

4

Add the white wine and bring to the boil, then let the liquid evaporate completely.

5

Add enough vegetable stock to just cover the rice, then cover the pan with a piece of baking parchment with a hole in the middle. Leave to cook over a gentle heat, adding the stock little by little and letting it be absorbed before adding more.

6

Take the risotto off the heat and remove the baking parchment. Add the Parmesan and a little butter. Mix in very gently, to avoid damaging the grains of rice.

7

Finish by stirring enough butter into the risotto to give it a meltingly soft texture.

8

The risotto should be very soft; for the best results, 'feed' it with plenty of butter.

For 4
Preparation time: 1 h
Chilling time: overnight
Cooking time: 1 h

}

Lamb confit and mint tortellini with crushed lemon courgettes

Making this filled pasta is very simple, but you need to do it carefully. The secret to its success lies in getting the texture of the meat filling just right, and balancing its richness with fresh herbs and lemon.

The pasta dough

500 g/1 lb 2 oz plain (all purpose) or '00' flour
2 whole eggs + 4 egg yolks
fine salt

The lamb confit

1 onion
knob of butter
splash of olive oil
½ boned shoulder of lamb (about 600 g/1 lb 5 oz)
500 ml/18 fl oz vegetable stock (see step-by-step method on p. 126)
sprig of thyme
sprig of bay leaves
1 garlic clove
sprig of mint
fine salt, freshly ground pepper

The crushed lemon courgettes

2 large courgettes (zucchini)
splash of olive oil
100 ml/3½ fl oz vegetable stock (see step-by-step method on p. 126)
zest of 1 unwaxed lemon
pinch of fine salt

Cooking the tortellini

50 ml/1¾ fl oz hot vegetable stock (see step-by-step method on p. 126)
50 g/1¾ oz butter
a few mint leaves

Equipment

food processor
8 cm/3¼ in round pastry cutter

1⁓ The pasta dough

Follow the recipe for ravioli dough on p. 346 (step 1).

2⁓ The lamb confit

Peel and finely chop the onion. Heat the butter and olive oil in a pressure cooker over a medium heat. Add the chopped onion and cook for 2–3 minutes without letting it colour, stirring all the time. Season the shoulder of lamb with salt and pepper. Increase the heat to high, add the lamb to the onion and brown it all over. Add the vegetable stock, thyme, bay and peeled garlic clove. Follow the manufacturer's instructions for bringing the cooker up to pressure, then cook for 40 minutes. At the end of the cooking time, remove from the heat and let the pressure drop slowly. Remove the meat from the cooker, then strain the cooking juices through a fine sieve. Shred the meat with a fork and place in a large bowl. Add a little of the cooking juices and the finely chopped mint and mix well. Season with salt and pepper if necessary, then set aside somewhere cool.

3⁓ The crushed lemon courgettes

Cut the courgettes in half lengthways, and then into quarters. Finely slice the quarters, then put in a saucepan with the olive oil and cook gently for about 3 minutes. Season with salt, add the vegetable stock and bring to the boil. When the stock has evaporated and the courgettes are soft, take the pan off the heat. Crush the courgettes with a fork, then add the grated lemon zest and a pinch of salt.

4⁓ Making the tortellini

Roll out the pasta dough very thinly and use a pastry-cutter to cut out 8 cm/3¼ in circles. Shape the tortellini following the step-by-step method on p. 358.

5⁓ Cooking the tortellini

Bring a pan of salted water to the boil, then cook the tortellini for 2–3 minutes. Carefully remove the tortellini from the pan with a slotted spoon. Put them in a large bowl with the stock and the butter and toss together gently.

6⁓ Plating up

Put a pastry cutter on each plate, fill with the crushed lemon courgettes to a depth of about 1–2 cm/½–¾ in, then remove the pastry cutter. Place the hot cooked tortellini on top and decorate with a few mint leaves.

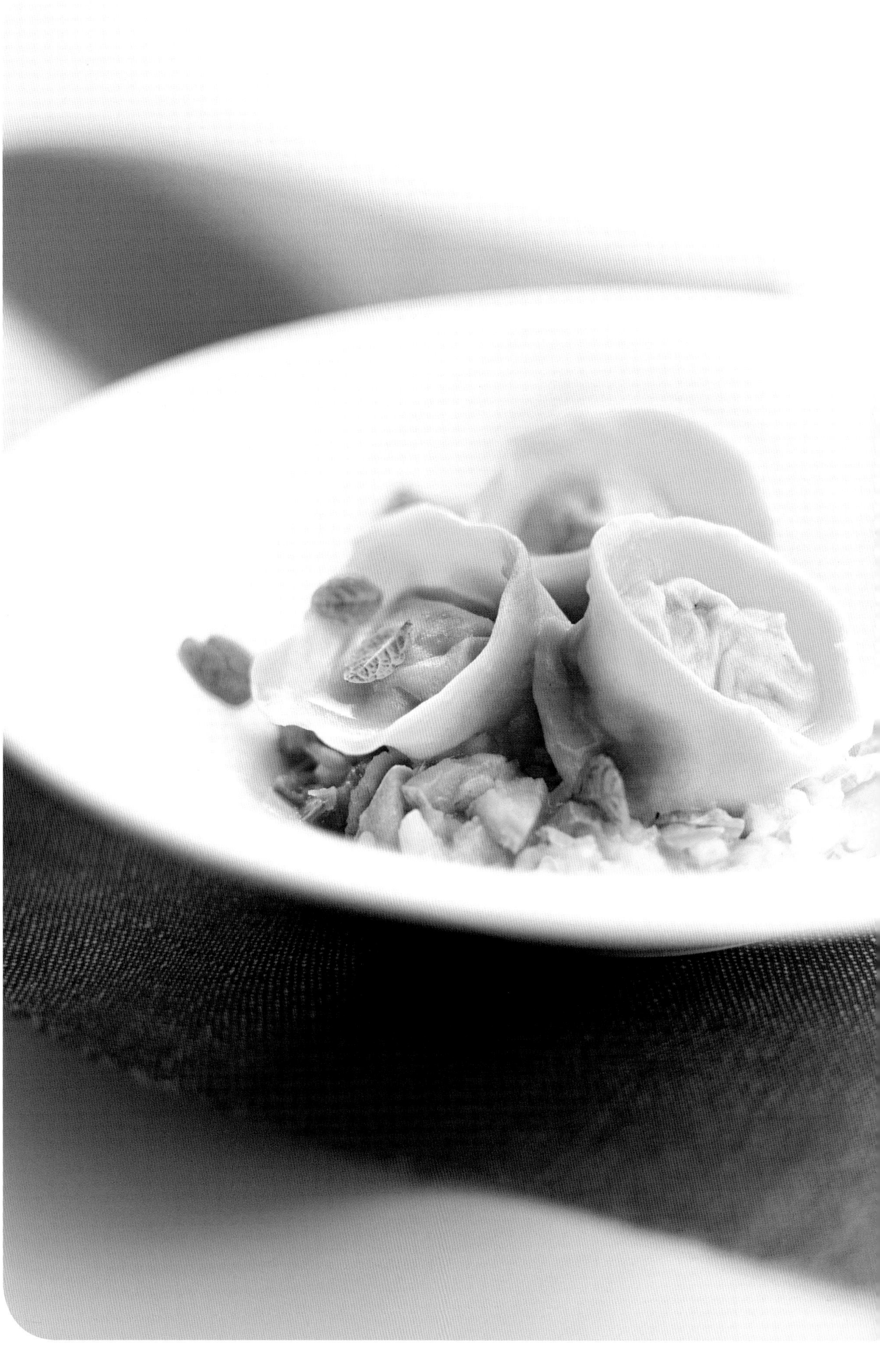

How to make tortellini

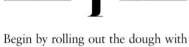

1

Begin by rolling out the dough with a rolling pin.

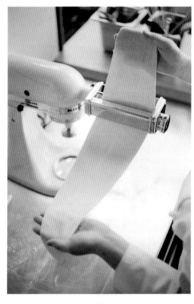

2

Use a pasta machine to roll out the dough more finely, until it is a very thin, almost translucent strip.

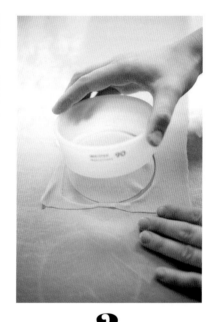

3

Put the strip of dough onto a lightly floured work surface, then cut out 8 cm/3¼ in circles using a pastry cutter.

4

Put a teaspoon of filling into the middle of each circle of dough. Use a pastry brush dipped in water to dampen the edges of the dough, then fold the circle over to make a semi-circle and enclose the filling.

5

Using your fingers, seal the edges together, pressing gently to get rid of as much air as possible before sealing completely.

6

Finally, to shape the tortellini, press the two ends of the semicircle firmly together as shown.

7

Make sure the two ends are securely pressed together, so they don't come apart while cooking.

8

Cook the tortellini immediately or freeze them.

For 4
Preparation time: 40 min
Cooking time: 20 min + 30 min
Pasteurizing time: 10 min

Tandoori beef bourguignon

Tandoori combined with beef bourguignon is not the odd combination it might at first appear to be. The tandoori spices up the classic bourguignon, and when cooked in this way, it has a superb melting texture. The secret is very simple – the meat is cooked twice in a pressure cooker. This can be eaten up to two weeks after being cooked.

2 carrots
1 onion
1 stalk celery
1 leek, white part only
splash of groundnut (peanut) oil
20 g/¾ oz butter
500 g/1 lb 2 oz diced braising steak
250 ml/9 fl oz red wine
500 ml/18 fl oz chicken stock
   (see step-by-step method on p. 246)
8 sprigs of thyme
4 bay leaves
1 teaspoon black peppercorns
1 tablespoon tandoori spices
fine salt, freshly ground pepper

Equipment

4 individual 'Le Parfait'
   or other sealable jars

1 - The flavourings

Peel and slice the carrots and onion. Wash the celery and leek, then dice them. Put all the vegetables to one side.

2 - The beef bourguignon

Heat the oil and butter over a high heat in a pressure cooker. Add the diced beef and brown all over, stirring now and again. Remove the meat from the pan and pour off most of the fat, leaving just a little, then return the meat to the pan with the diced vegetables and red wine. Bring to the boil, then use a match to light the wine and flambé everything. When the flames die down, add the chicken stock, along with the thyme, bay leaves and peppercorns. Following the manufacturer's instructions, bring the cooker up to pressure (on a 'vegetables' setting), then cook for 30 minutes. At the end of the cooking time, remove from the heat and let the pressure drop slowly. Opening the cooker too soon may cause a sharp drop in pressure, which can damage the texture of food. Once the pressure has dropped, open the cooker and, using a slotted spoon, remove the meat and vegetables. Bring the cooking juices to the boil and reduce for about 10 minutes, then add the tandoori spices and season with salt and pepper if necessary.

3 - Finishing off

Divide the meat and vegetables between the jars. Cover with the hot reduced sauce, then close and seal. Put the jars in the basket of the pressure cooker, then pour some water into the bottom of the cooker and bring to the boil. Follow the manufacturer's instructions for bringing the cooker up to pressure, then cook for 10 minutes. At the end of the cooking time, remove from the heat and let the pressure drop slowly. Open the pressure cooker, remove the jars and leave to cool. Store in the fridge until needed.

Tip | When the jars are cold, check that the vacuum seal is secure. To do this you just need to remove the metal closures; the rubber seal should still hold the lid in place.

For 4
Preparation time: 20 min
Cooking time: 20 min + 8 min
}

Red mullet
in aniseed escabeche

Using aniseed in the escabeche brings a real holiday flavour to this dish. Depending on what fish you can get, you could use other mullet or even mackerel, as its dense, well-flavoured flesh goes very well with the herbs and spices. Sterilizing jars in the pressure cooker is a great 'plan ahead' solution; this will keep for up to a week in the fridge

1 teaspoon aniseed
¼ fennel bulb
1 garlic clove
1 onion
1 carrot
250 ml/9 fl oz white wine
250 ml/9 fl oz water
pinch of coarse salt
juice of 1 lemon
sprig of thyme
1 bay leaf
75 ml/2½ fl oz olive oil
75 ml/2½ fl oz white balsamic vinegar
4 red mullet fillets

Equipment

boning tweezers (or normal tweezers)
1 x 500 ml/18 fl oz 'Le Parfait'
   or other sealable jar

1~ The escabeche

Crush the aniseed. Trim and finely slice the fennel, then peel and trim the garlic, removing any green sprout from its centre. Peel and slice the onion and carrot. Put all the ingredients except the fish into a large frying pan and bring to the boil. Lower the heat and leave to cook for 20 minutes.

2~ Preparing the red mullet

While the escabeche is cooking, prepare the red mullet fillets. Rinse them under cold running water and gently pat dry, then remove any remaining bones with tweezers.

3~ Cooking the dish

Put the red mullet fillets in the jar, then add the vegetables and spices from the escabeche, followed by the hot liquid. Close the jar and place in the basket of a pressure cooker, then pour some water into the bottom of the cooker and bring to the boil. Follow the manufacturer's instructions for bringing the pressure cooker up to pressure, then cook for 8 minutes. Remove from the heat, leaving the lid on, and let the pressure drop slowly. Open the pressure cooker and remove the jar, then leave to cool. Store in the fridge until needed. Serve the mullet in escabeche chilled, straight from the jar.

Tp | When the jar is cold, check that the vacuum seal is secure. To do this you just need to remove the metal closures; the rubber seal should still hold the lid in place.

For 4
Preparation time: 40 min
Infusing time: 1 h
Cooking time: 10 min
+ 25 min

}

Vegetable tian with bay leaf butter

Delicious, brightly coloured summer vegetables are served here in individual jars. In this recipe, the warm flavours of the south are cooked using an innovative and very practical method, which means you can store the vegetable tians in the fridge for up to 15 days after cooking them.

The bay leaf butter

100 g/3½ oz salted butter
2 dried bay leaves

The vegetable tian

1 green courgette (zucchini)
1 white courgette (zucchini)
1 aubergine (eggplant)
2 red (bell) peppers
4 garlic cloves
100 ml/3½ fl oz olive oil
fine salt

Equipment

pestle and mortar
4 individual 'Le Parfait'
  or other sealable jars

1~The bay leaf butter

Beat the butter until it is very soft and resembles a paste. Using a pestle and mortar, grind the bay leaves to a powder. Mix the butter and bay leaf powder together, then leave to infuse for 1 hour.

2~The vegetable tian

Wash, top and tail the courgettes and aubergines, then slice finely with a mandoline. Peel and deseed the peppers, then cut into strips. Peel and crush each garlic clove. Sauté the vegetables separately, adding a garlic clove and a splash of olive oil to each one. Season with a little salt. Put each sautéed vegetable on a plate to one side.

3~Cooking the dish

In 4 individual, sealable jars, arrange a layer of green courgette in a rosette shape, then a layer of red peppers, then a layer of white courgette, and finally a layer of aubergine. Put a large knob of bay leaf butter on the top, add a splash of olive oil, and then close the jars. Place the jars in the basket of a pressure cooker, then pour some water into the bottom of the cooker and bring to the boil. Follow the manufacturer's instructions for bringing the cooker up to pressure, then cook for 25 minutes. At the end of the cooking time, remove from the heat, leaving the lid on, and let the pressure drop slowly. Open the pressure cooker, remove the jars and leave to cool. Store in the fridge until needed. Serve the tians chilled, straight from the jar

Tip | *When the jars are cold, check that the vacuum seal is secure. To do this you just need to remove the metal closures; the rubber seal should still hold the lid in place.*

5

For children

FAST BUT GOOD FOOD

After a day at work, it sometimes feels like a real effort to come home and cook dinner. However, cooking can also be a very relaxing pleasure, one that helps you unwind after a busy day. The recipes in this chapter focus on that pleasure and relaxation, because none of them take that long. But, in order to be able to make good food without it taking hours, you need to plan. So it's important to have plenty of store-cupboard ingredients that are both simple and seasonal. It also helps to make a few dishes in advance (like ratatouille); to use the freezer for storage (as with the Drôme caillette turnovers); and to know how to make the most of leftovers (such as transforming stale bread into pain perdu with strawberry jam).

For 4
Preparation time: 30 min
Cooking time: 40 min

}

Boulangère potatoes with bacon

This is a very light gratin, as the potatoes are cooked in a simple vegetable stock, rather than in milk, cream or a béchamel sauce.

3 onions
splash of olive oil
30 g/1 oz salted butter
500 g/1 lb 2 oz potatoes, ideally Bintje
5 slices unsmoked streaky bacon
2 garlic cloves
sprig of thyme
juice of ½ lemon
250 ml/9 fl oz vegetable stock
  (see step-by-step method on p. 126)
large pinch of fine salt
freshly ground pepper (about one
  turn of the grinder)

1~ The cooking juices

Peel the onions, then cut them into the thinnest slices possible (using a mandoline or a food processor or, failing that, a very good knife). Heat the olive oil and butter in a saucepan over a gentle heat, then add the sliced onions, whole unpeeled garlic cloves and the thyme. Leave to cook, stirring all the time, until the onion and garlic have just coloured a little. Then add the lemon juice and, as soon as the juice has nearly evaporated, add half the vegetable stock and leave to cook slowly until the onions are really soft. Finally, remove the garlic and thyme and season lightly with salt.

2~ Making the gratin

Preheat the oven to 170°C (325°F; gas mark 3). Peel the potatoes, then rinse in cold water. Pat dry and cut into slices 2 mm/¹⁄₁₆ in thick. Line an ovenproof dish with baking parchment, then butter the paper. Add two layers of potatoes, season, then add a layer of onions, followed by a slice of bacon. Repeat until all the ingredients are used up, then pour the remainder of the stock over the top.

3~ Cooking the gratin

Cover the dish with baking parchment, then cook in the oven for about 30 minutes, or until the potatoes are tender. Remove from the oven and leave to rest for a few minutes before serving.

Tip | *Don't be tempted to wash the potato slices to remove the starch, because it is the starch that holds it all together.*

Variation | *For adults, you can replace the lemon juice with 50 ml/1¾ fl oz dry white wine.*

}

Drôme caillette turnovers

This speciality from the Valence region uses a coarse-textured spinach and pork pâté called Drôme caillette as a filling for savoury pastries. They are fun to make with children, who love shaping the turnovers. You can prepare these in advance and freeze them, but you'll need to increase the cooking time by about 20–25 minutes if cooking them from frozen.

The filling

500 g/1 lb 2 oz fresh spinach
200 g/7 oz pork loin
50 g/1¾ oz chicken livers
75 g/2¾ oz pork back fat
1 garlic clove
1 shallot
½ onion
1 egg
splash of Cognac
1 level tablespoon fine salt
freshly ground black pepper

The turnovers

2 sheets ready-made puff pastry
1 egg, lightly beaten

1~ The filling

Trim and thoroughly wash the spinach. Bring a pan of salted water to the boil, add the spinach and cook for 5 minutes. Drain, then refresh under cold running water. Drain again in a sieve, squeezing the spinach firmly with your hands to remove any excess water, then chop with a knife and put to one side. Cut the pork loin, chicken livers and back fat into small pieces (or ask your butcher to do this). Peel the garlic, shallot and onion, then chop them into a fine mince with the meats. Transfer to a bowl and mix in the drained spinach, followed by the egg, Cognac, salt and pepper.

2~ The turnovers

Preheat the oven to 180°C (350°F; gas mark 4). Lay the puff pastry sheets on a work surface and cut out four 14 cm/5½ in circles, then put 1–2 tablespoons of the filling on each one. Using a pastry brush, brush the edge of each circle with beaten egg. Fold the pastry over on itself to make a turnover shape, then seal the edges together, taking care to press out as much air as possible. Brush the tops of the turnovers with the rest of the beaten egg, then bake for 15 minutes. Eat hot.

Tip | Make the most of the leftovers! You can wrap any remaining filling in caul (which you can buy from a good butcher) to make meatballs; bake them at 220°C (425°F; gas mark 7) for 20 minutes, then eat either hot or cold. The filling can also be frozen, ready for when you next want to make turnovers.

For 4
Preparation time: 20 min
Cooking time: 7 min

}

Petits pois velouté with horseradish cream

I particularly love this delicate velouté because of its appetizing green colour. Horseradish has a very strong flavour, but mixed with crème fraîche it loses some of its heat and becomes smoother, which means even children will like it. One to try...

The petits pois velouté

600 g/1 lb 5 oz freshly shelled
 petits pois
150 ml/5 fl oz vegetable stock
 (see step-by-step method on p. 126)
coarse salt, fine salt

The horseradish cream

150 ml/5 fl oz chilled crème fraîche
 (sour cream)
20 g/¾ oz horseradish paste
pinch of fine salt
freshly ground pepper

1~ The petits pois velouté

Fill a saucepan with water, add a little coarse salt and bring to the boil. Add the petits pois and cook for 5–7 minutes, or until very tender. Refresh under cold water to stop them cooking any more and to preserve their bright green colour, then drain. Save a few peas to garnish the soup, then blend the rest with the vegetable stock until smooth. Check and adjust the seasoning.

2~ The horseradish cream

Whip the crème fraîche with the salt, either by hand or in a mixer, until thick. Fold in the horseradish paste and season with salt and pepper.

3~ Serving

Divide the velouté between 4 bowls or cups. Using a tablespoon, shape the cream into 'quenelles' and add one to each bowl of soup. It doesn't matter if you can't make quenelles; just scoop a spoonful of the cream into each bowl – it will still look lovely. Garnish with the reserved peas and serve immediately.

Tip | Use really fresh peas for this, to make sure you get the best light green colour. Buy them unshelled if you can, since they are the freshest.

For 4
Preparation time: 10 min
Cooking time: 25 min

}

Grandma Alice's bulgur wheat with vermicelli

Discover the marvellous contrast of soft bulgur wheat and crunchy vermicelli in this traditional Armenian dish. It's a perfect accompaniment for white meat, like chicken or pork, and a great alternative to rice.

The vermicelli

splash of olive oil
50 g/1¾ oz vermicelli pasta
½ onion
knob of salted butter

The bulgur wheat

250 g/8½ oz bulgur wheat
450 ml/15 fl oz vegetable stock
  (see step-by-step method on p. 126)
fine salt

Finishing off

a few knobs of butter
fine salt

1 - The vermicelli

Heat the oil in a saucepan over a gentle heat. Add the vermicelli and let it colour, stirring from time to time, until golden brown. Meanwhile, peel and finely chop the onion, then add to the pan, along with the butter. Cook over a gentle heat for another 2–3 minutes, stirring every so often.

2 - The bulgur wheat

Add the bulgur wheat and stir it in well with a wooden spoon, making sure it is covered with the melted butter and onions. Pour in the vegetable stock and add a little salt, then cover and leave to cook for 20 minutes over a gentle heat. Taste the bulgur: it should be soft and fragrant. If it is still chewy, add a little water, cover and cook for a minute or two longer.

3 - Finishing off

Take the pan off the heat and add a few knobs of butter. Mix in gently, then cover the pan and leave to rest for a few minutes. Fluff up the bulgur with a fork to break up any lumps, then taste and adjust the seasoning if necessary. Serve hot.

Tip | Bulgur wheat is a type of coarse grain derived from durum wheat. It has a delicate nutty flavour, and its high fibre and carbohydrate content makes it very nutritious.

For 4
Preparation time: 30 min
Cooking time: 30 min
}

My ratatouille

This is 'the' ratatouille recipe: baked in the oven, very simple to make and delicious. The secret lies in cutting the vegetables into very small pieces, then keeping the lid on throughout cooking so that all the steam is retained and the ratatouille stays juicy.

2 red (bell) peppers
3 tomatoes
1 aubergine (eggplant)
2 courgettes (zucchini)
1 onion
3 garlic cloves
50 ml/1¾ fl oz olive oil
sprig of thyme
sprig of summer savory
1 bay leaf
fine salt

1- Preparing the vegetables

Peel the peppers and remove their stalks, then deseed them and remove any white pith. Cut a cross in the base of the tomatoes. Bring a pan of water to the boil, then immerse the tomatoes in the boiling water for 15 seconds. Remove the tomatoes and refresh in cold water, then peel off the skins and remove the seeds. (See step-by-step method on p. 22.) Rinse the aubergine and courgettes and peel the onion. Dice all the vegetables (this is known as a 'brunoise'), keeping the dice as regular as possible and making sure all the pieces are separated from each other. Leave the garlic unpeeled, but squash each clove with the blade of a knife.

2- Cooking the ratatouille

Preheat the oven to 150°C (300°F; gas mark 2). Heat the oil in a flameproof casserole dish with a lid. Add the onion, peppers, garlic and herbs and cook, stirring all the time, for 5 minutes. Add the aubergine and courgette and cook for another 5 minutes, without letting them colour, then add the tomatoes. Mix together, cover and bake for 20 minutes. Remove from the oven and take out the thyme, summer savory, bay leaf and garlic, then cover the dish again and leave to cool. Season lightly before serving.

Tip | *In summer, try this ratatouille cold, either on its own or alongside some firm white fish like cod or pollock.*

For 4
Preparation time: 40 min
Cooking time: 30 min

}

Grandma Suzanne's stuffed tomatoes

This is my mother's recipe, and I have always loved it. The secret lies in using good, firm tomatoes and a richly flavoured stuffing made with lamb, mushrooms and herbs, but no bread.

The stuffing

1 shallot
4 large white button mushrooms
knob of butter
250 g/8½ oz lamb shoulder
   or minced (ground) lamb
100 g/3½ oz ham, diced
1 garlic clove, chopped
1 tablespoon finely chopped parsley
20 g/¾ oz grated Parmesan
1 egg
pinch of fine salt
freshly ground pepper

The tomatoes

4 large firm tomatoes
pinch of fine salt
splash of olive oil

Equipment

mincer (optional)

1~ The stuffing

Preheat the oven to 180°C (350°F; gas mark 4). Peel and finely slice the shallot. Trim the mushrooms, if necessary, then cut into very small dice. Melt the butter in a large pan over a gentle heat, add the shallot and mushrooms and sweat slowly for 2–3 minutes without letting them colour, stirring often. Take off the heat and leave to cool. Mince the lamb, if necessary – in a mincer or with a knife – then add to the pan, along with the ham, garlic, parsley, Parmesan and egg. Mix well and season.

2~ Cooking the stuffed tomatoes

Using a serrated knife (this will make it easier), cut off the top of the tomatoes, then scoop out the seeds with a spoon. Lightly salt the inside of the tomatoes, then place them upside down on a wire rack and leave to sweat for about 15 minutes. Use a tablespoon to fill the tomatoes generously with the stuffing, replace their tops, then place on an oiled baking sheet and bake for 30 minutes. Serve hot, perhaps with plain white rice.

Tip | It is important to allow time for the tomatoes to sweat – this draws out some of their liquid, so they don't go too soft in the oven and collapse.

For 4
Preparation time: 45 min
Infusing time: 15 min
Cooking time: 30 min
Resting time: 1 h

Goat's cheese and peppermint blancmange with aubergine caviar

This very Provençal dish, with its delicate texture, will delight your children – they will especially love watching the gelatine dissolve and disappear. I serve the blancmange with an aubergine caviar, made in this instance without garlic.

The aubergine caviar

2 aubergines (eggplants)
50 ml/1¾ fl oz olive oil
1 tablespoon chopped mint
large pinch of fine salt

The blancmange

200 ml/7 fl oz milk
2 sprigs of peppermint
50 g/1¾ oz fresh goat's cheese
10 g/⅓ oz gelatine leaves
80 ml/2½ fl oz very cold double
   (heavy) cream
pinch of fine salt

1- The aubergine caviar

Preheat the oven to 180°C (350°F; gas mark 4). Rinse the aubergines and remove their stalks, then cut in half lengthways and season with fine salt. Put the olive oil in a frying pan over a high heat and add the aubergines, cut-side down. Brown them for 3–4 minutes, then remove from the heat and transfer to a baking sheet, this time skin-side down, and bake for 30 minutes. Remove the aubergines from the oven, then scoop out their flesh with a spoon and chop it finely. Put in a bowl with the mint and mix well, then check and adjust the seasoning as necessary. Put to one side.

2- The blancmange

Heat the milk in a saucepan and add the finely chopped peppermint. Remove from the heat, cover and leave to infuse for 15 minutes, then strain through a fine sieve, discarding the mint. Add the goat's cheese to the infusion and blend until smooth. Soak the gelatine leaves in cold water for 4–5 minutes. Stir the drained and squeezed-out gelatine into the blancmange mixture while it is still warm, then whip the cream to firm peaks and fold into the mixture before it sets. Check and adjust the seasoning as necessary, then pour into hemispherical moulds or glasses and leave to set in the fridge for at least 1 hour.

3- Serving

Once the blancmange is set, serve with the aubergine caviar.

Variation | *This is a perfect spring dish. In winter, try replacing the aubergines with parsnips – just remember you'll need to cook them for longer.*

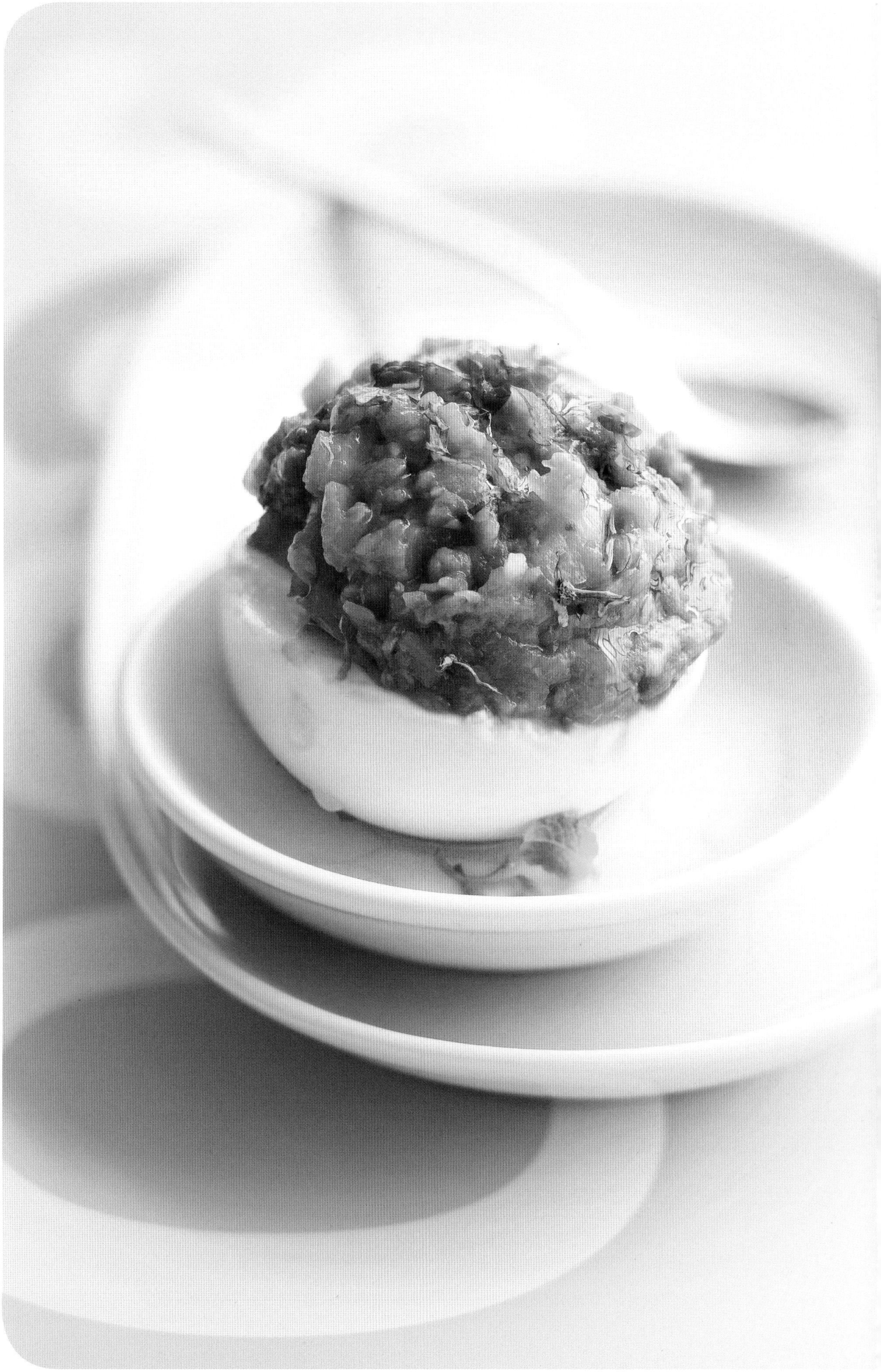

NURTURING A LOVE OF FINE FOOD

Contrary to popular belief, children will love
and appreciate sophisticated food, as long as they
are used to tasting unfamiliar things. I hope the
next few pages will tempt you to try more complex
combinations, with spices, herbs, unusual vegetables
and recipes that use lots of different ingredients.
If you involve your children in the preparation, they
will understand how ingredients are transformed
by being mixed together and cooked. This will
help them to identify flavours and tastes,
as well as nurturing an adventurous palate.

For 4
Preparation time: 45 min
Cooking time: 50 min

}

Poached sole and potatoes with sweet spices

The mild spices used in this dish — cloves, star anise, cinnamon and nutmeg — are ideal for children. They give a lovely sweetness to potatoes, with no trace of bitterness or heat. The sole is lightly poached at a low temperature in a delicate herby vegetable stock, which makes it really tender and juicy.

The crushed potatoes

2 cloves
2 star anise
1 tablespoon ground cinnamon
½ tablespoon grated nutmeg
200 g/7 oz Charlotte potatoes
1 kg/2¼ lb coarse salt
50 g/1¾ oz butter
splash of olive oil
fine salt

The sole

1 lemon
50 g/1¾ oz salted butter
1 garlic clove
sprig of thyme
2 tablespoons olive oil
4 x 100 g/3½ oz sole fillets
fine salt

Equipment

pestle and mortar (optional)

1~ The crushed potatoes

Preheat the oven to 180°C (350°F; gas mark 4). Crush the cloves and star anise using a pestle and mortar (or in a bowl, using the end of a rolling pin), then mix with all the other spices and put to one side. Wash the potatoes, then season with salt and roll in the spice mixture. Put a layer of coarse salt in an ovenproof dish, put the potatoes on top and bake for about 45 minutes. Remove from the oven and, when they are cool enough to handle, peel the potatoes. Add the butter and olive oil, then crush the potatoes with a fork. Put them to one side and keep warm.

2~ The sole

Juice the lemon. Pour the juice into a sauté pan (or just a normal frying pan), along with 50 ml/1¾ fl oz of water. Add the butter, peeled and crushed garlic, thyme and olive oil, then bring to a simmer. Season the sole fillets with fine salt, then immerse them in the simmering liquid. Cover and cook over a gentle heat for 2 minutes, then turn the fillets and cook for another 2 minutes.

3~ Serving

Divide the crushed potatoes between 4 shallow bowls. Put the sole fillets on top and serve immediately.

Variation | *You can use other equally delicious but less expensive fish for this, such as cod or black sea bream.*

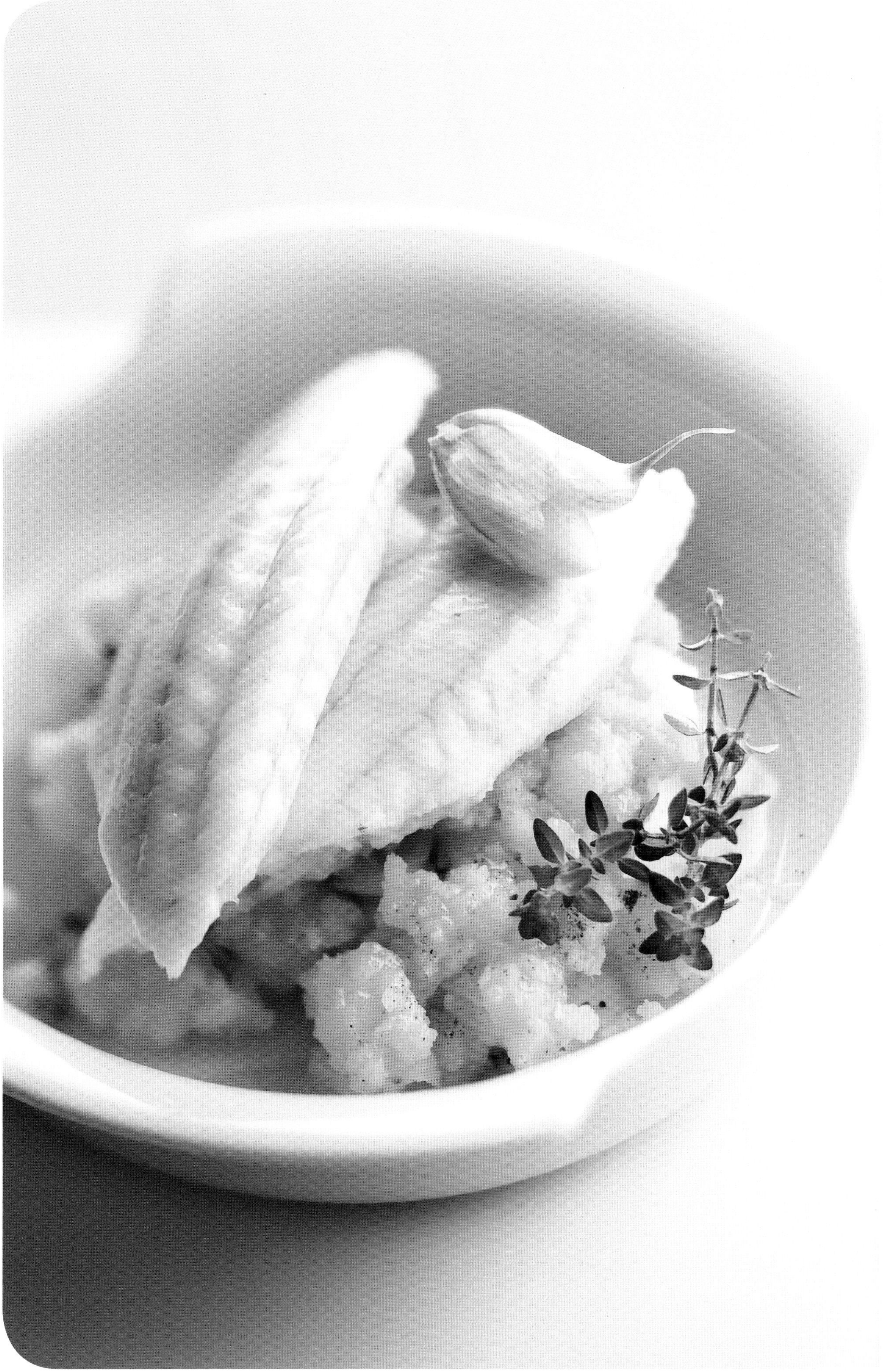

For 4
Preparation time: 1 h
Soaking time 20 min
Cooking time: 18 min
}

Mussel risotto

Do your children eat rice without really enjoying it? Well, try making them this soft, creamy risotto. Packed with slowly digested carbohydrates and the protective benefits of turmeric, it's a complete dish that will give a child all the energy they need. Making a risotto with vegetable stock means it can be used as a base for lots of other variations. Here I use just mussels, but you could also add cockles or clams.

The risotto

½ onion
2 knobs of butter
200 g/7 oz Arborio rice
100 ml/3½ fl oz white wine
500 ml /18 fl oz vegetable stock
   (see step-by-step method on p. 126)
1 teaspoon ground turmeric
fine salt

The shellfish

400 g/14 oz mussels
1 shallot
splash of olive oil
40 ml/1½ fl oz dry white wine
1 bay leaf
sprig of thyme
100 ml/3½ fl oz double (heavy) cream

Finishing off

60 g/2¼ oz grated Parmesan
250 ml/9 fl oz double (heavy) cream
1 tablespoon finely chopped parsley

1 ~ The risotto

Finely chop the onion. Melt the butter in a saucepan over a low heat, then add the chopped onion and cook for 2–3 minutes, stirring constantly, without letting it colour. Add the rice and cook for another 2–3 minutes, stirring all the time. Pour in the white wine and bring to the boil, then reduce until nearly all of the wine has evaporated. Add enough vegetable stock to just cover the rice and leave to cook over a gentle heat. As soon as the stock has been absorbed, add more, ladleful by ladleful, stirring often. The whole process should take about 18 minutes. Finally, stir in the turmeric and season the risotto with a little salt. Remove from the heat, cover and put to one side.

2 ~ The mussels

While the risotto is cooking, soak the mussels in cold water for 20 minutes to purge them of any grit or sand, then drain in a sieve or colander. Peel and finely chop the shallot. Heat the olive oil in a large lidded saucepan over a low heat. Add the shallot and cook for about a minute, stirring all the time. Add the mussels, white wine, bay and thyme, then cover and cook for 2–3 minutes, or until the mussels have opened. Take off the heat and leave to cool, then shell most of the mussels (save a few in their shells for garnish), reserving the cooking liquid. Strain the mussel-cooking liquid through a muslin (cheesecloth)-lined sieve into a saucepan, then bring to the boil and reduce to almost nothing. Add the cream, bring to the boil and reduce again, this time by half. Add the shelled mussels, then take off the heat and stir to coat the mussels in the sauce.

3 ~ Finishing off

Whip the cream until stiff, then carefully stir it into the risotto with the Parmesan and the mussels in their sauce. Divide between 4 bowls and decorate with a couple of mussels in their shells and the finely chopped parsley.

Tip | Arborio is a short-grain rice that is rich in starch, making it perfect for risotto. It is easy to find in supermarkets and delicatessens. If you want to get a head start, you can prepare the risotto and mussels in advance, which means the dish takes very little time to finish off – and you can still keep an eye on the children!

For 8
Preparation time: 30 min
Cooking time: 25 min

}

Praline cream choux buns

To save time on the day you want to serve these, prepare the choux buns and praline cream in advance, then all you need to do is put them together at the last minute. Get your children to help: depending on their age, they could put the raw dough onto the baking sheet or fill the cooked choux buns with cream using a piping bag. You should be able to find pearl sugar and ready-made hazelnut praline in some delicatessens and specialist food shops or online.

The choux pastry

100 ml/3½ fl oz milk
100 ml/3½ fl oz water
1 tablespoon caster (superfine) sugar
80 g/3 oz butter
1 teaspoon salt
120 g/4¼ oz plain (all-purpose)
   flour, sifted
3 eggs

The choux decoration

1 egg yolk
small handful of chopped almonds
small handful of pearl sugar
icing (confectioners') sugar

The praline chantilly

2.5 g/0.09 oz gelatine leaves
45 ml/1¾ fl oz double (heavy) cream
150 g/5½ oz hazelnut praline
300 ml/10 fl oz chilled double
   (heavy) cream

Equipment

piping bag

1- The choux pastry

Preheat the oven to 165°C (320°F; gas mark 2–3). Put the milk, water, caster sugar, butter and salt into a saucepan and bring to the boil, then remove from the heat. Add the flour and mix in with a spatula, then return the saucepan to a medium heat and cook, stirring rapidly, until the pastry dries out and comes away from the sides. This will take 1–2 minutes. Tip the pastry into a bowl and add the eggs one by one, mixing each one in well before adding the next.

2- Decorating the choux

Put the dough into a piping bag fitted with a 2–3 cm/1 in round nozzle then, using your hands to squeeze the bag, pipe regular dome-like choux bun shapes onto a baking sheet. Mix the egg yolk with 3 tablespoons of water and use a pastry brush to glaze the buns with this eggwash. Sprinkle on the chopped almonds and pearl sugar, then bake for 25 minutes. Remove from the oven and transfer to a wire rack to cool.

3- The praline chantilly

Soak the gelatine leaves in cold water for 5 minutes to soften. In a small saucepan, gently heat the double cream, then remove from the heat and add the drained and squeezed-out gelatine, stirring to dissolve. Put the hazelnut praline into a large bowl, then pour the hot cream over the top and stir until smooth. With an electric whisk, beat the cold double cream to stiff peaks, then slowly fold it into the praline cream. Put the mixture into another piping bag, this time one fitted with a crenellated nozzle, then chill it in the fridge.

4- Finishing off

Using a serrated knife, cut off the top quarter of the choux buns and then, using the piping bag, fill them with the praline chantilly. Replace the tops of the buns and sprinkle with icing sugar (or hazelnut praline, if you have some left). Serve immediately.

}

Little chocolate pots

This recipe is only limited by your imagination. Instead of cocoa, try orange flower water, vanilla, coffee or praline. Ideally, make these the day before you want to serve them and let them rest overnight in the fridge: they will be even better.

80 ml/2½ fl oz milk
15 g/½ oz cocoa powder
4 egg yolks
70 g/2½ oz caster (superfine) sugar
350 ml/12 fl oz double (heavy) cream

Equipment
6 ramekins

1~ Preparing the chocolate mixture

Preheat the oven to 100–110°C (210–225°F; gas mark ¼ or lower). Put the milk and cocoa into a saucepan, place over a medium heat and whisk to dissolve the cocoa, then take off the heat. In a large bowl, briefly mix the egg yolks with the sugar, then pour in the cocoa milk and the cream. Mix well, without making it too frothy, and then strain through a fine sieve.

2~ Cooking the chocolate mixture

Fill the ramekins two-thirds full with the cocoa mixture. Put the ramekins into a roasting tin or baking dish, then pour in enough hot water to come two-thirds of the way up the sides of the ramekins. Cover with baking parchment and cook in the oven for 1½ hours.

3~ Finishing off

Carefully remove the ramekins from the oven and the bain-marie. Leave them to cool, then chill for at least 4 hours in the fridge before eating them very cold, straight from the pot.

Tip | *Use a good-quality unsweetened cocoa powder for this, not drinking chocolate. Though they seem similar, in reality they have nothing in common. The first has complex and delicious chocolatey notes, whereas the second is often very low in cocoa content. So be sure to read the label before buying!*

For 4
Preparation time: 1 h
Cooking time: 1 h 15

}

Braised beef with red pepper and tomato sauce

Children love sharp flavours as long as they are not overwhelming. Unlike bought ketchup, the pepper and tomato sauce in this recipe has a much more subtle, less sugary taste. The other great advantage of this braised beef is that it practically prepares itself!

2 onions
2 shallots
2 red (bell) peppers
2 garlic cloves
2 tomatoes
1 tablespoon olive oil + a little extra
50 g/1¾ oz salted butter
500 g/1 lb 2 oz braising beef or beef cheek, cut into 30–40 g/1–1½ oz pieces
sprig of summer savory
sprig of thyme + extra to garnish
1 bay leaf
100 ml/3½ fl oz vegetable stock (see step-by-step method on p.126)
splash of sherry vinegar
fine salt, freshly ground pepper

1~ The vegetables

Preheat the oven to 180°C (350°F; gas mark 4). Peel the onions and shallots. De-stalk and quarter the peppers, then remove the seeds and any white pith. Finely chop the onions, shallots and peppers. Peel the garlic. De-stalk the tomatoes and cut into quarters.

2~ Preparing the meat and the vegetables

In a flameproof casserole with a lid, heat the tablespoon of olive oil with the butter. Season the beef all over with salt and brown on all sides for about 8 minutes, then remove from the pan. Pour off most of the fat, then add the onions, shallots, peppers and tomatoes. Add a little extra olive oil and cook the vegetables over a gentle heat for about 5 minutes, stirring now and again.

3~ Braising and finishing off

Place the browned meat on top of the vegetables in the casserole, then add the garlic, summer savory, thyme, bay leaf and vegetable stock. Cover and cook in the oven for 1 hour. Remove the casserole from the oven and take the meat out of the sauce. Discard the summer savory, thyme and bay leaf, then blend the cooked vegetables until you have a smooth sauce. Season with salt and pepper, then stir in the vinegar. Divide the beef and sauce between 4 bowls, garnish with a sprig of thyme and serve.

Tip | Check on the vegetables every so often while they are in the oven to be sure that they are not burning. If they seem to be drying out, add a little more vegetable stock.

For 4
Preparation time: 30 min
Marinating time: 15 min
Cooking time: 1 h

Scallops with buttered green cabbage

Cabbage may not be your children's favourite thing, but this might persuade them to try it. Cooked in butter, cabbage becomes very sweet and is an ideal accompaniment to fish or seafood. Here I serve it with scallops for a sweet, yet salty taste. If you can't find scallops, cubes of cod would work just as well.

The scallops

10 g/⅓ oz lemon coriander seeds
400 g/14 oz fresh or defrosted
   trimmed scallops
100 ml/3½ fl oz olive oil

**The buttered cabbage
and potato**

200 g/7 oz potatoes
500 g/1 lb 2 oz coarse salt
½ green cabbage
100 g/3½ oz unsalted butter
fine salt

Finishing off

10 g/⅓ oz salted butter
fine salt

1~ The scallops

Roughly crush the coriander seeds with a rolling pin or the flat side of a knife to bring out their flavour. Put the scallops in a bowl with the crushed coriander and olive oil, then leave to marinate somewhere cool for at least 15 minutes.

2~ The buttered cabbage and potato

Preheat the oven to 180°C (350°F; gas mark 4). Wash the potatoes, then cook on a bed of coarse salt in the oven for 45 minutes. Leave to cool, then peel them. Remove the outer leaves from the cabbage and discard. Break off the rest of the leaves and cut away the central ribs, then shred finely. Cook the cabbage in boiling salted water for 5 minutes. Drain, immerse in cold water, then drain again. Melt a little butter in a frying pan or large saucepan over a gentle heat, add the cabbage and cook for 5 minutes. Crush the potatoes with a fork and add to the pan, then remove from the heat. Dice the rest of the butter and stir thoroughly into the cabbage and potato. Season with a little salt.

3~ Finishing off

Lightly salt the scallops. Put a little of the marinade into a hot frying pan with the salted butter, then add the scallops and cook for 3 minutes. Remove from the heat. Divide the buttered cabbage and potato between 4 shallow bowls, top with the just-cooked scallops and serve immediately.

Variation | *You can also make this using scallops with coral attached, but the cooking time will be longer. Don't overcook the scallops, though, or they will become tough. If you can't find lemon coriander seeds, substitute ground coriander and the finely chopped zest of half a lemon.*

CHILDHOOD FAVOURITES

Childhood memories have a big influence
on our attitude to cooking. Whether it was my
father, whose kitchen I walked through every day
after school; or my mother, who was an excellent
cook too, but focused on fast, healthy food; or
my grandmother in the Provençale countryside,
who taught me about tasty, local food, I am a
combination of all these influences, and of all the
love they transmitted through their cooking.
In this section I have collected some of my fondest
culinary memories from childhood – simple recipes
that I hope your children will like, and that will
feed their imagination.

For 8
Preparation time: 30 min
Cooking time: 10 min
Resting time: 24 h + 3 h

}

Raspberry Swiss roll

This is a great cake to make with children. First, they get to make a sponge, then bake and roll it up, learning as they go — and then they get to taste the results with their fingers. And by changing the jam, you can change the flavour.

The raspberry jam

300 g/10½ oz raspberries
200 g/7 oz caster (superfine) sugar

The Swiss roll

60 g/2¼ oz cornflour (cornstarch)
60 g/2¼ oz plain (all-purpose) flour
6 eggs, separated
110 g/3¾ oz caster (superfine) sugar

Finishing off

icing (confectioners') sugar
raspberries

1~ The raspberry jam

In a large, non-metallic bowl, mix together the raspberries and sugar, then leave to rest somewhere cool for 24 hours. The next day, tip the mixture into a saucepan, bring to the boil and cook over a high heat (to preserve the colour of the fruit) for 4–5 minutes, stirring all the time to prevent the jam catching. Remove from the heat and leave to cool, then chill in the fridge for at least 1 hour.

2~ The Swiss roll

Mix the cornflour and flour together, then sift into a bowl. Preheat the oven to 200°C (400°F; gas mark 6). Whisk the egg whites in an electric mixer. When they start to firm up, add the sugar little by little, whisking after each addition. Once the egg whites are stiff, gently fold in the egg yolks and the sifted flours, being careful not to knock too much air out of the mixture. Line a baking sheet with baking parchment, then spread the mixture evenly across it and bake for 5 minutes. Lift the paper and dough together off the baking tray and place on a work surface. Cover with cling film to keep the sponge soft, then allow to cool before removing the cling film and carefully peeling off the baking parchment.

3~ Finishing off

Using the back of a spoon, spread the jam over the sponge as evenly as possible, without pressing too hard, then use your hands to gently roll it up. Chill in the fridge for 2 hours, then sprinkle with icing sugar and decorate with fresh raspberries just before serving.

Tip | The secret to keeping the sponge soft and easy to roll lies in the cooking. It needs to be cooked in a hot oven and not for too long or the dough dries out and becomes impossible to roll. Ideally, make the sponge a maximum of 1–2 hours before adding the jam, then it won't have time to dry out.

For 4–6
Preparation time: 20 min
Resting time: 2 h

}

Chocolate mousse

There is no secret to this mousse: you just need really fresh eggs and very good dark chocolate, preferably with 52–70% cocoa solids to give it real depth. Serve this with shortbread, a banana smoothie, almond biscuits...

The chocolate ganache

200 g/7 oz dark (bittersweet)
   chocolate
90 ml/3 fl oz double (heavy) cream
2 egg yolks

The egg white

120 g/4¼ oz egg white
   (from about 4–5 eggs)
40 g/1½ oz caster (superfine) sugar

1 ~ The chocolate ganache

Break the chocolate into pieces, then chop it finely with a knife and put into a heat-proof bowl. Pour the cream into a saucepan and bring to the boil, then immediately pour over the chocolate. Mix well with a spatula until smooth and glossy, then add the egg yolks, mix again and put to one side.

2 ~ The egg white

Put the egg white into a large bowl or an electric mixer (the bowl used should be very clean, since any trace of fat will make it harder to whisk the egg white), then whisk. As soon as peaks begin to form, start to add the sugar, little by little. Don't over-whisk the egg white, or it will be difficult to fold in the chocolate ganache.

3 ~ Finishing off

Gently fold the whisked egg white into the chocolate ganache, keeping as much air in the egg white as possible. Don't over-mix: you need to just incorporate the two mixtures, no more. Leave the mousse in the mixing bowl, or decant into ramekins or smaller bowls, then chill in the fridge for 2 hours. Serve as it is – set, yet meltingly soft.

Tip | *For the mousse to be properly light and airy, the chocolate ganache and the egg white mixtures need to have the same consistency. If you have a cooking thermometer, check the temperature of the chocolate ganache before you add the whisked egg white: it should be around 35–40°C/95–104°F.*

Variation | *Try adding mint or cinnamon to the mixture, or infuse the cream with orange zest.*

For 4
Preparation time: 20 min
Cooking time: 30 min

}

Glacé fruit cake

This is a very classic and moist cake, ideal for a child's teatime, though adults will love this comforting and tasty cake too. Get the children to help you make the mixture.

1 vanilla pod (bean)

zest of 1 orange

zest of 1 lemon

125 g/4½ oz soft butter + a little extra for the tin

125 g/4½ oz caster (superfine) sugar

2 eggs

150 g/5½ oz plain (all-purpose) flour + a little extra for the glacé fruits and sultanas

5 g/¼ oz baking powder

75 g/2¾ oz glacé fruits (see the recipe for glacé grapefruit on p. 406)

75 g/2¾ oz golden sultanas

Equipment

20 cm/8 in loaf tin

1 - The cake mixture

Preheat the oven to 170°C (325°F; gas mark 3). Split the vanilla pod in half lengthways, then scrape out and reserve the seeds (save the pod for another use). Finely chop the orange and lemon zest and put to one side. Mix the soft butter and the sugar with a spatula. Beat the eggs very lightly with a fork, then gradually mix into the sugar and butter mixture. Finally, sift together the flour and baking powder, then add to the rest of the mixture and mix until smooth.

2 - Finishing off

Dice the glacé fruits, if necessary, then mix with the sultanas, zests, a teaspoon of extra flour and the vanilla seeds. Stir into the cake mixture. Butter the loaf tin, fill it with the mixture and bake for 25–30 minutes. Remove from the oven, unmould from the tin while still hot and leave to cool on a wire rack. Serve in thick slices.

For 4 grapefruit
Preparation time: 40 min
Cooking time: 40 min
Resting time: 5 days

}

Glacé grapefruit

This recipe requires a bit of effort and time, but it is very easy. In the restaurant I often serve glacé grapefruit with game, such as venison.

4 unwaxed pink grapefruit
4 kg/9 lb caster (superfine) sugar

1~ Preparing the grapefruit

Put the grapefruit in a large saucepan and cover with cold water. Bring to the boil and cook for 10 minutes. In another saucepan, bring 2 litres/3½ pints of water to the boil with 2 kg/4½ lb of sugar. Halve the grapefruit, then immerse them in this syrup. Bring back to a simmer and leave the grapefruit to poach for 30 minutes, without letting the syrup boil. Drain them in a colander (reserving the syrup), place in a dish and leave to cool, then chill in the fridge for 24 hours. Transfer the grapefruit to a bowl big enough to hold them and the reserved syrup.

2~ The glacé grapefruit

On the first day, strain the reserved syrup into a saucepan, add 500 g/1 lb 2 oz sugar and bring to the boil, then pour over the grapefruit. Leave to cool, then chill in the fridge for another 24 hours. The second day, do exactly the same: strain the syrup into a saucepan, add another 500 g/1 lb 2 oz sugar, then bring to the boil and pour over the grapefruit; cool, then chill for 24 hours. Repeat these steps again on the next two days, so four times in total.

Tip | Use this delicious glacé grapefruit in cakes (see the recipe on p. 404) and fruit salads, or to bring a really different touch to poached fish like sole or pollock – just dice the grapefruit and add it to the fish at the last minute.

Variation | This is a very easy recipe, even it does demand a little time, and it can be used for other citrus fruits, such as clementines or oranges. It is important to use unwaxed fruit.

407

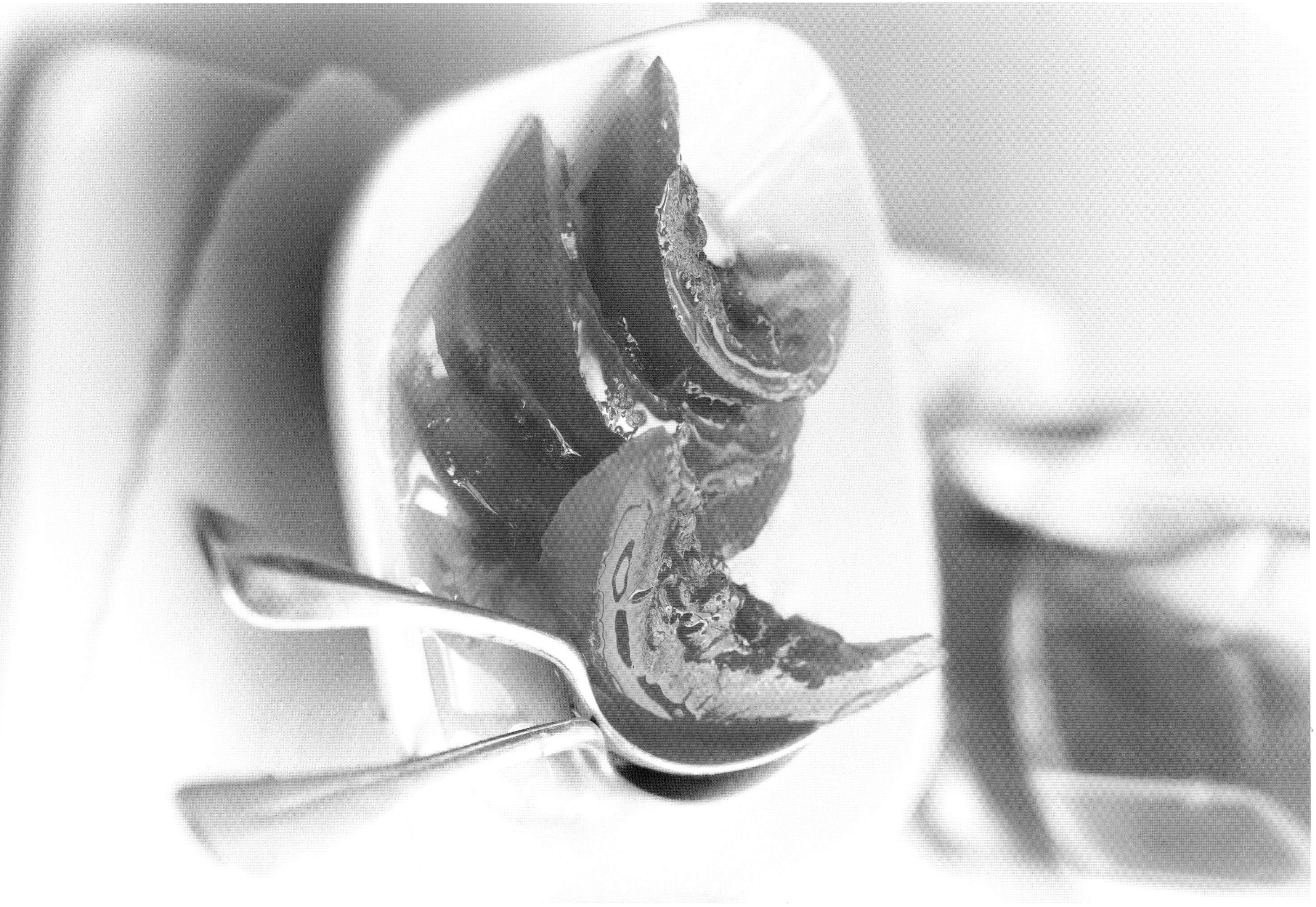

For 4
Preparation time: 25 min
Resting time: 4 h
Cooking time: 5 min

}

Lyonnaise Mardi Gras doughnuts

A traditional treat for Mardi Gras. Children love helping to make the dough and cutting out the doughnuts.

zest of 1 unwaxed lemon
100 g/3½ oz butter
250 g/8½ oz plain (all-purpose) flour
5 g/¼ oz baking powder
6 egg yolks
75 g/2¾ oz caster (superfine) sugar
¼ teaspon fine salt
2 teaspoons vanilla sugar
25 ml/1 fl oz rum
2 litres/3½ pints groundnut (peanut)
  or sunflower oil for deep-frying
icing (confectioners') sugar

Equipment
cooking thermometer

1~ The dough

Finely chop the lemon zest. Melt the butter in a saucepan over a gentle heat. Sift the flour into a bowl, then mix in the baking powder. In another bowl, mix together the egg yolks, sugar, salt, vanilla sugar and lemon zest, then add the rum, the sifted flour and baking powder and, finally, the melted butter. Mix just long enough to form a smooth dough, then cover the bowl with cling film and leave the dough to chill in the fridge for 4 hours.

2~ Cooking the doughnuts

In a saucepan or deep-fryer, heat the oil to 180°C/350°F. While it is heating, roll out the dough on a work surface to a thickness of 2–3 mm/⅛ in and cut into lozenge shapes. Drop the doughnuts into the hot oil and cook for 3 minutes, then turn them over and cook for about another 3 minutes, or until crisp and golden. Remove with a slotted spoon and drain on kitchen paper to remove the excess oil. Sprinkle with icing sugar and serve hot.

Tip | *If you don't have a cooking thermometer to check the temperature of the oil, drop a small piece of bread into it: it should sizzle and colour rapidly. If it doesn't, let the oil heat up a little more and then check it again.*

Be careful | *You can prepare the dough with the children in the kitchen, but for safety reasons it's best to keep them out of the way when cooking the doughnuts in the hot oil.*

For 8
Preparation time: 30 min
Resting time: 24 h
Cooking time: 15 min

}

Pain perdu with strawberry jam

Don't throw out stale bread! Turn it into a light dessert instead. This is a gourmand's delight – a tasty dessert and, at the same time, a bargain. You could also make it with slices of brioche.

The strawberry jam

300 g/10½ oz strawberry jam
200 g/7 oz caster (superfine) sugar

The pain perdu

4 eggs
20 g/¾ oz caster (superfine) sugar
100 ml/3½ fl oz milk
1 vanilla pod (bean)
8 thick slices stale bread
butter for frying

1~ The strawberry jam

In a large, non-metallic bowl, mix the strawberries with the sugar and leave to rest somewhere cool for 24 hours. The next day, put the fruit and sugar in a saucepan (preferably a copper one), bring to the boil and cook over quite a high heat for about 10 minutes, stirring often so the mixture doesn't catch or burn. Do this gently, to avoid crushing the strawberries – you want to keep them whole, if possible. Pour the jam into a small dish and set aside to cool.

2~ The pain perdu

Whisk the eggs and sugar by hand, then add the milk and vanilla pod and mix together. Soak the slices of bread in this mixture for a few minutes. Meanwhile, heat some butter in a frying pan. Drain the slices of bread, then cook in the hot butter until golden, turning them once or twice. Serve hot with the jam.

Tip | *Fresh bread is not what you want in this recipe; stale is best here, and this is an easy way to use it up. You could use other fruits, such as strawberries, blackcurrants or figs, for the jam.*

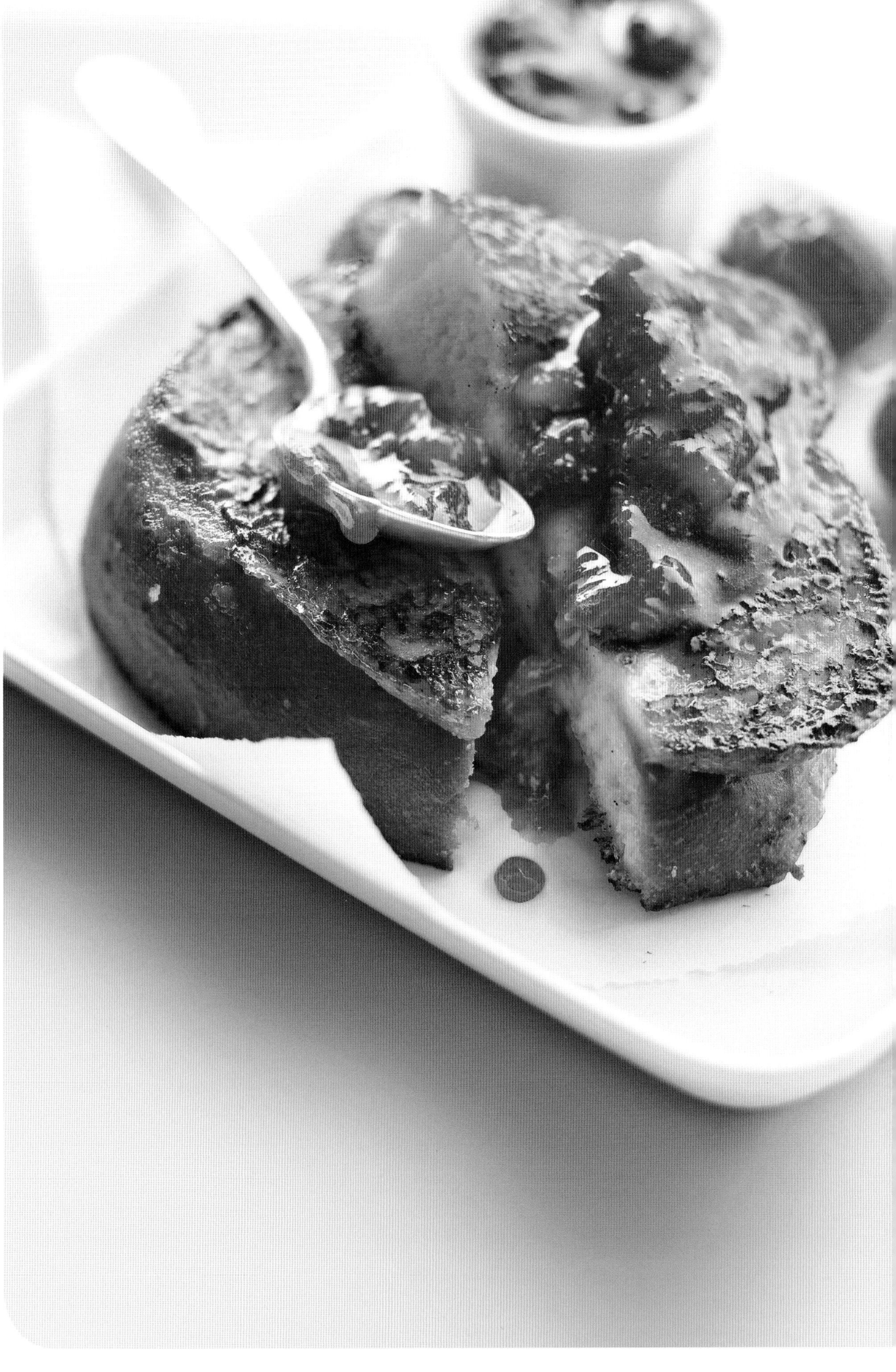

Index

A

almonds: almond milk *70*
  almond pannacotta *342*
anchovies: herb-salt marinated
    anchovies *296*
  the new pissaladière *48*
apricot macaroons *172*
artichokes: poached egg with snail foam,
    galangal and artichokes *158*
asparagus: asparagus vichyssoise with
    fennel seeds *112*
  green asparagus with mint hollandaise
    sauce *224*
aubergines (eggplant): aubergine and
    coconut milk custard *134*
  aubergine caviar *382*
  grilled aubergine caviar with
    turmeric *294*
  my ratatouille *378*

B

baba, rum *264*
banana-passionfruit foam *80*
béarnaise sauce *123*
béchamel sauce *36, 210, 214*
  nutmeg béchamel *118*
beef: braised beef with red pepper and
    tomato sauce *394*
  my spaghetti bolognese *34*
  oxtail Parmentier *102*
  pot-au-feu *228*
  tandoori beef bourguignon *360*
beetroot: beetroot salad with Arabica
    coffee salt *300*
  six-minute foie gras with beetroot *106*
biscuits: raspberry shortbread *326*
  shortbread *90*
blanquette of veal revisited *252–5*
blinis *56*
bouillabaisse jus, black rice risotto
  with *352*
boulangère potatoes with bacon *370*
bread: melba toast *28, 30–1*
  melba toast with lardo di Colonnata
    and Comté cheese *292*
  pain perdu with strawberry jam *410*
  surprise sandwich loaf ('pain surprise')
    288–91
brioche *164–5*
  grandmother's brioche with chocolate
    hazelnut spread *162*
  pogne de Romans *332–5*
bulgur wheat with vermicelli *376*
butter: aniseed butter *288*
  bay leaf butter *364*
  beurre monté *54, 148, 150–1, 272*
  brown butter *26*
  buttering soufflé dishes *68–9*
  Choron sauce *120–3*
  clarified butter *16, 68*

green Szechuan pepper butter *288*
juniper butter *114*
maître d'hôtel butter *230*
mint hollandaise sauce *224*
saffron and tomato butter *288*
smoked tea butter *288*

C

cabbage, buttered green *396*
cakes: chocolate financiers *328*
  glacé fruit cake *404*
  raspberry Swiss roll *400*
cauliflower: cauliflower cream *28*
  Du Barry velouté with orange *226*
celeriac: brown shrimp and citrus
    verrine *52*
  gravadlax and celeriac remoulade *306*
celery: lobster and celery with
    red fruits *146*
  vodka-citron beurre monté *54*
chard: chard gratin *12*
  chard, sheep's cheese and ricotta
    ravioli *346*
cheese: buffalo mozzarella
    pannacotta *310*
  chard gratin *12*
  chard, sheep's cheese and ricotta
    ravioli *346*
  cheese royale *204*
  eggs Florentine with Beaufort
    cheese *214*
  fresh morels with tarragon and
    Parmesan cream *14*
  goat's cheese and peppermint
    blancmange *382*
  goat's cheese cream *302*
  green Szechuan pepper butter with
    Parmesan *288*
  melba toast with lardo di Colonnata
    and Comté cheese *292*
  Mimolette cheese soufflé *66*
  oyster tartare with cheese fondue
    revisited *152*
  Parmesan pastry *188*
  Saint-Marcellin cheese croquettes *36*
  tomato and mozzarella revisited *46*
  young Parmesan cream *276*
cherries: cinnamon and cherry
    clafoutis *88*
  roast duck breast with black cherry
    compote *56*
chestnuts: baked eggs with turmeric,
    mushrooms and chestnuts *26*
  chestnut cream with pineapple *168*
  cream of chestnut soup *38*
  rum baba with chestnut sauce *264*
chicken: chicken cream sauce
    with lemon *220*
  stock *246–7*
  tarragon chicken with rice pilaf *116*

chicory with ham *204*
chocolate: chocolate financiers *328*
  chocolate hazelnut spread *162*
  chocolate-mint profiteroles *280*
  chocolate mousse *402*
  chocolate sauce *84*
  little chocolate pots *392*
  passionfruit and chocolate coulis *166*
  white chocolate foam *90*
  white chocolate fondant *166*
Choron sauce *120–3*
choux pastry *260, 280*
  Paris-Valence with red fruits *170*
  praline cream choux buns *390*
chutney, plum *156*
clafoutis, cinnamon and cherry *88*
coconut and lime îles flottantes *80–3*
coconut milk: aubergine and coconut
    milk custard *134*
cod: sous-vide cod with lentils *98–101*
coffee: beetroot salad with Arabica
    coffee salt *300*
  coffee fondant *86*
  pumpkin soup with Blue Mountain
    coffee *312*
courgettes (zucchini): courgette and
    bay leaf custard *134*
  crushed lemon courgettes *356*
  my ratatouille *378*
  sardine tempura *120*
crayfish: Nantua sauce *258*
cream: almond pannacotta *342*
  brown shrimp cream *96*
  buffalo mozzarella pannacotta *310*
  chocolate mousse *402*
  cinnamon cream *88*
  little chocolate pots *392*
  praline chantilly *390*
  pumpkin soup with Blue Mountain
    coffee *312*
  turmeric cream *26*
  vanilla chantilly *170*
  vanilla whipped cream *264*
crème caramel with muscovado sugar *16*
croquettes, Saint-Marcellin cheese *36*
cucumber: John Dory with cucumber
    pickle and purée *272*

D

doughnuts, Lyonnaise Mardi Gras *408*
Drôme caillette turnovers *372*
Du Barry velouté with orange *226*
duck: duck confit with lavender
    and spices *350*
  roast duck breast with black cherry
    compote *56*
  roast duckling with saffron-spiced
    apple *154*
duck foie gras terrine *190*
duck liver with seared melon *70*

E

eel: mixed vegetables with
    smoked eel *194*
eggplant *see* aubergines
eggs: baked eggs with turmeric,
    mushrooms and chestnuts *26*
    eggs Florentine with Beaufort
        cheese *214*
    poached egg and piperade with
        cloves *324*
    poached egg with snail foam, galangal
        and artichokes *158*
    poached egg with tomato ketchup,
        capers and black olives *62*
    poaching *64–5*
    soft-boiled egg in lemon jelly with
        foie gras royale *182*
'en papillote': cooking vegetables *42–3*
    sea bass 'en papillote' *114*
escabeche: mackerel *248*
    red mullet in aniseed *362*

F

filleting fish *250–1*
financiers, chocolate *328*
fish: black rice risotto with bouillabaisse
        jus *352*
    filleting *250–1*
    fish terrine with brown shrimp
        cream *96*
    see also monkfish, salmon etc
foam: banana-passionfruit *80*
    mozzarella *46*
    orange *52*
    snail *158*
    tomato *62*
    warm vodka and lemon *54*
    white chocolate *90*
foie gras: cooking in a pressure
        cooker *108–9*
    duck foie gras terrine *190*
    foie gras royale *182*
    foie gras terrine *192–3*
    game terrine *188*
    six-minute foie gras with beetroot *106*
fondue: cheese fondue revisited *152*
fruit: lobster and celery with
        red fruits *146*
    Paris-Valence with red fruits *170*
    see also apples, strawberries etc

G

game terrine *188*
glacé fruit cake *404*
glacé grapefruit *406*
gnocchi *16*
    Roman gnocchi revisited *124*
goat: shoulder of kid goat with
        sorrel *270*
goat's cheese: goat's cheese cream *302*

goat's cheese and peppermint
    blancmange *382*
Grand Marnier soufflé *278*
Grandma Alice's bulgur wheat with
    vermicelli *376*
Grandma Suzanne's stuffed
    tomatoes *380*
grandmother's brioche with chocolate
    hazelnut spread *162*
grapefruit, glacé *406*
gratins: boulangère potatoes with
        bacon *370*
    chard gratin *12*
    ravioli gratin with caramelized
        onions *118*
gravadlax *308–9*
    gravadlax and celeriac remoulade *306*
guinea fowl: guinea fowl supremes
        with walnut crust *140*
    poached guinea fowl supremes with
        wakame seaweed cream *72*

H

ham: creamy chicory with ham *204*
    jellied ham and parsley terrine *200*
hazelnuts: chocolate hazelnut
        spread *162*
    praline chantilly *390*
hollandaise sauce: mint hollandaise *224*
    tarragon hollandaise *16*
horseradish cream *228, 374*

I

ice cream: mint *280*
    vanilla *238*
îles flottantes, coconut and lime *80–3*

J

jam: raspberry *326, 400*
    strawberry *410*
jellied ham and parsley terrine *200*
jelly: mushroom *136, 200*
    pineapple *84*
    saffron tomato *184*
    tomato *46*
John Dory with cucumber pickle
    and purée *272*
jus: bouillabaisse jus *352*
    quick jus *142–3*

K

kid goat: shoulder of kid goat with
        sorrel *270*
kidneys: veal kidneys with gin
        and pepper *40*

L

lamb: Grandma Suzanne's stuffed
        tomatoes *380*
    lamb confit and mint tortellini *356*

roast saddle of lamb with basil *12*
    spring navarin of lamb *244*
langoustines, mint-marinated *268*
leeks: sea bass 'en papillote' with
        baby leeks *114*
lemon: chicken cream sauce
        with lemon *220*
    lemon tart with Italian meringue *176*
    seared red tuna with warm vodka
        and lemon foam *54*
    soft-boiled egg in lemon jelly *182*
lentils, sous-vide cod with *98*
lime: coconut and lime îles
        flottantes *80–3*
    lime-marinated scallop carpaccio *136*
    vodka-citron beurre monté *54*
liver: calves' liver soufflé *210*
    duck liver with seared melon *70*
    game terrine *188*
    see also foie gras
lobster *186–7*
    lobster and celery with red fruits *146*
    lobster 'bellevue' with saffron
        tomato jelly *184*
Lyonnaise Mardi Gras doughnuts *408*

M

macaroons *174–5*
    apricot macaroons *172*
mackerel escabeche *248*
marshmallows, peanut *286*
mayonnaise *196*
    brown shrimp and citrus verrine *52*
    smoked eel mayonnaise *194*
    tomato mayonnaise *320*
meat: quick jus *142–3*
    see also beef, lamb etc
melba toast *28, 30–1*
    with lardo di Colonnata and
        Comté cheese *292*
melon: duck liver with seared melon *70*
    melon soup with aniseed and
        goat's cheese cream *302*
meringue: coconut and lime îles
        flottantes *80–3*
    French meringue *240–1*
    lemon tart with Italian meringue *176*
    vacherin *238*
Mimolette cheese soufflé *66*
monkfish terrine *320*
mousse, chocolate *402*
mushrooms: baked eggs with turmeric,
        mushrooms and chestnuts *26*
    cream of chestnut soup with seasonal
        mushrooms *38*
    fresh morels with tarragon and
        Parmesan cream *14*
    Grandma Suzanne's stuffed
        tomatoes *380*
    mushroom jelly *136, 200*

mushrooms (*continued*)

mushroom-stuffed squid *132*

Nantua sauce *258*

sole bonne femme *256*

stock *138–9*

veal paupiettes with mushrooms *206*

vol-au-vent *220*

mussels: mussel risotto *388*

mussel royale with pumpkin cream *130*

mustard: gravadlax and celeriac remoulade with Meaux mustard *306*

roast saddle of lamb with basil and mustard *12*

N

Nantua sauce *258*

Nathan's favourite fruits in syrup *336*

navarin of lamb *244*

O

onions: boulangère potatoes with bacon *370*

ravioli gratin with caramelized onions *118*

onion pickles *48*

poached egg and piperade with cloves *324*

red onion pickles *188*

oranges: brown shrimp and citrus verrine *52*

Du Barry velouté with orange *226*

iced Grand Marnier soufflé *278*

oxtail Parmentier *102*

oyster tartare with cheese fondue revisited *152*

P

pain perdu with strawberry jam *410*

'pain surprise' *288–91*

pannacotta: almond *342*

buffalo mozzarella *310*

parfait, iced vanilla *84*

Paris-Valence with red fruits *170*

passionfruit: banana-passionfruit foam *80*

passionfruit and chocolate coulis *166*

pasta: chard, sheep's cheese and ricotta ravioli *346*

ravioli gratin *118*

lamb confit and mint tortellini *356*

mushroom-stuffed squid with creamy tagliatelle *132*

my spaghetti bolognese *34*

pollock with turnip ravioli *148*

ravioli *348–9*

roast scallops with spaghettini *274*

tortellini *358–9*

pastries: chocolate-mint profiteroles *280*

Drôme caillette turnovers *372*

Paris-Valence with red fruits *170*

vol-au-vent *220*

see also tarts

pastry: choux *170, 260, 280, 390*

Parmesan *188*

puff *236–7*

shortcrust *176, 276*

peaches: Nathan's favourite fruits in syrup *336*

peanut marshmallows *286*

pears: Nathan's favourite fruits in syrup *336*

poached vanilla pear with cassis and coffee fondant *86*

peas *see* petits pois

peppers (bell): braised beef with red pepper and tomato sauce *394*

my ratatouille *378*

poached egg and piperade with cloves *324*

pork fillet with red pepper confit and pineapple *58*

vegetable sauce vierge *198*

petits pois: petits pois cream *268*

petits pois and wasabi mousseline *32*

petits pois velouté *374*

rabbit in white wine with liquorice and petits pois *104*

pike quenelles with Nantua sauce *258*

pilaf, rice *116*

pineapple: chestnut cream with pineapple and piña colada sorbet *168*

iced vanilla parfait with pineapple *84*

pork fillet with red pepper and pineapple confit *58*

piperade: poached egg and piperade with cloves *324*

pissaladière with crunchy fennel and onion pickles *48*

pogne de Romans *332–5*

pollock with turnip ravioli and rum sauce *148*

pommes dauphine *260–3*

pommes soufflées re-invented *74–7*

pork: Drôme caillette turnovers *372*

game terrine *188*

pork fillet with red pepper confit and pineapple *58*

pot-au-feu *228*

potatoes: asparagus vichyssoise *112*

boulangère potatoes with bacon *370*

buttered green cabbage *396*

crushed potatoes and snails *256*

fondant potatoes *270*

gnocchi *16*

my pommes dauphine *260–3*

poached sole and potatoes *386*

pommes soufflées re-invented *74–7*

potato mousseline *156*

sweet potato mash *102*

prawns: monkfish terrine with prawns and saffron *320*

see also shrimp

profiteroles, chocolate-mint *280*

pumpkin: mussel royale with pumpkin cream *130*

pumpkin soup with Blue Mountain coffee *312*

Q

quinoa salad with minted yogurt *304*

R

rabbit: rabbit in white wine with liquorice and petits pois *104*

rabbit rillettes with chorizo and mint *322*

raspberries: raspberry confit *342*

raspberry shortbread biscuits *326*

raspberry Swiss roll *400*

ratatouille *378*

ravioli *348–9*

chard, sheep's cheese and ricotta ravioli *346*

ravioli gratin with caramelized onions *118*

pollock with turnip ravioli *148*

red mullet in aniseed escabeche *362*

rhubarb: rhubarb and tarragon compote *190*

rhubarb and tarragon tart *90*

rice: black rice risotto with bouillabaisse jus *352*

mussel risotto *388*

rice pilaf *116*

risotto *354–5*

rillettes: rabbit with chorizo and mint *322*

salmon *316–19*

sardine *28*

risotto *354–5*

black rice risotto with bouillabaisse jus *352*

mussel risotto *388*

Roman gnocchi revisited *124*

rum baba *264*

S

Saint-Marcellin cheese croquettes *36*

salmon: fillets of marinated salmon with petits pois and wasabi mousseline *32*

gravadlax *308–9*

gravadlax and celeriac remoulade *306*

salmon rillettes *318–19*

salmon rillettes with tonka bean and green apple *316*

salt: Arabica coffee salt *300*

herb-salt marinated anchovies *296*

sea bass in a sea salt crust *16–19*

sardines: sardine rillettes with whisky *28*

sardine tempura *120*

sauces: béarnaise sauce *123*
  béchamel sauce *36, 210, 214*
  beurre monté *54, 148, 150–1, 272*
  chestnut sauce *264*
  chicken cream sauce with lemon *220*
  chocolate sauce *84*
  chocolate-mint sauce *280*
  Choron sauce *120–3*
  mayonnaise *196*
  mint hollandaise sauce *224*
  Nantua sauce *258*
  nutmeg béchamel *118*
  passionfruit and chocolate coulis *166*
  pepper sauce *40*
  quick jus *142–3*
  sauce gribiche *196*
  sauce vierge *20*
  tarragon hollandaise *16*
  tartare sauce *198*
  tomato coulis *210*
  vegetable sauce vierge *198*
scallops: lime-marinated scallop
    carpaccio *136*
  roast scallops with spaghettini *274*
  scallops with buttered green
    cabbage *396*
sea bass: sea bass 'en papillote' with
    baby leeks *114*
  sea bass in a Guérande sea salt
    crust *16*
shrimp: brown shrimp and citrus
    verrine *52*
  fish terrine with brown shrimp
    cream *96*
  see also prawns
six-minute foie gras with beetroot *106*
snails: crushed potatoes and snails *256*
  poached egg with snail foam *158*
sole: poached sole and potatoes *386*
  sole bonne femme with crushed
    potatoes and snails *256*
sorbets: piña colada *168*
  strawberry *238*
soufflés *212–13*
  buttering soufflé dishes *68–9*
  calves' liver soufflé *210*
  iced Grand Marnier soufflé *278*
  Mimolette cheese soufflé *66*
soups: asparagus vichyssoise *112*
  cream of chestnut soup *38*
  Du Barry velouté with orange *226*
  melon soup with aniseed and
    goat's cheese cream *302*
  petits pois velouté *374*
  pumpkin soup with Blue Mountain
    coffee *312*
sous-vide cod with lentils *98–101*
spaghetti bolognese *34*
spaghettini, roast scallops with *274*
spinach: Drôme caillette turnovers *372*

eggs Florentine with Beaufort
    cheese *214*
spring onions, minted liquorice *268*
squid, mushroom-stuffed *132*
stock: chicken *246–7*
  mushroom *138–9*
  vegetable *38, 126–7*
strawberries: pain perdu with
    strawberry jam *410*
  strawberry sorbet *238*
surprise sandwich loaf *288–91*
sweet potato mash *102*
sweetbreads *222–3*
  vol-au-vent *220*
sweetcorn: blinis *56*
Swiss roll, raspberry *400*

T
tagliatelle: mushroom stuffed squid
    with creamy tagliatelle *132*
tandoori beef bourguignon *360*
tartare sauce *198*
tarts: lemon tart with Italian
    meringue *176*
  the new pissaladière *48*
  rhubarb and tarragon tart *90*
  tarte tatin with tonka bean *232–5*
  tuna tartlet with sauce vierge *20*
  vegetable tart with young Parmesan
    cream *276*
tempura, sardine *120*
terrines: duck foie gras terrine *190*
  fish terrine *96*
  foie gras terrine *192–3*
  game terrine *188*
  jellied ham and parsley terrine *200*
  monkfish terrine *320*
tomatoes: braised beef with red pepper
    and tomato sauce *394*
  Grandma Suzanne's stuffed
    tomatoes *380*
  herb-salt marinated anchovies with
    Green Zebra tomatoes *296*
  heritage tomatoes with buffalo
    mozzarella pannacotta *310*
  lobster 'bellevue' with saffron tomato
    jelly and rainbow tomatoes *184*
  my ratatouille *378*
  my spaghetti bolognese *34*
  the new pissaladière *48*
  peeling and dicing *22–3*
  Roman gnocchi revisited *124*
  saffron and tomato butter *288*
  sauce vierge *20*
  tomato and mozzarella revisited *46*
  tomato concassé *20, 34, 48, 50–1, 124*
  tomato coulis *210*
  tomato ketchup *62*
tonka bean: salmon rillettes with tonka
    bean and green apple *316*

tarte tatin with tonka bean *232–5*
tortellini *358–9*
  lamb confit and mint tortellini *356*
tuiles, vanilla *86*
tuna: seared red tuna with warm
    vodka and lemon foam *54*
  tuna tartlet with sauce vierge *20*
turnip ravioli *148*
turnovers, Drôme caillette *372*

V
vacherin with vanilla ice cream
  and strawberry sorbet *238*
vanilla: iced vanilla parfait with
    pineapple *84*
  poached vanilla pear with cassis *86*
  vanilla chantilly *170*
  vanilla ice cream *238*
  vanilla tuiles *86*
  vanilla whipped cream *264*
veal: blanquette of veal revisited *252–5*
  roast veal with potato mousseline *156*
  veal paupiettes *208–9*
  veal paupiettes with mushrooms *206*
veal kidneys with gin and pepper *40*
vegetables: blanquette of veal
    revisited *252*
  cooking 'en papillote' *42–3*
  fried vegetables *230*
  mixed vegetables with smoked eel *194*
  my ratatouille *378*
  pot-au-feu *228*
  spring navarin of lamb *244*
  stock *126–7*
  vegetable sauce vierge *198*
  vegetable stock *38*
  vegetable tart with young Parmesan
    cream *276*
  vegetable tian with bay leaf butter *364*
  see also peppers, tomatoes etc
vermicelli, Grandma Alice's bulgur
    wheat with *376*
verrine, brown shrimp and citrus *52*
vichyssoise, asparagus with fennel
    seeds *112*
vol-au-vent *220*

W
walnuts: guinea fowl supremes with
    walnut crust *140*
whiting: breaded whiting with maître
    d'hôtel butter and fried vegetables *230*

Y
yogurt: homemade yogurts *338–41*
  minted yogurt *304*

Z
zucchini *see* courgettes

✳

First published in the UK, USA and Australia in 2015 by:
Jacqui Small LLP
7–77 White Lion Street
London N1 9PF

First published by Hachette Livre, Paris, 2013

Publisher: Jacqui Small
Translator: Louise Tucker
Photography: Michaël Roulier
Styling: Emmanuel Turiot

ISBN 9781909342866

A catalogue record for this book is available from the British Library.

10 9 8 7 6 5 4 3 2 1

Printed in China

Editor's note
The times given for keeping a dish are only a guide and cannot be guaranteed, since safe storage
times will depend on the quality of the ingredients, and whether all the steps of the recipe have been
followed accurately. Make sure you put any finished dishes you want to keep in the fridge promptly,
and eat as soon as possible after cooking.